# STUDY GUIDE

**Dean Croushore**
*Federal Reserve Bank of Philadelphia*

**Angela E. Trimarchi**
*Wilfrid Laurier University*

# Macroeconomics

## Third Canadian Edition

Andrew B. Abel
*University of Pennsylvania*

Ben S. Bernanke
*Princeton University*

Gregor W. Smith
*Queen's University*

Toronto

ISBN 0-321-11525-2

Acquisitions Editor: Gary Bennett
Developmental Editor: Paul Donnelly
Production Editor: Marisa D'Andrea
Production Coordinator: Janette Lush

1 2 3 4 5   07 06 05 04 03

Printed and bound in Canada.

# Contents

# Introduction

The goal of the Study Guide is to help students learn the material in the textbook efficiently and effectively. The best way to learn material that is analytical or numerical in nature, as is the case with much of the textbook, is to work as many problems as possible. So, much of this Study Guide consists of multiple-choice questions, review questions, numerical problems, and analytical questions to help students prepare. Students may want to work some of the problems after they have read the chapter and attended their class lecture, or they many want to simulate exam conditions, trying to answer the questions without looking at their notes. In all cases, the answers are given to students, though they may also need to refer back to the textbook where the material appears.

In addition, each chapter includes an introduction and a detailed chapter outline. The chapter outline will help students see how the chapter fits together and where particular material is located. Some students find it useful to bring the chapter outline to class, highlight the material covered by the instructor, then add additional notes. The outline may also provide a quick review as students prepare for an exam. However, the outline does not look at the topics in much detail, so students should refer often to the textbook.

If, after studying the textbook, class notes, and this Study Guide, a student does not understand a concept, he or she should be sure to see the class instructor or teaching assistant.

# CHAPTER 1: INTRODUCTION TO MACROECONOMICS

## INTRODUCTION

The purpose of this chapter is to give you a general introduction to the main concepts in macroeconomics. In Section 1.1, the major issues in economics are discussed—growth, business cycles, unemployment, inflation, the international economy, macroeconomic policy, and aggregation. Section 1.2 discusses the major things that macroeconomists do—forecasting, analysis, research, and data development. Then Section 1.3 covers the subject of why economists disagree and talks about the textbook's approach to covering material, given that there's so much disagreement.

Though many instructors will blow through this chapter quickly, you shouldn't. You should spend some time looking at all the data in this chapter and trying to understand what it's all about. This will help you later on when you go through the rest of the textbook. You should know that most macroeconomists are very motivated by looking at data. They want to explain how the world works and why the data behave the way they do. Figures like those shown in Section 1.1 provide economists with what they call "stylized facts" about how the economy behaves. Then the economists try to think up models that are consistent with the data.

## CHAPTER OUTLINE

I.   What Macroeconomics Is About (Sec. 1.1)
   A.   Long-run economic growth
      1.   Growth of output in Canada over time
      2.   Sources of growth—population, average labour productivity growth
   B.   Unemployment; Canadian experience
   C.   Business cycles
   D.   Inflation
      1.   Canadian experience
      2.   Deflation (falling prices)
      3.   Inflation rate
   E.   The international economy
      1.   Open vs. closed economies
      2.   Trade imbalances; the trade deficit
   F.   Macroeconomic policy
      1.   Fiscal policy
      2.   Monetary policy; the Bank of Canada
   G.   Aggregation; from microeconomics to macroeconomics
II.  What Macroeconomists Do (Sec. 1.2)
   A.   Macroeconomic forecasting
      1.   Relatively few economists make forecasts
      2.   Forecasting is very difficult
   B.   Macroeconomic analysis
      1.   Private and public sector economists—analyze current conditions
      2.   Does having lots of economists ensure good macroeconomic policies? No, since politicians, not economists, make major decisions
   C.   Macroeconomic research

        1.   Goal:  to make general statements about how the economy works
        2.   Theoretical and empirical research are necessary for forecasting and economic analysis
        3.   Economic theory: a set of ideas about the economy, organized in a logical framework
        4.   Economic model: a simplified description of some aspect of the economy
        5.   Usefulness of economic theory or models depends on reasonableness of assumptions, possibility of being applied to real problems, empirically testable implications, theoretical results consistent with real-world data
    D.   Data development—very important for making data more useful
III.   Why Macroeconomists Disagree (Sec. 1.3)
    A.   Positive vs. normative analysis
    B.   Classicals vs. Keynesians
        1.   The classical approach
        2.   The Keynesian approach
        3.   The evolution of the classical-Keynesian debate
    C.   A unified approach to macroeconomics
        1.   Textbook uses a single model to present both classical and Keynesian ideas
        2.   Three markets:  goods, assets, labour
        3.   Model starts with microfoundations:  individual behavior
        4.   Long run:  wages and prices are perfectly flexible
        5.   Short run:  Classical case—flexible wages and prices; Keynesian case—wages and prices are slow to adjust

## MULTIPLE-CHOICE QUESTIONS

1.  Which of the following is *not* a principal issue of macroeconomics?
    a.  business cycles
    b.  inflation
    c.  fiscal policies
    d.  competitiveness of firms in the steel industry

2.  Which of the following is *not* a topic of macroeconomics?
    a.  why nations have different rates of growth
    b.  what causes inflation and what can be done about it
    c.  what factors contribute to the presence of monopolies in the economy
    d.  why unemployment periodically reaches very high levels

3.  The most direct effect of an increase in the growth rate of average labour productivity would be an increase in
    a.  the inflation rate.
    b.  the unemployment rate.
    c.  the long-run economic growth rate.
    d.  imported goods.

4.  In analyzing macroeconomic data during the past year, you have discovered that average labour productivity fell, but total output increased.  What was most likely to have caused this?
    a.  There is nothing unusual in this outcome because this is what normally occurs.
    b.  The capital/output ratio probably rose.
    c.  There was an increase in labour input.
    d.  Unemployment probably increased.

5.  The term *business cycle* describes the
    a.  long-run growth rate of the economy.
    b.  short-run movements in inflation.
    c.  long-run growth of the labour force.
    d.  short-run movements in economic activity.

6.  The business cycle describes the
    a.  progression of an industry's structure from monopoly to perfect competition.
    b.  progression of an industry's structure from perfect competition to monopoly.
    c.  expansion and contraction of an individual industry within the economy.
    d.  expansion and contraction of economic activity in the economy as a whole.

7.  Recessions
    a.  don't occur in developed countries, like Canada.
    b.  cause the unemployment rate to increase.
    c.  never last more than two consecutive quarters.
    d.  are always followed by long periods of high rates of real economic growth.

8. The unemployment rate is the
   a. number of unemployed divided by the number of employed.
   b. number of employed divided by the number of unemployed.
   c. number of unemployed divided by the labour force.
   d. labour force divided by the number of unemployed.

9. During the Great Depression the unemployment rate for Canada peaked at approximately
   a. 10%.
   b. 70%.
   c. 45%.
   d. 25%.

10. The average price of goods in Canada
    a. was relatively constant over the 1800–1945 period.
    b. was relatively constant over the decade of the 1980s.
    c. declined over the decade of the 1970s.
    d. is always constant in the long run.

11. Historical evidence shows that consumer prices in Canada
    a. deflated between the 1920s and World War II, but inflated afterward.
    b. inflated between the 1920s and World War II, but deflated afterward.
    c. have shown a continuous inflationary pattern since the 1920s.
    d. have displayed no clear-cut trend since the 1920s.

12. A closed economy is a national economy that
    a. doesn't interact economically with the rest of the world.
    b. has a stock market that is not open to traders from outside the country.
    c. has extensive trading and financial relationships with other national economies.
    d. has not established diplomatic relations with other national economies.

13. In most years during the 1980s and 1990s, the Canadian trade balance
    a. was in equilibrium.
    b. was a trade deficit.
    c. was a trade surplus.
    d. was cyclical, fluctuating annually between trade deficits and  trade surpluses.

14. Canadian exports are goods and services
    a. produced abroad and sold to Canadians.
    b. produced in Canada and sold to Canadians.
    c. produced abroad and sold to foreigners.
    d. produced in Canada and sold to foreigners.

15. Canadian imports are goods and services
    a. produced abroad and sold to Canadians.
    b. produced in Canada and sold to Canadians.
    c. produced abroad and sold to foreigners.
    d. produced in Canada and sold to foreigners.

16. In 1999, a country had imports of $50 billion, exports of $60 billion, and GDP of $300 billion.  The trade surplus was what percent of GDP in 1999?
    a.    3.3%
    b.    10.0%
    c.    16.7%
    d.    20.0%

17. A country's monetary policy is controlled by
    a.    private citizens.
    b.    the central bank.
    c.    large banks.
    d.    the legislature.

18. Critics of the government's fiscal policies have argued that government deficits
    a.    prevent capital from flowing into Canada.
    b.    are linked to the excess of imports over exports that occurred in the 1980s.
    c.    caused the level of unemployment in Canada to increase during the 1980s.
    d.    have directly contributed to a decline in the level of demand in the Canadian economy.

19. Which of the following fiscal policies do Keynesians recommend to help the economy recover from a recession?
    a.    an increase in government spending
    b.    an increase in taxes
    c.    an increase in the money supply
    d.    an increase in saving

20. Since the Great Depression, the share of national income collected in taxes and spent by the federal government in Canada has
    a.    increased from less than 10% to more than 20%.
    b.    remained relatively stable at 15%.
    c.    remained relatively stable at 35%.
    d.    declined from about 40% to less than 15%.

21. In 1999, a government of Anchovy collected receipts of $100 billion and had expenditures of $125 billion. Its GDP was $400 billion.  The government's deficit was what percent of GDP in 1999?
    a.    6.25%
    b.    12.50%
    c.    25.00%
    d.    100.00%

22. Aggregation is the process of
    a.    calculating real GDP based on nominal GDP and the price index.
    b.    summing individual economic variables to obtain economywide totals.
    c.    forecasting the components of GDP.
    d.    predicting when recessions will occur.

23. Assumptions for economic theories and models should be
    a. rejected if they are not totally realistic.
    b. logical rather than empirically testable.
    c. simple and reasonable rather than complex.
    d. maintained until overwhelming evidence to the contrary occurs.

24. The principal distinction between positive analysis and normative analysis is that
    a. positive analysis is useful and normative analysis is not useful.
    b. positive analysis is optimistic and normative analysis is neutral.
    c. economists always agree on the conclusions of positive analysis but could disagree on the conclusions of normative analysis.
    d. positive analysis tells us "what is," but normative analysis tells us "what ought to be."

25. The two most comprehensive, widely accepted macroeconomic models are
    a. the classical model and the supply-side model.
    b. the supply-side model and the real business cycle model.
    c. the classical model and the Keynesian model.
    d. the Austrian model and the Keynesian model.

26. Adam Smith's idea of the "invisible hand" tries to convey the idea that if there are free markets and people conduct their economic affairs in their own best interests,
    a. any country can become an advanced, industrialized nation.
    b. markets will eliminate problems of hunger and dissatisfaction.
    c. most inequalities between the rich and the poor will be eliminated.
    d. the overall economy will work well.

27. Classical economists who assume the "invisible hand" works reasonably well do *not* argue that
    a. the government should have a limited role in the economy.
    b. government policies will be ineffective and counterproductive.
    c. the government should actively intervene in the economy to eliminate business cycles.
    d. wages and prices adjust quickly to bring the economy back to equilibrium.

28. Equilibrium in the economy means
    a. unemployment is zero.
    b. quantities demanded and supplied are equal in all markets.
    c. prices aren't changing over time.
    d. tax revenues equal government spending, so the government has no budget deficit.

29. John Maynard Keynes disagreed with the classical economists in assuming that
    a. wages and prices adjusted slowly.
    b. international trade played a major role in the macroeconomy.
    c. government intervention in the economy could not reduce business cycles.
    d. unemployment would be eliminated quickly by the invisible hand of the market.

# REVIEW QUESTIONS

1. Identify and briefly describe six major topics studied by macroeconomists.

2. What is a recession?  Briefly state the effect of a recession on the unemployment rate.  Identify and briefly describe two macroeconomic policies that might be used to help pull the macroeconomy out of a recession.  In the absence of government intervention, do classical or Keynesian economists believe the economy would recover quickly from a recession?  Briefly explain.

3. Briefly describe the following tasks of macroeconomists:  forecasting; analysis; research; and data development.

4. What are the four major areas in which macroeconomists work?  Give an example of a job in each.

5. Compare and contrast the classical and Keynesian schools of thought for the following economic issues:
   a.   the flexibility of wages and prices
   b.   the importance of macroeconomic policies

6. Discuss the major differences between classical and Keynesian economists.  Be sure to explain how they differ with regard to how quickly equilibrium is restored in the economy as well as what role they see for government action in restoring equilibrium.

7. Describe the evolution of the classical-Keynesian debate since World War II.

# NUMERICAL PROBLEMS

1. Starting from a year in which gross domestic product for the economy is $8,000 billion, calculate how much output the national economy would produce in the next five years if it continued to grow at its potential real growth rate of 3%.

   How much output would the economy produce if it grew by 4% the first year, 2% the second year, 1% the third year, -1% the fourth year, and -3% the fifth year?  (Note:  A negative growth rate means output is declining.)

   By the fifth year, how far is output below its potential level?

2. Suppose there are 125 million people in the labour force.
   a.   Calculate the unemployment rate if 10 million people are unemployed.
   b.   Calculate the unemployment rate if the number of unemployed falls to 6 million.
   c.   If the unemployment rate is 6%, how many unemployed people are there?

3. Using the CPI measure of the price level, which is 100 in the base year of 1996, calculate the annual inflation rates for: a) 1997, when the index is 103.5;  b) 1998, when the index is 104.5; c) 1999, when the index is 105.2.

# ANALYTICAL QUESTIONS

1.  Determine whether each of the following is a positive or normative statement.
    a.  The Bank of Canada should lower interest rates to increase economic growth, because we're in a recession.
    b.  Higher government budget deficits cause higher interest rates.
    c.  The trade deficit should decline because of the fall in the value of the dollar.
    d.  Because of our high inflation rate, we must reduce the rate of money growth.
    e.  A generous unemployment insurance system is a primary cause of high unemployment in Europe.
    f.  Increased average labour productivity in a country should lead to faster growth.
    g.  Government budget deficits are too high in Canada and should be reduced.

# ANSWERS TO MULTIPLE-CHOICE QUESTIONS

| Number | Answer | Number | Answer | Number | Answer |
|--------|--------|--------|--------|--------|--------|
| 1 | d | 11 | a | 21 | a |
| 2 | c | 12 | a | 22 | b |
| 3 | c | 13 | b | 23 | c |
| 4 | c | 14 | d | 24 | d |
| 5 | d | 15 | a | 25 | c |
| 6 | d | 16 | a | 26 | d |
| 7 | b | 17 | b | 27 | c |
| 8 | c | 18 | b | 28 | b |
| 9 | d | 19 | a | 29 | a |
| 10 | a | 20 | a | | |

# ANSWERS TO REVIEW QUESTIONS

1. Macroeconomists study the causes and effects of the following macroeconomic events.

    (1) Long-run economic growth. Economists examine increases in real GDP (national output) over extended periods of time, living standards, and productivity growth.

    (2) Business cycles. Economists study the alternating periods of contraction and expansion in economic activity.

    (3) Unemployment. Unemployment is the inability of some people to find jobs, even though they are willing to work at market wages.

    (4) Inflation. Inflation is the rate of growth in the average price of goods and services.

    (5) The international economy. Economists study patterns of international trade and borrowing among nations, as well as trade imbalances.

    (6) Macroeconomic policy. Economists examine both fiscal and monetary policy. Fiscal policy consists of changes in government spending and taxation. Monetary policy represents changes in the money supply.

2. A recession is a time when the economy's output is growing very slowly or falling. The unemployment rate increases during recessions. Two macroeconomic policies that might be used to help pull the macroeconomy out of a recession are fiscal policy (increases in government spending or reductions in taxes) and monetary policy (increases in the money supply). Both classical and Keynesian economists believe the economy will recover from a recession in the absence of government intervention. However, classical economists believe the recovery will occur fairly quickly; Keynesians believe the recovery will occur slowly.

3. (a) Forecasting. Macroeconomists develop models to predict the future values of macroeconomic variables in one or more markets. These models are usually based on economic theory but are statistical in form and estimated using macroeconomic data.

(b)    Analysis.  Macroeconomists analyze changes in macroeconomic policies as well as other changes in macroeconomic market conditions.  This analysis is based on economic theory, uses analytic reasoning techniques, and may rely on forecasting models.

(c)    Research.  The goal of macroeconomic research is to make general statements about how the economy works.  Research economists formulate and test theories.

(d)    Data development.  Macroeconomic data development provides the data needed in macroeconomic research, analysis, and forecasting.  Most macroeconomic data are collected and published by the government.

4.    Forecasting, analysis, research, and data development. Forecasting: forecasting the stock market on Bay Street; analysis: analyzing the economy for the Bank of Canada; research: investigating the link between the trade deficit and the government budget deficit as a university professor; data development: working at the Ministry of Labour  to develop better ways to measure unemployment.

5.    The flexibility of wages and prices is a principal point of disagreement between classical economists and Keynesians.  Classical economists believe that wages and prices are quite flexible; in response to some change in market conditions, wages and prices adjust quickly to their new market-clearing levels. Keynesians believe that wages and prices are rigid or, at least, sticky; in response to changes in the economy, wages and prices adjust slowly to their new market-clearing levels.

Classicals and Keynesians also disagree about the use of macroeconomic policies.  Given wage-price flexibility, classical economists believe that the market economy normally provides for full employment. They believe that government intervention in the form of macroeconomic fiscal and monetary policies is not needed to prevent recessions.  Given slow adjustments in wages and prices, Keynesians believe that recessions could plague the economy for several years.  They believe that efficient use of macroeconomic policies could return the economy to equilibrium more quickly.

6.    Classical and Keynesian economists differ most with regard to how quickly they see wages and prices adjusting to restore equilibrium in the economy.  Classical economists think that when the economy is out of equilibrium, wages and prices adjust quickly to restore equilibrium.  As a result, there shouldn't be long periods of abnormally high unemployment.  The quick return to equilibrium means there is no reason for government action.  Keynesians, on the other hand, think wages and prices are slow to adjust.  As a result, the economy may be out of equilibrium for some time, perhaps with high unemployment.  To restore equilibrium quickly may necessitate some government action, such as increasing the government's demand for goods and services.

7.    The Keynesian approach dominated macroeconomic theory and policy from World War II until about 1970. But stagflation in the 1970s undermined faith in the Keynesian approach, and classical macroeconomics made a comeback.  Currently, excellent research is being conducted with both approaches.

## ANSWERS TO NUMERICAL PROBLEMS

1.

| Potential output | Actual output |
|---|---|
| Year 1: $8,000 billion x 1.03 = $8,240 billion | $8,000 billion x 1.04 = $8,320 billion |
| Year 2: $8,240 billion x 1.03 = $8,487 billion | $8,320 billion x 1.02 = $8,486 billion |
| Year 3: $8,487 billion x 1.03 = $8,742 billion | $8,486 billion x 1.01 = $8,571 billion |
| Year 4: $8,742 billion x 1.03 = $9,004 billion | $8,571 billion x 0.99 = $8,486 billion |
| Year 5: $9,004 billion x 1.03 = $9,274 billion | $8,486 billion x 0.97 = $8,231 billion |

[Note: Don't worry about rounding differences that arise in problems like this, because such differences depend on how many digits you carry over from one calculation to the next.]

Output is below potential output by $[(9,274 - 8,231)/9,274] \times 100\% = 11.2\%$.

2. Use the formula: unemployment rate = number of people unemployed/number of people in labour force x 100%.

   a. $10/125 \times 100\% = 8\%$.

   b. $6/125 \times 100\% = 4.8\%$.

   c. Solve for $y$ in the equation: $6\% = y/125 \times 100\%$, or $y = 125 \times 6/100 = 125 \times .06 = 7.5$ million.

3. The annual inflation rate = (price level in the current year - price level in the previous year)/price level in the previous year

   (a) inflation in 1997 = $(103.5 - 100)/100 \times 100\% = 3.5\%$.

   (b) inflation in 1998 = $(104.5 - 103.5)/103.5 \times 100\% = 1.0\%$.

   (c) inflation in 1999 = $(105.2 - 104.5)/104.5 \times 100\% = 0.7\%$.

## ANSWERS TO ANALYTICAL QUESTIONS

1. a. normative; b. positive; c. positive; d. normative; e. positive; f. positive; g. normative

# CHAPTER 2: THE MEASUREMENT AND STRUCTURE
# OF THE CANADIAN ECONOMY

## INTRODUCTION

Chapter 2 is all about numbers—those that describe the economy.  First, Section 2.1 discusses the general idea of the national income accounts and talks about the relationships between key macroeconomic variables. Section 2.2 then goes into a detailed discussion of GDP (the main measure of output) and its components.  Then, Section 2.3 talks about measures of saving and wealth, both for the private sector and for the government. Section 2.4 covers real GDP, price indexes, and inflation.  Interest rates are discussed in Section 2.5.

You might think that all this accounting business is pretty dull, routine stuff, but it's been the focus of a lot of attention recently.  As you'll learn in the chapter, counting all the economy's output, and especially calculating the inflation rate, is very tricky business.  Many economists are convinced that we've been mismeasuring many of the macroeconomic variables, especially inflation.  And that, in turn, has policymakers concerned.

As you go through this chapter, you may find some of the details of national income accounting somewhat tedious.  But it helps to know how economic goods and services are counted in order to understand the concepts used later in the textbook.  So immerse yourself in some of the details; it will pay off later.

## CHAPTER OUTLINE

I.   National Income Accounting: The Measurement of Production, Income, and Expenditure (Sec. 2.1)
    A.   Three alternative approaches give the same measurements
        1.   Product approach: the amount of output produced
        2.   Income approach: the incomes generated by production
        3.   Expenditure approach: the amount of spending by purchasers
    B.   Juice business example shows that all three approaches are equal
        1.   Important concept in product approach: value added = value of output minus value of intermediate inputs
    C.   Why are the three approaches equivalent?
        1.   They must be, by definition
        2.   Any output produced (product approach) is purchased by someone (expenditure approach) and results in income to someone (income approach)
        3.   The fundamental identity of national income accounting:
        total production = total income = total expenditure
II.  Gross Domestic Product (Sec. 2.2)
    A.   The product approach to measuring GDP
        1.   GDP is the market value of final goods and services newly produced within a nation during a fixed period of time
        2.   Market value: allows adding together unlike items by valuing them at their market prices
            a.   Problem: misses nonmarket items such as homemaking, the value of environmental quality, and natural resource depletion
            b.   There is some adjustment to reflect the underground economy

    c.   Government services (that aren't sold in markets) are valued at their cost of production

  3.  Newly produced: counts only things produced in the given period; excludes things produced earlier

  4.  Final goods and services
    a.  Don't count intermediate goods and services
    b.  Capital goods (goods used to produce other goods) are final goods since they aren't used up in the same period that they are produced
    c.  Inventory investment (the amount that inventories of unsold finished goods, goods in process, and raw materials have changed during the period) is also treated as a final good
    d.  Adding up value added works well, since it automatically excludes intermediate goods

  5.  GNP vs. GDP
    a.  GNP = output produced by domestically owned factors of production
    b.  GDP = output produced within a nation
    c.  GDP = GNP - NFP (net factor payments from abroad)
    d.  NFP = payments to domestically owned factors located abroad minus payments to foreign factors located domestically
    e.  Example: Engineering revenues for a road built by a Canadian company in Saudi Arabia is part of Canadian GNP (built by a Canadian factor of production), not Canadian GDP, and is part of Saudi GDP (built in Saudi Arabia), not Saudi GNP
    f.  Difference between GNP and GDP is small for Canada, about 2%, but higher for countries that have many citizens working abroad

B.  The expenditure approach to measuring GDP
  1.  Measures total spending on final goods and services produced within a nation during a specified period of time
  2.  Four main categories of spending: consumption ($C$), investment ($I$), government purchases of goods and services ($G$), and net exports ($NX$)
  3.  $Y = C + I + G + NX$, the income-expenditure identity
  4.  Consumption: spending by domestic households on final goods and services (including those produced abroad)
    a.  About 60% of Canadian GDP
    b.  Three categories
      (1)  Consumer durables (examples: cars, TV sets, furniture, major appliances)
      (2)  Nondurable goods (examples: food, clothing, fuel)
      (3)  Services (examples: education, health care, financial services, transportation)
  5.  Investment: spending for new capital goods (fixed investment) plus inventory investment
    a.  About 1/6 of Canadian GDP
    b.  Business (or nonresidential) fixed investment: spending by businesses on structures and equipment
    c.  Residential fixed investment: spending on the construction of houses and apartment buildings
    d.  Inventory investment: increases in firms' inventory holdings
  6.  Government purchases of goods and services: spending by the government on goods or services
    a.  About 1/5 of Canadian GDP
    b.  Most by provincial and local governments, not federal government
    c.  Not all government expenditures are purchases of goods and services
      (1)  Some are payments that are *not* made in exchange for current goods and services
      (2)  One type is transfers, including Old Age Security payments, welfare, and unemployment benefits
      (3)  Another type is interest payments on the government debt

        d.   Some government spending is for capital goods that add to the nation's capital stock, such as highways, airports, bridges, and water and sewer systems

    7.   Net exports: exports minus imports

        a.   Exports: goods produced in the country that are purchased by foreigners

        b.   Imports: goods produced abroad that are purchased by residents in the country

        c.   Imports are subtracted from GDP, as they represent goods produced abroad, and were included in consumption, investment, and government purchases

C.   The income approach to measuring GDP

    1.   Adds up income generated by production (including profits and taxes paid to the government)

        a.   National income = compensation of employees (including benefits) + proprietor's income + rental income of persons + corporate profits + net interest

        b.   National income + indirect business taxes = net national product

        c.   Net national product + depreciation = gross national product (GNP)

        d.   GNP - net factor payments ($NFP$) = GDP

    2.   Private sector and government sector income

        a.   Private disposable income = income of the private sector = private sector income earned at home ($Y$ or GDP) and abroad ($NFP$) + payments from the government sector (transfers, $TR$, and interest on government debt, $INT$) - taxes paid to government ($T$) = $Y + NFP + TR + INT - T$

        b.   Government's net income = taxes - transfers - interest payments = $T - TR - INT$

        c.   Private disposable income + government's net income = GDP + $NFP$ = GNP

III.  Saving and Wealth (Sec. 2.3)

  A.   Wealth

    1.   Household wealth = a household's assets minus its liabilities

    2.   National wealth = sum of all households', firms', and governments' wealth within the nation

    3.   Saving by individuals, businesses, and government determine wealth

  B.   Measures of aggregate saving

    1.   Saving = current income - current spending

    2.   Saving rate = saving / current income

    3.   Private saving = private disposable income - consumption

$$S_{pvt} = (Y + NFP - T + TR + INT) - C$$

    4.   Government saving = net government income - government purchases of goods and services

$$S_{govt} = (T - TR - INT) - G$$

        a.   Government saving = government budget surplus = government receipts - government outlays

        b.   Government receipts = tax revenue ($T$)

        c.   Government outlays = government purchases of goods and services ($G$) + transfers ($TR$) + interest payments on government debt ($INT$)

        d.   Government budget deficit = $-S_{govt}$

        e.   Despite Statistics Canada's change in methods that explicitly recognize government investment, the text simplifies matters by counting government investment as government purchases, not investment. This avoids complications when the concepts are introduced and can be modified for further analysis later.

    5.   National saving

        a.   National saving = private saving + government saving

        b.   $S = S_{pvt} + S_{govt}$

$$= [Y + NFP - T + TR + INT - C] + [T - TR - INT - G]$$
$$= Y + NFP - C - G = \text{GNP} - C - G$$

    C.  The uses of private saving
       1.  $S = I + (NX + NFP) = I + CA$
          Derived from $S = Y + NFP - C - G$ and $Y = C + I + G + NX$
          $CA = NX + NFP$ = current account balance
       2.  $S_{pvt} = I + (-S_{govt}) + CA$   {using $S = S_{pvt} + S_{govt}$}
          The uses-of-saving identity—saving is used in three ways:
         a.  investment ($I$)
         b.  government budget deficit ($-S_{govt}$)
         c.  current account balance ($CA$)
       3.  Text Fig. 2.1 illustrates the uses-of-saving identity for Canada, plotting private saving, investment, the government deficit, and the current account balance for Canada from 1926 to 2000
    D.  Relating saving and wealth
       1.  Stocks and flows
         a.  Flow variables: measured per unit of time (GDP, income, saving, investment)
         b.  Stock variables: measured at a point in time (quantity of money, value of houses, capital stock)
         c.  Flow variables often equal rates of change of stock variables
       2.  Wealth and saving as stock and flow (wealth is a stock, saving is a flow)
       3.  National wealth
         a.  Country's domestic physical assets (capital goods and land)
         b.  Country's net foreign assets = foreign assets (foreign stocks, bonds, and capital goods owned by domestic residents) minus foreign liabilities (domestic stocks, bonds, and capital goods owned by foreigners)
         c.  Changes in national wealth
           (1)  Change in value of existing assets and liabilities (change in price of financial assets, or depreciation of capital goods)
           (2)  National saving ($S = I + CA$) raises wealth
         d.  Comparison of Canadian saving and investment with other countries
           (1)  Canadian saving rates are close to the averages for industrialized countries; Japan is a high-saving country
           (2)  Canadian investment exceeds Canadian saving, so we have a negative current-account balance

IV.  Real GDP, Price Indexes, and Inflation (Sec. 2.4)
    A.  Real GDP
       1.  Nominal variables (in dollar terms)
       2.  Problem: Do changes in nominal values reflect changes in prices or quantities?
       3.  Real variables: adjust for price changes; reflect only quantity changes
       4.  Example of computers and bicycles
       5.  Nominal GDP is the dollar value of an economy's final output measured at current market prices
       6.  Real GDP is an estimate of the value of an economy's final output, adjusting for changes in the overall price level
    B.  Price Indexes
       1.  A price index measures the average level of prices for some specified set of goods and services, relative to the prices in a specified base year
       2.  GDP deflator = nominal GDP / real GDP
       3.  Note that base year $P = 1$ or $P = 100$
       4.  Consumer Price Index (CPI)
         a.  Monthly index of consumer prices
         b.  Based on basket of goods in base year
         c.  Need for base year to be revised frequently

      5.   Box 2.2 on the computer revolution and chain-weighted GDP
         a.   Choice of base year matters for GDP when prices and quantities of a good, such as computers, are changing rapidly
         b.   Statistics Canada compromised by developing chain-weighted GDP
         c.   Now, however, components of real GDP don't add up to real GDP, but discrepancy is usually small

C.   Inflation
      1.   Calculate inflation rate: $\pi_{t+1} = (P_{t+1} - P_t)/P_t = \Delta P_{t+1}/P_t$
      2.   Text Fig. 2.2 shows the Canadian inflation rate for 1951–2000 for the GDP deflator
      3.   The CPI may overstate increases in the cost of living
         a.   In the United States, a government commission reported that the CPI was biased upwards by as much as one to two percentage points per year
         b.   One problem is that adjusting the price measures for changes in the quality of goods is very difficult
         c.   Another problem is that price indexes with fixed sets of goods don't reflect the substitution by consumers that goes on when one good becomes relatively cheaper than another; this problem is known as substitution bias
      4.   If inflation is overstated, then real incomes are higher than we thought and we've overindexed payments like Old Age Security

V   Interest rates (Sec. 2.5)
A.   Real vs. nominal interest rates
      1.   Real interest rate: real return to an asset
      2.   Nominal interest rate: nominal return to an asset
      3.   Real interest rate $= i - \pi$
         Text Fig. 2.3 plots nominal and real interest rates for Canada from 1951 to 2001
B.   The expected real interest rate
      1.   $r = i - \pi^e$
      2.   If $\pi = \pi^e$, real interest rate = expected real interest rate

## MULTIPLE-CHOICE QUESTIONS

1.  The *value added* of a producer is the
    a.   total amount for which all its products sell minus its change in inventories.
    b.   value of its total sales once externalities are accounted for.
    c.   value of its output minus the value of the inputs it purchases from other producers.
    d.   quality-adjusted amount of its total sales less any commissions paid.

2.  The product approach to calculating GDP
    a.   adds together the market values of final goods and services produced by domestic and foreign-owned factors of production within the nation in some time period.
    b.   includes the market value of goods and services produced by households for their own consumption but excludes the value of the underground economy.
    c.   is superior to the income approach because, unlike the income approach, it gives us the real value of output.
    d.   adds together the market values of final goods, intermediate goods, and goods added to inventories.

3.  The A company collects bushels of wild berries, which it sells for $2 million to the B company to be made into jam. The B company's wild berry jam is sold for a total of $6 million. What is the value added of company B?
    a.   $2 million
    b.   $4 million
    c.   $6 million
    d.   $8 million

4.  The fundamental identity of national income accounting tells us that
    a.   total production = total income = total expenditure.
    b.   total production = total income - total expenditure.
    c.   total production = total income + total expenditure.
    d.   total production < total income + total expenditure.

5.  One problem with using market values to measure GDP is that
    a.   you cannot compare completely heterogeneous goods by using their dollar values.
    b.   some useful goods and services are not sold in markets.
    c.   prices for some goods change every year.
    d.   market values of exported goods are usually priced in foreign currencies.

6.  Unlike final goods and services, intermediate goods and services
    a.   are purchased by businesses.
    b.   are purchased by government.
    c.   are not exported.
    d.   are completely used up in the current time period.

7.  Underground activities in the economy are
    a.   excluded from measurements of the GDP because they are not beneficial to the nation.
    b.   excluded from measurements of GDP because there is no way of measuring them.
    c.   included in GDP if legal and excluded from GDP if illegal.
    d.   estimated and included in measurements of GDP.

8. Capital goods are
   a. not counted in GDP as final goods.
   b. not used to produce other goods.
   c. used up in the same period that they are produced.
   d. goods used to produce other goods.

9. Inventories are
   a. included in the measurement of capital goods.
   b. included in the measurement of intermediate goods.
   c. fully included in annual measurements of GDP.
   d. included in measurements of GDP only if they have changed from the preceding year.

10. Suppose Toyota built a new automobile plant in Mexico using Japanese management practices, Canadian capital, and Mexican labour. Which of the following statements would be true?
    a. The portion of output contributed by Canadian capital would be included in Canadian GDP.
    b. The portion of output contributed by Japanese management would be included in both Japanese GNP and GDP.
    c. The portion of output contributed by Japanese management would be included in neither Japanese GNP nor GDP.
    d. The portion of output contributed by Mexican labour would be included in both Mexican GNP and GDP.

11. If gross national product (GNP) is $500 billion, net factor payments (NFP) are $50 billion, and net exports (NX) are $75 billion, then gross domestic product (GDP) is
    a. $375 billion.
    b. $450 billion.
    c. $550 billion.
    d. $625 billion.

12. In using the expenditure approach to GNP, consumption includes
    a. all final and intermediate goods consumed by domestic households and firms.
    b. all final and intermediate goods consumed by domestic households produced at home, but not those produced abroad.
    c. all final goods consumed by domestic households produced at home, but not those produced abroad.
    d. all final goods consumed by domestic households produced at home and abroad.

13. Business fixed investment includes purchases of
    a. capital equipment and structures.
    b. land and energy.
    c. long-term bonds.
    d. inventories.

14 Government purchases
    a. account for about one fifth of Canadian GDP.
    b. are larger than private sector purchases in the post-World-War-II Canadian economy.
    c. do not include purchases of foreign goods.
    d. are less than government outlays.

15. National income is equal to
    a.    GNP minus depreciation.
    b.    GNP minus depreciation and indirect business taxes.
    c.    net national product minus depreciation and indirect business taxes.
    d.    net national product minus indirect business taxes and employer contributions to Old Age Security.

16. Monica grows coconuts and catches fish.  Last year she harvested 1500 coconuts and 600 fish. She values one fish as worth three coconuts. She gave Rachel 300 coconuts and 100 fish for helping her to harvest coconuts and catch fish, all of which were consumed by Rachel. Monica set aside 200 fish to help with next year's harvest. In terms of fish, consumption would equal
    a.    700 fish.
    b.    900 fish.
    c.    1100 fish.
    d.    2700 fish.

17. Private saving is defined as
    a.    private disposable income minus consumption.
    b.    net national product minus consumption.
    c.    private disposable income minus consumption plus interest.
    d.    private disposable income minus consumption plus interest plus transfer payments.

18. Which of the following equations describes a government budget deficit?
    a.    $T - TR - INT < G$
    b.    $T - TR - INT > G$
    c.    $T + TR + INT < G$
    d.    $T + TR + INT > G$

19. Assume that the government of Tantallon, Nova Scotia, has taxes of $500, government purchases of $350, transfer payments of $150, and interest expenses of $50.  The government budget would
    a.    show a surplus of $100.
    b.    show a surplus of $50.
    c.    be in balance with neither a surplus nor a deficit.
    d.    show a deficit of $50.

20. The government budget surplus equals
    a.    government purchases plus transfers.
    b.    government receipts minus outlays.
    c.    government outlays minus receipts.
    d.    government purchases minus transfers.

21. In 1992 private saving was $986.9 billion, investment was $796.5 billion, and the current account balance was -$55.1 billion. From the uses-of-saving identity, how much was government saving?
    a.    -$245.5 billion
    b.    -$135.3 billion
    c.    $135.3 billion
    d.    $245.5 billion

22. Which of the following equals national saving (S)?
    a.  $(Y + NFP - T + TR) - C$
    b.  $Y + NFP - (C + G)$
    c.  $T - (G + TR + INT)$
    d.  $Y - (C + I + G + NX)$

23. The uses-of-saving identity shows that net foreign investment is financed by
    a.  a budget deficit.
    b.  a trade deficit.
    c.  domestic investment.
    d.  an excess of national saving over investment.

24. Saving is a _____ variable, and wealth is a _____ variable.
    a.  stock, flow
    b.  stock, stock
    c.  flow, flow
    d.  flow, stock

25. National wealth is the value of
    a.  domestic and foreign physical and financial assets.
    b.  domestic physical and financial assets.
    c.  domestic physical assets plus net foreign physical and financial assets.
    d.  net foreign assets.

26. Use the following information to answer this question about the country of Polity:

| Good | Quantity (1999) | Price (1999) | Quantity (2000) | Price (2000) |
|------|----------|-------|----------|-------|
| Guns | 4000 | $4 | 4500 | $6 |
| Butter | 5000 | $3 | 5200 | $2 |

Using 1999 as the base year, what is the percent change in real output from 1999 to 2000?
    a.  8%
    b.  10%
    c.  12%
    d.  15%

27. Nominal GDP in 1970 was $1,015.5 billion, and in 1980 it was $2,732.0 billion. The GDP deflator is 42.0 for 1970 and 85.7 for 1980, where 1982 is the base year. Calculate the percent change in real GDP in the decade from 1970 to 1980. Round off to the nearest percentage point.
    a.  32%
    b.  104%
    c.  132%
    d.  169%

28. Nominal personal consumption expenditures in Canada were $1,748.1 billion in 1980 and rose to $3,742.6 billion in 1990. The implicit price deflator for personal consumption expenditures is 71.4 for 1980 and 114.7 for 1990, where 1987 is the base year. Calculate the percent change in real personal consumption expenditures (rounded to the nearest percentage point) in the decade.
    a.   33%
    b.   61%
    c.   114%
    d.   133%

29. Nominal GDP was $6,038.5 billion in 1992 and $5,722.9 billion in 1991, while the GDP deflator was 121.1 in 1992 and 117.7 in 1991. What was the growth rate of real GDP between 1991 and 1992?
    a.   5.5%
    b.   2.9%
    c.   2.6%
    d.   1.0%

30. The nominal interest rate equals the
    a. real interest rate minus the expected rate of inflation.
    b. real interest rate minus the rate of inflation.
    c. expected real interest rate plus the rate of inflation.
    d. expected real interest rate plus the expected rate of inflation.

## REVIEW QUESTIONS

1.   Identify and briefly describe the three approaches to measuring GDP.

2.   State the fundamental identity of national income accounting.

3.   Give an example of each of the following:
     (1) consumer durables
     (2) nondurable goods
     (3) services

4.   Approximately what share of GDP do personal consumption expenditures represent?

5.   Give an example of each of the following types of business fixed investment:
     (1) equipment
     (2) structures

6.   Briefly describe the role that inventory investment plays in the income-expenditure identity.

7.   Why are net exports added into the expenditure calculation of GDP?

8.   How are net exports, net factor payments from abroad, and the current account balance related?

9.   State the "uses-of-saving identity" and tell what it means.

10.  What is chain-weighted real GDP?  Why did the government switch to using chain-weighted indexes?

11.  Does the CPI provide an accurate estimate of the cost of living?  Discuss.

## NUMERICAL PROBLEMS

1.  Use the following data to calculate national output using the expenditure approach and the income approach for the economy, and show that GDP has the same value when calculated by either approach.

| | | | |
|---|---|---|---|
| consumption | $4480 billion | compensation to employees | $4200 billion |
| investment | 980 | proprietors' income | 420 |
| government purchases | 1400 | rental income of persons | 70 |
| net exports | 140 | corporate profits | 490 |
| | | net interest | 420 |
| | | indirect business taxes | 700 |
| | | consumption of fixed capital | 770 |
| | | factor income received from rest of world | 140 |
| | | payments of factor income to rest of world | 70 |

2.  Pete the Pizza Man produced $87 thousand worth of pizzas in the past year. He paid $39 thousand to employees, paid $11 thousand for vegetables and other ingredients, and paid $5 thousand in taxes. He began the year with ingredient inventories valued at $1 thousand, and ended the year with inventories valued at $2 thousand. What was Pete's (and his employees') total contribution to GDP this year?

3.  Use the following data to calculate private saving, government saving, and national saving.

| | |
|---|---|
| GDP | $7000 billion |
| net factor payments from abroad | - 70 |
| consumption | 4480 |
| government purchases | 1400 |
| interest payments on government debt | 210 |
| taxes | 2450 |
| transfers | 1050 |

4.  For 1992 the Canadian economy had the following nominal quantities (in billions of dollars) and price indexes (1987 = 100) for each category of expenditure:

| | Nominal Value | Price Index |
|---|---|---|
| Consumption | 4139.9 | 123.9 |
| Fixed investment | 789.1 | 108.6 |
| Government purchases | 1131.8 | 119.7 |
| Exports | 640.5 | 110.8 |
| Imports | 670.1 | 109.6 |
| Inventory investment | 7.3 | 112.3 |

a.  Calculate the real quantity for each category (to one decimal point).
b.  Calculate nominal and real GDP (you may assume the real components add up to real GDP).
c.  Find the implicit price deflator (1987 = 100).

5.  Nominal GDP in Canada was $8,759.9 billion in 1998 and $9.254.6 billion in 1999. The GDP deflator was 102.86 for 1998 and 104.37 for 1999.
    a.  What is the growth rate of nominal GDP between 1998 and 1999?
    b.  What is the inflation rate from 1998 to 1999?
    c.  What is the growth rate of real GDP from 1998 to 1999?

6.  The country of Old Jersey produces milk and butter, and it has published the following macroeconomic data, where quantities are in gallons and prices are dollars per gallon:

| Good | 1999 | | 2000 | |
|------|----------|-------|----------|-------|
|      | Quantity | Price | Quantity | Price |
| Milk | 500 | $2 | 900 | $3 |
| Butter | 2000 | $1 | 3000 | $2 |

What was the growth rate of real GDP between 1999 and 2000?  What was the inflation rate (using 1999 as the base year)?

7.  If the CPI was 125 one year ago and increased to 150 today, what would be the inflation rate over the past year?

8.  Calculate the real interest rate if the nominal interest rate is 8% and the inflation rate is 5%.

## ANALYTICAL QUESTIONS

1.  Would an increase in goods imported from a foreign subsidiary of a Canadian multinational firm, produced mostly with Canadian-owned capital and labour, increase GDP for Canada?  Briefly explain.

2.  Could GDP increase while GNP declined?  Briefly explain.

3.  If net exports were equal to 1 percent of a nation's GDP, is it fair to say that international trade is unimportant?  Briefly explain.

# ANSWERS TO MULTIPLE-CHOICE QUESTIONS

| Number | Answer | | Number | Answer | | Number | Answer |
|--------|--------|---|--------|--------|---|--------|--------|
| 1 | c | | 11 | b | | 21 | a |
| 2 | a | | 12 | d | | 22 | b |
| 3 | b | | 13 | a | | 23 | d |
| 4 | a | | 14 | d | | 24 | d |
| 5 | b | | 15 | b | | 25 | c |
| 6 | d | | 16 | b | | 26 | b |
| 7 | d | | 17 | a | | 27 | a |
| 8 | d | | 18 | a | | 28 | a |
| 9 | d | | 19 | d | | 29 | c |
| 10 | d | | 20 | b | | 30 | d |

# ANSWERS TO REVIEW QUESTIONS

1.  The three approaches to measuring GDP are called the product approach, the income approach, and the expenditure approach. The product approach adds together the market values of the goods and services produced within the borders of the nation's domestic economy during a specified time period (e.g., one-quarter of a year or one year). The income approach adds together the compensation to employees, interest income, rental income of persons, proprietors' income, and corporate profits earned from domestic production before taxes and depreciation, less net factor payments from abroad. The expenditure approach adds together consumption, investment, government purchases, and net exports to measure spending on all domestically produced goods and services.

2.  The fundamental identity of national income accounting is total production = total income = total expenditure.

3.  (1)  Consumer durables are long-lived consumer goods, such as family automobiles, refrigerators, lawn mowers, home computers, and household furniture.
    (2)  Nondurable goods are short-lived consumer goods, such as food, clothing, fuel, cosmetics, and prescription drugs.
    (3)  Services include such things as education, medical services, legal advice, accounting, travel, and restaurant and hotel services.

4.  Personal consumption expenditures currently represent approximately 60% of GDP for Canada.

5.  (1)  Equipment includes tools and machines, such as harvesters for farms, printing presses for newspaper businesses, tractors for construction companies, cash registers for retail stores, office equipment, furniture, company-owned vehicles, and so on.

    (2)  Structures include construction of facilities such as factory buildings, warehouses, retail store buildings, and so on.

6.  The income-expenditure identity states that $Y = C + I + G + NX$. This equation suggests that all the goods and services produced are sold. If all the goods and services produced are not sold during the year, inventory investment increases by the amount of the unsold goods. From an accounting viewpoint the unsold goods are recorded as being sold to the firms that produced them, and they are counted as investment.

7.    Net exports = exports - imports. Exports are added to the expenditure calculation of GDP because they represent foreign spending on goods and services produced in the domestic economy. Imports are subtracted because they were included in the figures for consumption, investment, or government purchases. Since GDP represents how much is produced by a country, we add exports to $C + I + G$ to represent goods produced domestically and sold to foreigners, and we subtract imports from $C + I + G$ since they represent goods produced abroad and purchased by domestic consumers, firms, or governments. So, total production equals $C + I + G + NX$.

8.    $NX + NFP = CA$.

9.    The following equation is the "uses-of-saving identity":   $S_{pvt} = I + (-S_{govt}) + CA$.  It means that private saving can be used for domestic investment, financing the government deficit, or investing abroad.

10.   Chain-weighting methods calculate the growth of real output by averaging growth rates of real GDP using both the prior year and the current year as the base year. Statistics Canada switched to a chain-weight index primarily because there's no clear "right" year to choose as the base year. Also, chain weighting avoids the problem of historical growth rates being revised when the base year changes, as had been the case before 1996.

11.   The CPI overstates increases in the cost of living because of changes in the quality of goods and services and because of substitution bias.

## ANSWERS TO NUMERICAL PROBLEMS

1.    In the expenditure approach, national output is $Y = C + I + G + NX$,  which totals $7000 billion. The income approach is calculated by adding all the payments received by domestic resource suppliers (the first seven numbers in the last column), then subtracting the $70 billion of net factor payments from abroad ($140 billion factor income received minus $70 billion payments to the rest of the world), which also totals $7000 billion.

2.    $87 thousand - $11 thousand paid for intermediate goods + $1 thousand change in inventories = $77 thousand.

3.    The values of these variables can be calculated by plugging the appropriate data values into the following equations (where $Y$ = GDP).

$S_{pvt} = (Y + NFP - T + TR + INT ) - C =$  $1260 billion.

$S_{govt} = (T - TR - INT) - G = -$ $210 billion.

$S = S_{pvt} + S_{govt} = Y + NFP - C - G =$  $1050 billion.

4.    a.    Real $C = 4139.9/1.239 = 3341.3$; real fixed $I = 789.1/1.086 = 726.6$; real $G = 1131.8/1.197 = 945.5$; real exports $= 640.5/1.108 = 578.1$; real imports $= 670.1/1.096 = 611.4$; real $II = 7.3/1.123 = 6.5$.

      b.    Add up the nominal quantities (but subtract imports) to get 6038.5. Add up the real quantities (but subtract imports) in part a to get 4986.6.

c.    The implicit deflator is nominal GDP/real GDP x 100 = 6038.5/4986.6 x 100 = 121.1.

5.    a.    9,254.6/8,759.9 x 100 = 5.6%

b.    [(104.37/102.86) - 1] x 100 = 1.5%

c.    real GDP (1998) = 8759.9/1.0286 = 8516.3
real GDP (1999) = 9254.6/1.0437 = 8867.1
growth rate = [(8867.1/8516.3) - 1] x 100% = 4.1%
Note that the growth rate of nominal GDP (5.6%) equals the inflation rate (1.5%) plus the growth rate of real GDP (4.1%).

6.    Real GDP (1999) = 1999 quantities at 1999 prices = (500 x $2) + (2000 x $1) = $3000
Real GDP (2000) = 2000 quantities at 1999 prices = (900 x $2) + (3000 x $1) = $4800
Growth rate of real GDP = [(4800/3000) - 1] x 100% = 60%
Nominal GDP (2000) = 2000 quantities at 2000 prices = (900 x $3) + (3000 x $2) = $8700
GDP deflator (2000) = (8700/4800) x 100 = 181.3
Inflation rate = [(181.3/100) - 1] x 100% = 81.3%

7.    If the CPI increased from 125 to 150, the inflation rate would be [(150 - 125)/125] x 100% = 20%.

8.    Real interest rate = nominal interest rate - inflation rate = 8% - 5% = 3%.

## ANSWERS TO ANALYTICAL QUESTIONS

1.    No.  Goods produced abroad, including goods produced with Canadian-owned factors of production, are not part of the GDP of Canada.

2.    Yes.  GDP = GNP - NFP, so GDP would increase if a decline in NFP exceeded the decline in GNP.

3.    Even though net exports represent just 5% of GDP, net exports equal exports minus imports.  A better measure of the importance of international trade would be to examine exports or imports separately. Exports and imports might each be a substantial fraction of GDP.  So international trade in goods and services could be an important component of the economy, even though net exports aren't large.

# CHAPTER 3: PRODUCTIVITY, OUTPUT, AND EMPLOYMENT

## INTRODUCTION

This chapter's main goal is to provide the background of a theoretical model of the economy that is developed throughout the textbook. The discussions of the labour market and production function developed in this chapter are the basic building blocks of everything that comes later. Section 3.1 begins the chapter by introducing the production function—the main determinant of output. Then, Section 3.2 discusses the demand for labour, showing how firms decide on how much labour to use based on the wage and the marginal product of labour. Section 3.3 then shows how people decide how much labour to supply. Demand and supply together determine equilibrium in the labour market, as Section 3.4 discusses. The section also shows how labour-market equilibrium then determines the economy's rate of full-employment output and what happens when there's a change in either the demand or supply of labour. Section 3.5 provides an introduction to unemployment—how it's measured, how long it lasts, and why it occurs.

This is a long and very important chapter. It's the first chapter in which the main analytic device used throughout the chapter appears—a diagram in which equilibrium is found where two curves cross. You'll find the same basic diagram that appears here for the labour market also appears in other chapters for other markets. So be sure you understand why the labour-demand and labour-supply curves have the slopes they do, what shifts them, and how equilibrium is determined. You'll see a similar pattern in many other places in the textbook.

If you have trouble understanding some of the math in the chapter, be sure to work many of the numerical problems in this study guide and in the textbook. The more you work with things like calculating output using a production function.

## CHAPTER OUTLINE

I. How Much Does the Economy Produce? The Production Function (Sec. 3.1)
   A. Factors of production
      1. Capital
      2. Labour
      3. Others (raw materials, land, energy)
      4. Productivity of factors depends on technology and management
   B. The production function
      1. $Y = AF(K,N)$
      2. Parameter $A$ is "total factor productivity"

Figure 3.1

C.   Application: The production function of the Canadian economy and Canadian productivity growth
   1.   Cobb-Douglas production function works well for Canadian economy:
$$Y = A\,K^{0.3}\,N^{0.7}$$
   2.   Data for Canadian economy—Table 3.1
   3.   Productivity growth calculated using production function
     a.   Productivity moves sharply from year to year
     b.   Productivity grew slowly in the 1980s

D.   The shape of the production function
   1.   Two main properties of production functions
     a.   Slopes upward: more of any input produces more output
     b.   Slope becomes flatter as input rises: diminishing marginal product as input increases
   2.   Graph production function ($Y$ vs. one input; hold other input and $A$ fixed)
     a.   Marginal product of capital, $MPK = \Delta Y/\Delta K$ (Fig. 3.1; Key Diagram 1; like text Fig. 3.2)
       (1)   Equal to slope of production function graph ($Y$ vs. $K$)
       (2)   $MPK$ always positive
       (3)   Diminishing marginal productivity of capital
     b.   Marginal product of labour, $MPN = \Delta Y/\Delta N$ (Fig. 3.2; like text Fig. 3.3)
       (1)   Equal to slope of production function graph ($Y$ vs. $N$)
       (2)   $MPN$ always positive
       (3)   Diminishing marginal productivity of labour

E.   Supply shocks
   1.   Supply shocks affect the amount of output that can be produced for a given amount of inputs
   2.   Shocks may be positive (increasing output) or negative (decreasing output)
   3.   Examples:  weather, inventions and innovations, government regulations, oil prices (for example, OPEC)
   4.   Supply shocks shift graph of production function
     (Fig. 3.3; like text Fig. 3.4)
     a.   Negative (adverse) shock: Usually slope of production function decreases at each level of input (for example, if shock causes parameter A to decline)
     b.   Positive shock: Usually slope of production function increases at each level of output (for example, if parameter A increases)

Figure 3.2

II.   The Demand for Labour (Sec. 3.2)
A.   How much labour do firms want to use?
   1.   Assumptions
     a.   Hold capital stock fixed—short-run analysis
     b.   Workers are all alike
     c.   Labour market is competitive
     d.   Firms maximize profits

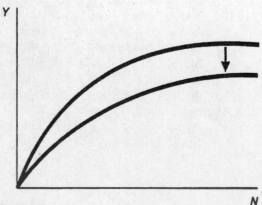

Figure 3.3

2.  Analysis at the margin: costs and benefits of
    hiring one extra worker (Fig. 3.4; like text
    Fig. 3.5)
    a.  If real wage ($w$) > marginal product of
        labour ($MPN$), the firm is paying the
        marginal worker more than the worker
        produces, so the firm should reduce the
        number of workers to increase profits
    b.  If $w < MPN$, the marginal worker
        produces more than he or she is being
        paid, so the firm should increase the
        number of workers to increase profits
    c.  Firms' profits are highest when $w =$
        $MPN$

Figure 3.4

B.  The marginal product of labour and labour
    demand
    1.  Example: The Clip Joint—setting the
        nominal wage equal to the marginal revenue
        product of labour ($MRPN = P \times MPN$)
    2.  $W = MRPN$ is the same condition as $w =$
        $MPN$, since $W = P \times w$ and $MRPN = P \times$
        $MPN$
    3.  A change in the wage
        a.  Begin at equilibrium where $W = MRPN$
        b.  A rise in the wage rate means $W >$
            $MRPN$, unless $N$ is reduced so the $MRPN$ rises
        c.  A decline in the wage rate means $W < MRPN$, unless $N$ rises so the $MRPN$ falls
C.  The marginal product of labour and the labour demand curve
    1.  Labour demand curve shows relationship
        between the real wage rate and the quantity of
        labour demanded
    2.  It is the same as the $MPN$ curve, since $w =$
        $MPN$ at equilibrium
    3.  So the labour demand curve is downward
        sloping; firms want to hire less labour, the
        higher the real wage
D.  Factors that shift the labour demand curve
    1.  Note: A change in the wage causes a
        movement along the labour demand curve,
        not a shift of the curve
    2.  Supply shocks: Beneficial supply shock raises
        $MPN$, so shifts labour demand curve to the
        right; opposite for adverse supply shock
    3.  Size of capital stock. Higher capital stock
        raises $MPN$, so shifts labour demand curve to
        the right; opposite for lower capital stock
E.  Aggregate labour demand (Fig. 3.5)
    1.  Aggregate labour demand is the sum of all
        firms' labour demand

Figure 3.5

       2.   Same factors (supply shocks, size of capital stock) that shift firms' labour demand cause shifts in aggregate labour demand

III.  The Supply of Labour (Sec. 3.3)

    A.   Supply of labour is determined by individuals

       1.   Aggregate supply of labour is sum of individuals' labour supply

       2.   Labour supply of individuals depends on labour-leisure choice

    B.   The income-leisure trade-off

       1.   Utility depends on consumption and leisure

       2.   Need to compare costs and benefits of working another day

          a.   Costs: Loss of leisure time

          b.   Benefits: More consumption, since income is higher

       3.   If benefits of working another day exceed costs, work another day

       4.   Keep working additional days until benefits equal costs

    C.   Real wages and labour supply

       1.   An increase in the real wage has offsetting income and substitution effects

          a.   Substitution effect of a higher real wage: Higher real wage encourages work, since the reward for working is higher

          b.   Income effect of a higher real wage: Higher real wage increases income for the same amount of work time, and with higher income, the person can afford more leisure, so will supply less labour

       2.   A pure substitution effect: a one-day rise in the real wage

          A temporary real wage increase has just a pure substitution effect, since the effect on wealth is negligible

       3.   A pure income effect: winning the lottery

          a.   Winning the lottery doesn't have a substitution effect, because it doesn't affect the reward for working

          b.   But winning the lottery makes a person wealthier, so a person will both consume more goods and take more leisure; this is a pure income effect

       4.   The substitution effect and the income effect together: a long-term increase in the real wage

          a.   The reward to working is greater: a substitution effect toward more work

          b.   But with a higher wage, a person doesn't need to work as much: an income effect toward less work

          c.   The longer the high wage is expected to last, the stronger the income effect; thus labour supply will increase by less or decrease by more than for a temporary reduction in the real wage

       5.   Empirical evidence on real wages and labour supply

          a.   Overall result: Labour supply increases with a temporary rise in the real wage

          b.   Labour supply falls with a permanent increase in the real wage

    D.   Application: weekly hours of work and the wealth of nations

       1.   In 1900 the average workweek in manufacturing was 55 hours; it's now about 38

       2.   The main reason for the decline is a permanent increase in the real wage, due to technological innovation and increased productivity

       3.   Although the workweek has been about 40 hours since the end of World War II, lifetime labour supply has declined as workers now retire earlier and take more vacation time

       4.   Looking across countries, those with higher real GDP per capita tend to have lower average workweeks than those with lower real GDP per capita

       5.   These results are all consistent with the income effect dominating the substitution effect for a permanent increase in the real wage

    E.   The labour supply curve (Fig. 3.6); like text Fig. 3.7

       1.   Increase in the current real wage should raise quantity of labour supplied

        2. Labour supply curve relates quantity of labour supplied to real wage

        3. Labour supply curve slopes upward because higher wage encourages people to work more

  F. Factors that shift the labour supply curve

        1. Wealth: Higher wealth reduces labour supply (shifts labour supply curve to the left)

        2. Expected future real wage: Higher expected future real wage is like an increase in wealth, so reduces labour supply (shifts labour supply curve to the left)

  G. Aggregate labour supply

        1. Aggregate labour supply rises when current real wage rises

          a. Some people work more hours

          b. Other people enter labour force

          c. Result: Aggregate labour supply curve slopes upward

Figure 3.6

        2. Factors increasing labour supply

          a. Decrease in wealth

          b. Decrease in expected future real wage

          c. Increase in working-age population (higher birth rate, immigration)

          d. Increase in labour force participation (increased female labour participation, elimination of mandatory retirement)

IV. Labour Market Equilibrium (Sec. 3.4)

  A. Equilibrium: Labour supply equals labour demand (Fig. 3.7; Key Diagram 2; like text Fig. 3.11)

        1. Classical model of the labour market—real wage adjusts quickly

        2. Determines full-employment level of employment $\bar{N}$ and market-clearing real wage $\bar{w}$

        3. Factors that shift labour supply or labour demand affect $\bar{N}$ and $\bar{w}$

        4. Problem with classical model: can't study unemployment

  B. Full-employment output

        1. $\bar{Y} = AF(K, \bar{N})$

        2. $\bar{Y}$ affected by changes in $\bar{N}$ or production function (example: supply shock)

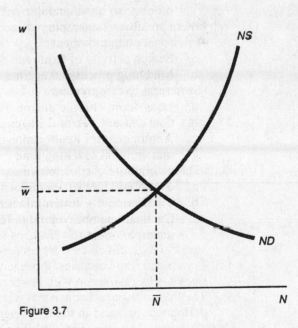

Figure 3.7

  C. Application: output, employment, and the real wage during oil price shocks

        1. Sharp oil price increases in 1973-74, 1979-80, 1990

        2. Adverse supply shock—lowers labour demand, employment, the real wage, and the full-employment level of output

        3. All three cases: Canadian economy entered recessions

    D.   Application: Technical Change And Wage Inequality
        1.   Two important features of Canadian real wages since 1970
            a.   Slowdown in growth of real wages
            b.   Increased wage inequality
        2.   Slowdown in productivity growth combined with increased labour force participation has kept real wages from rising as much as they did before 1970
        3.   Skill-biased technical change (such as computerization) has increased real wages of highly educated workers, but reduced real wages of unskilled workers (shown graphically)

V.   Unemployment (Sec. 3.5)
    A.   Measuring unemployment
        1.   Categories:  employed, unemployed, not in the labour force
        2.   Labour Force = Employed + Unemployed
        3.   Unemployment Rate = Unemployed / Labour Force
        4.   Participation Rate = Labour Force / Adult Population
        5.   Employment Ratio = Employed / Adult Population
    B.   Changes in employment status
        1.   Flows between categories
    C.   How long are people unemployed?
        1.   Most unemployment spells are of short duration
            a.   Unemployment spell = period of time an individual is continuously unemployed
            b.   Duration = length of unemployment spell
        2.   Most unemployed people on a given date are experiencing unemployment spells of long duration
        3.   Reconciling 1 and 2—numerical example:
            a.   Labour force = 100; on the first day of every month, two workers become unemployed for one month each; on the first day of every year, four workers become unemployed for one year each
            b.   Result:  28 spells of unemployment during year; 24 short (one month), four long (one year); so most spells are short
            c.   At any date, unemployment = six; four have long spells (one year), two have short spells (one month); so most unemployed people on a given date have long spells
    D.   Why there are always unemployed people
        1.   Frictional unemployment
            a.   Search activity of firms and workers due to heterogeneity
            b.   Matching process takes time
        2.   Structural unemployment
            a.   Long-term, chronic unemployment
            b.   One cause: Lack of skills prevents some workers from finding long-term employment
            c.   Another cause: Reallocation of workers out of shrinking industries or depressed regions; matching takes a long time
        3.   The natural rate of unemployment
            a.   $\bar{u}$ = natural rate of unemployment; when output and employment are at full-employment levels
            b.   $\bar{u}$ = frictional + structural unemployment
            c.   Cyclical unemployment: difference between actual unemployment rate and natural rate of unemployment ($\bar{u}$ - $\bar{u}$)

4.  In touch with the macroeconomy: labour market data
    a.  Statistics Canada
        (1)  Labour Force Information
        (2)  Employment, Earnings and Hours

## MULTIPLE-CHOICE QUESTIONS

1.   Equilibrium in the labour market determines
     a.   inflation and employment.
     b.   inflation and the real wage.
     c.   the real wage and employment.
     d.   productivity and employment.

2.   Suppose the economy's production function is $Y = A K^{0.3} N^{0.7}$. If $K = 1000$ and $N = 50$, then $Y = 2000$.
     What is $Y$ if $K = 2000$ and $N = 100$?
     a.   4000
     b.   3500
     c.   3400
     d.   3000

3.   The factors of production include
     a.   capital, labour, energy, and materials.
     b.   households, firms, and government.
     c.   supply factors and demand factors.
     d.   wages, interest, rents, and profits.

4.   The production function shows the effect on
     a.   labour employment when output is increased.
     b.   labour employment when capital is increased.
     c.   goods production when production of services declines.
     d.   output when labour is increased.

5.   An increase in total factor productivity will
     a.   increase the unemployment rate.
     b.   increase the full-employment level of output.
     c.   lower the rate of return to capital.
     d.   shift the production function down.

6.   In the production function $Y = AF(K,N)$, $A$ is
     a.   labour productivity.
     b.   total factor productivity.
     c.   capital productivity.
     d.   the marginal productivity of capital.

7.   In a graph of the production function relating output to capital, it is *not* true that
     a.   labour supply increases as capital increases.
     b.   the marginal product of capital can be measured as the slope of the production function.
     c.   the marginal product of capital falls as the capital stock increases.
     d.   the shape of the production function reflects diminishing marginal productivity.

8. Because of diminishing marginal productivity
   a.  the labour supply curve is not vertical.
   b.  nominal wages are sticky in a downward direction.
   c.  the labour demand curve is negatively sloped.
   d.  households save only a small share of their income.

9. The marginal product of labour
   a.  equals the output produced per unit of labour employed.
   b.  decreases as more capital is added to the production process.
   c.  depends on the product price.
   d.  declines as more labour is added to the production process.

10. In the diagram of the production function, a beneficial supply shock is shown by
    a.  an upward shift in the production function.
    b.  a movement up along the production function.
    c.  a downward shift in the production function.
    d.  an increase in the convexity of the curve.

11. The real wage
    a.  is the nominal wage divided by the price level.
    b.  automatically increases with the cost of living.
    c.  is the price level divided by the nominal wage.
    d.  is the nominal wage multiplied by the price level.

12. Which of the following statements is true?
    a.  Changes in the total capital stock of the economy and in the amount of labour that firms employ occur quickly.
    b.  Changes in the total capital stock of the economy and in the amount of labour that firms employ occur slowly.
    c.  Changes in the total capital stock of the economy occur slowly, while changes in the amount of labour that firms employ occur quickly.
    d.  Changes in the total capital stock of the economy occur quickly, while changes in the amount of labour that firms employ occur slowly.

13. A favourable supply shock would
    a.  shift the production function up and decrease marginal products at every level of employment.
    b.  shift the production function down and decrease marginal products at every level of employment.
    c.  shift the production function down and increase marginal products at every level of employment.
    d.  shift the production function up and increase marginal products at every level of employment.

14. For the economy of Lower Volta, the *MPN* is given by
    $$MPN = 400 - 0.2N$$
    where $N$ is aggregate employment. The aggregate quantity of labour supplied is $500 + 10(1 - t)w$ where $t$ is the income tax rate and $w$ is the real wage. Assume that the income tax rate is 50%. What is the before-tax real wage?
    a.  150
    b.  200
    c.  250
    d.  1250

15. Suppose the marginal product of labour for unskilled labour is given by
    $$MPN = 200 - 0.5N$$
    The supply of unskilled labour is given by $100 + 4w$. The government imposes a minimum wage of 60.
    How much unemployment will this create among unskilled labour?
    a.    0
    b.    60
    c.    80
    d.    100

16. The Grungo Company has the following production function:

| Number of Workers | Number of Grungos Produced |
|---|---|
| 0 | 0 |
| 1 | 10 |
| 2 | 19 |
| 3 | 26 |
| 4 | 31 |
| 5 | 34 |

    If the real wage rate is 6, how many workers will the company hire?
    a.    0
    b.    1
    c.    3
    d.    5

17. A favourable supply shock, such as a fall in the price of oil, would
    a.    cause firms to demand less labour at any given real wage.
    b.    cause the labour demand curve to shift to the left.
    c.    increase the marginal product of labour.
    d.    decrease the real wage.

18. Suppose the banking industry were to fail, leaving the federal government (through its deposit guarantee
    programs) to pay for trillions of dollars in losses; they do so by imposing a tax of 50% on all
    individuals' wealth. What happens to current employment and the real wage rate?
    a.    Both employment and the real wage rate would increase.
    b.    Both employment and the real wage rate would decrease.
    c.    Employment would increase and the real wage would decrease.
    d.    Employment would decrease and the real wage would increase.

19. A beneficial supply shock increases labour demand. What happens to current employment and the real
    wage rate?
    a.    Both employment and the real wage rate would increase.
    b.    Both employment and the real wage rate would decrease.
    c.    Employment would increase and the real wage would decrease.
    d.    Employment would decrease and the real wage  would increase.

20. One's supply of labour depends primarily on
    a.   one's marginal productivity.
    b.   the quantity of capital one can work with.
    c.   the amount of human capital one can supply on the job.
    d.   the trade-off between labour income and leisure.

21. The labour force participation rate is the percentage of the adult population that is
    a.   employed.
    b.   willing to work but unable to find jobs.
    c.   unemployed.
    d.   working or actively looking for work.

22. Discouraged workers are discouraged because
    a.   their employers continue to underpay them.
    b.   they are working part-time, but they want full-time work.
    c.   they don't have jobs and are pessimistic about their chances of finding a suitable job.
    d.   their employers are too demanding.

23. In Canada, the duration of most unemployment spells is
    a.   less than two weeks.
    b.   about two months or less.
    c.   approximately one year.
    d.   two or three years.

24. The type of unemployment for which the net economic costs are most likely to be small is
    a.   structural unemployment.
    b.   frictional unemployment.
    c.   chronic unemployment.
    d.   cyclical unemployment.

25. Most of the chronically unemployed workers in the Canadian economy are unemployed because
    a.   they are too old or too young to work.
    b.   they are too sick or too disabled to work.
    c.   they do not want to work; they would rather live on welfare.
    d.   they do not have the job skills and personal attributes that employers demand.

26. The kind of unemployment created by technological progress and by changes in competition is called
    a.   progressive unemployment.
    b.   competitive unemployment.
    c.   frictional unemployment.
    d.   structural unemployment.

27. What is the employment ratio (in percentage terms) if there are 170 million people employed, 25 million people unemployed, and 35 million not in the labour force?
    a.   74%
    b.   83%
    c.   87%
    d.   100%

28. Cyclical unemployment is caused by
    a.  people entering the labour force to search for jobs.
    b.  technological progress, which causes some industries to expand employment and others to reduce employment.
    c.  reducing international trade barriers, which causes some industries to expand employment and others to reduce employment.
    d.  business cycle fluctuations.

## REVIEW QUESTIONS

1.  Why does the labour demand curve slope downward?

2.  Identify two variables that shift the labour demand curve and state whether labour demand is positively related or negatively related to each of these variables.

3.  Why does the labour supply curve slope upward?

4.  Identify four variables that shift the labour supply curve and state whether labour supply is positively related or negatively related to each of these variables.

5.  What are structural unemployment and frictional unemployment, and how do they differ?  Does the duration of a typical unemployment spell depend on the type of unemployment?  How does the natural rate of unemployment relate to structural and frictional unemployment?

## NUMERICAL PROBLEMS

1.  Using $Y = A K^{0.5} N^{0.5}$ as the production function for the national economy, calculate total factor productivity ($A$), where:
    (a)  $Y = \$4878$ billion, $K = \$4773$ billion, and $N = 117.9$ million workers
    (b)  $Y = \$4821$ billion, $K = \$4824$ billion, and $N = 116.9$ million workers.

2.  Suppose the production function is $Y = A K^{0.3} N^{0.7}$. Suppose in 1980, $K = 1000$, $N = 100$, and $A = 1$. In 1990, capital and labour have doubled (so $K = 2000$ and $N = 200$), while $A$ has remained constant.
    a.   By what percentage did output grow from 1980 to 1990?
    b.   If total factor productivity had risen 10 percent instead of remaining constant, and capital and labour doubled, by what percentage would output have grown from 1980 to 1990?

3.  In August 2001, Canada had a labour force of 16,200,000, employment of 15,100,000, and there were 8,400,000 people not in the labour force (all numbers rounded to the nearest 1000).
    a.   Calculate the unemployment rate.
    b.   Calculate the participation rate.
    c.   Calculate the employment ratio.

## ANALYTICAL QUESTIONS

1.  What are the real effects on the labour market of a temporary beneficial supply shock that arises because of an increase in productivity?

2.  Would an increase in the capital stock create an increase in the level of employment?  Why?

## ANSWERS TO MULTIPLE-CHOICE QUESTIONS

| Number | Answer | Number | Answer | Number | Answer |
|--------|--------|--------|--------|--------|--------|
| 1 | c | 11 | a | 21 | d |
| 2 | a | 12 | c | 22 | c |
| 3 | a | 13 | d | 23 | b |
| 4 | d | 14 | a | 24 | b |
| 5 | b | 15 | b | 25 | d |
| 6 | b | 16 | c | 26 | d |
| 7 | a | 17 | c | 27 | a |
| 8 | c | 18 | c | 28 | d |
| 9 | d | 19 | a | | |
| 10 | a | 20 | d | | |

## ANSWERS TO REVIEW QUESTIONS

1.   The labour demand curve is the same as the marginal product of labour curve, since firms are willing to employ the amount of labour needed to equate the real wage and the marginal product of labour.  The marginal product of labour declines as labour increases because of diminishing returns.

2.   Two variables that shift labour demand are total factor productivity and the capital stock.

(1)   Labour demand is positively related to total factor productivity.  A beneficial productivity shock will shift the labour demand curve to the right because it increases the marginal product of labour.  An adverse productivity shock will decrease labour demand, shifting the curve to the left.

(2)   Labour demand is positively related to the capital stock.  Increasing the capital stock will increase the demand for labour because it raises the marginal product of labour.  A decline in the level of the capital stock will decrease labour demand, shifting the labour demand curve to the left.

3.   The labour supply curve is positively sloped, indicating that more labour time will be supplied at a higher real wage.  Along a given labour supply curve, an increase in the real wage increases the reward to working, which causes workers to increase the amount of labour time they are willing to work; as the real wage increases, workers substitute away from leisure and toward work.

4.   Variables that shift the labour supply curve include wealth, the expected future real wage, the size of the working-age population, and the labour force participation rate.
(1)   Labour supply is negatively related to wealth.  People who are wealthy don't want to work as much, so an increase in workers' wealth will reduce labour supply, shifting the labour supply curve to the left.
(2)   Labour supply is negatively related to workers' expected future real wage.  An increase in the expected future real wage will reduce labour supply because people will want to work less today and work more in the future, so the labour supply curve shifts to the left.
(3)   Labour supply is positively related to the working-age population.  An increase in the number of working-age people in the economy will increase labour supply, shifting the labour supply curve to the right.
(4)   Labour supply is positively related to the participation rate.  An increase in the participation rate will increase labour supply, shifting the labour supply curve to the right.

5.  Structural unemployment is caused by changes in the economy that create a mismatch in the job skills
    of unemployed workers and those skills required by firms looking for workers to fill vacancies.
    Examples of structural changes that create structural unemployment include technological advances and
    changes in foreign competition.  Structurally unemployed labour must often relocate or acquire further
    education or technical training to gain employment.

    Frictional unemployment is created by people entering the labour force to search for a job and by people
    quitting one job to search for a better one.  Unemployment spells for the frictionally unemployed are
    usually of short duration, since these people have the job skills and personal attributes needed to fill
    available vacancies.

    The duration of a typical unemployment spell for frictional unemployment is relatively short; the
    duration of a typical unemployment spell for structural unemployment is relatively long.

    The natural rate of unemployment equals the amount of frictional unemployment plus structural
    unemployment as a fraction of the labour force.

## ANSWERS TO NUMERICAL PROBLEMS

1.  Given that $Y = A K^{0.5} N^{0.5}$, then $A = Y / K^{0.5} N^{0.5}$.

    (a)  $A = 4878/[(4773)^{0.5}(117.9)^{0.5}] = 4878/[(69.09)(10.86)] = 6.50$.

    (b)  $A = 4821/[(4824)^{0.5}(116.9)^{0.5}] = 4821/[69.46)(10.81)] = 6.42$.

2.  a.  Output doubles (increases 100%), since the inputs doubled and the production function has
        constant returns to scale.  You can calculate output in 1980 equal to 199.5 and output in 1990 is
        399.
    b.  Since output doubles in the absence of a change in $A$, the 10% increase in $A$ increases output by a
        total of 120%.  Calculating output gives 439, which is 120% higher than the output of 199.5 in
        1980.

3.  a.  Unemployment = labour force - employment =  16, 200,000 – 15,100,000 = 1,100,000, so the
        unemployment rate is 1,100,000/16,200 000 = 6.8%.
    b.  The participation rate is the fraction of the adult population in the labour force. The adult
        population is the labour force + the number not in the labour force = 16,2000,000 + 8,400,000 =
        24,600,000.  The participation rate is then 16,200,000/24,600,000 = 65.9%.
    c.  The employment ratio is the employed fraction of the adult population, which is 15,100,000 /
        24,600,000 = 61.4%

## ANSWERS TO ANALYTICAL QUESTIONS

1.  A temporary beneficial supply (productivity) shock causes the slope of the production function (the marginal product of labour) to increase at every level of employment, as Figure 3.8 shows. Since the labour demand curve is the marginal product of labour schedule, the labour demand curve also shifts upward, as shown in Figure 3.9. As a result, the real wage rises and employment increases.

2.  An increase in the capital stock increases the slope of the production function at every level of employment, as shown in Figure 3.8. This increases the marginal product of labour and causes the labour demand curve to shift to the right, as shown in Figure 3.9. As a result, the equilibrium level of employment increases, as does the real wage.

Figure 3.8

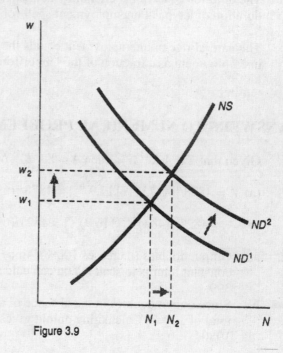

Figure 3.9

# CHAPTER 4: CONSUMPTION, SAVING, AND INVESTMENT

## INTRODUCTION

In this chapter, we examine equilibrium in the goods market by looking carefully at the two most important sectors of the economy—consumption and investment. Section 4.1 begins by giving you a detailed description of how people choose to spend and save. It also discusses how the government's budget deficit plays a major role in affecting national saving. Next, Section 4.2 talks about investment, showing how firms decide how much to invest, depending on the user cost of capital and the interest rate. Saving and investment together determine equilibrium in the goods market, as Section 4.3 discusses. Appendix 4.A presents an interesting two-period economic model that's worth your time to learn—it will really help you understand the important economic theory presented in the chapter.

In this chapter, there are two key analytical ideas that you need to understand. The first is how firms decide on their capital stock, as shown in Figure 4.3 in the textbook (reproduced below as Figure 4.1 in this study guide). It's important for you to understand why each curve in the figure looks the way it does, what shifts each curve, and why equilibrium occurs where it does. The other important idea is that of equilibrium in the goods market, shown in textbook Figure 4.7 and textbook Key Diagram 3 (reproduced below as Figure 4.2 in this study guide). You need to understand how saving and investment depend on the real interest rate and what other factors affect each curve. This chapter also introduces the Ricardian equivalence proposition; be sure that you understand what it means, because you'll see it again later in the textbook.

## CHAPTER OUTLINE

I.  Consumption and Saving (Sec. 4.1)
    A.  The importance of consumption and saving
        1.  Desired consumption: consumption amount desired by households
        2.  Desired national saving: level of national saving when consumption is at its desired level
            $S^d = Y - C^d - G$  (4.1)
    B.  The consumption and saving decision of an individual
        1.  A person can consume less than current income (saving is positive)
        2.  A person can consume more than current income (saving is negative)
        3.  Trade-off between current consumption and future consumption
            a.  The price of 1 unit of current consumption is $1 + r$ units of future consumption, where $r$ is the real interest rate
            b.  Consumption-smoothing motive: the desire to have a relatively even pattern of consumption over time
    C.  Effect of changes in current income
        1.  Increase in current income: both consumption and saving increase (vice versa for decrease in current income)
        2.  Marginal propensity to consume ($MPC$) = fraction of additional current income consumed in current period; between 0 and 1
        3.  Aggregate level: When current income ($Y$) rises, $C^d$ rises, but not by as much as $Y$, so $S^d$ rises
    D.      Effect of changes in expected future income
        1.  Higher expected future income leads to more consumption today, so saving falls

2. Application: consumer sentiment and the 1990–91 recession; sharp contraction in consumer sentiment in 1990 led to fall in consumer spending

E. Effect of changes in wealth
   1. Increase in wealth raises current consumption, so lowers current saving
   2. Application: the 1987 stock market crash and consumer spending
      a. When the stock market crashed in 1987, wealth declined by about $100 billion
      b. Consumption fell somewhat less than might be expected, and it wasn't enough to cause a recession
      c. There was a temporary decline in confidence about the future, but it was quickly reversed
      d. The small response may have been because there had been a large run-up in stock prices between January 1987 and August 1987, so the crash mostly erased this run-up
      e. In the 1990s, the boom in the stock market led to increased consumption, but much (4/5) of the increase in consumption was because of other factors

F. Effect of changes in real interest rat
   1. Increased real interest rate has two opposing effects
      a. Substitution effect:  Positive effect on saving, since rate of return is higher; greater reward for saving elicits more saving
      b. Income effect
         (1) For a saver:  Negative effect on saving, since it takes less saving to obtain a given amount in the future (target saving)
         (2) For a borrower:  Positive effect on saving, since the higher real interest rate means a loss of wealth
      c. Empirical studies have mixed results; probably a slight increase in aggregate saving
   2. Taxes and the real return to saving
      a. Expected after-tax real interest rate: $r_{a-t} = (1 - t)i - \pi^e$  (4.2)
      b. Simple examples: $i = 5\%$, $\pi^e = 2\%$; if $t = 30\%$, $r_{a-t} = 1.5\%$; if $t = 20\%$, $r_{a-t} = 2\%$
   3. In touch with the macroeconomy: interest rates
      a. Discusses different interest rates, default risk, term structure (yield curve), and tax status
      b. Since interest rates often move together, we frequently refer to "the" interest rate

G. Fiscal policy
   1. Affects desired consumption through changes in current and expected future income
   2. Directly affects desired national saving, $S^d = Y - C^d - G$
   3. Government purchases (temporary increase)
      a. Higher $G$ financed by higher current taxes reduces after-tax income, lowering desired consumption
      b. Even true if financed by higher future taxes, if people realize how future incomes are affected
      c. Since $C^d$ declines less than $G$ rises, national saving ($S^d = Y - C^d - G$) declines
      d. So government purchases reduce both desired consumption and desired national saving
   4. Taxes
      a. Lump-sum tax cut today, financed by higher future taxes
      b. Decline in future income may offset increase in current income; desired consumption could rise or fall
      c. Ricardian equivalence proposition
         (1) If future income loss exactly offsets current income gain, no change in consumption
         (2) Tax change affects only the timing of taxes, not their ultimate amount (present value)
         (3) In practice, people may not see that future taxes will rise if taxes are cut today; then a tax cut leads to increased desired consumption and reduced desired national saving

II.  Investment (Sec. 4.2)
   A.  Why is investment important?
      1.  Investment fluctuates sharply over the business cycle, so we need to understand investment to understand the business cycle
      2.  Investment plays a crucial role in economic growth
   B.  The desired capital stock

      1.  Desired capital stock is the amount of capital that allows firms to earn the largest expected profit
      2.  Desired capital stock depends on costs and benefits of additional capital
      3.  Since investment becomes capital stock with a lag, the benefit of investment is the future marginal product of capital ($MPK^f$)
      4.  The user cost of capital
         a.  Example of Tony's Bakery: cost of capital, depreciation rate, and expected real interest rate
         b.  User cost of capital = real cost of using a unit of capital for a specified period of time
         c.  $uc = rp_K + dp_K = (r + d)p_K$   (4.3)

Figure 4.1

      5.  Determination of the desired capital stock (Fig. 4.1; like text Fig. 4.3)
         a.  Desired capital stock is the level of capital stock at which $MPK_f = uc$
         b.  $MPK^f$ falls as $K$ rises due to diminishing marginal productivity
         c.  uc doesn't vary with $K$, so is a horizontal line
         d.  If $MPK^f > uc$, profits rise as $K$ is added (marginal benefits > marginal costs)
         e.  If $MPK^f < uc$, profits rise as K is reduced (marginal benefits < marginal costs)
         f.  Profits are maximized where $MPK^f = uc$
   C.  Changes in the desired capital stock
      1.  Factors that shift the $MPK^f$ curve or change the user cost of capital cause the desired capital stock to change
      2.  These factors are changes in the real interest rate, depreciation rate, price of capital, or technological changes that affect the $MPK^f$ (text Fig. 4.4 shows effect of change in $uc$)
      3.  Taxes and the desired capital stock
         a.  With taxes, the return to capital is only $(1 - \tau)MPK^f$
         b.  Setting the return equal to the user cost gives
            $MPK^f = uc/(1 - \tau) = (r + d)p_K/(1 - \tau)$
         c.  Tax-adjusted user cost of capital is $uc/(1 - \tau)$
         d.  An increase in $\tau$ raises the tax-adjusted user cost and reduces the desired capital stock
         e.  In reality, there are complications to the tax-adjusted user cost
           (1)  We assumed that firm revenues were taxed
              (a)  In reality, profits, not revenues, are taxed
              (b)  So depreciation allowances reduce the tax paid by firms, because they reduce profits
           (2)  Investment tax credits reduce taxes when firms make new investments

(3)   Summary measure: the effective tax rate—the tax rate on firm revenue that would have the same effect on the desired capital stock as do the actual provisions of the tax code

(4)   Table 4.2 shows effective tax rates for nine different countries; some are negative, implying a subsidy to capital

    f.   Application: measuring the effects of taxes on investment

      (1)   Do changes in the tax rate have a significant effect on investment?

      (2)   A 1994 study by Cummins, Hubbard, and Hassett found that after major tax reforms, investment responded strongly; elasticity about -0.66 (of investment to user cost of capital)

D.   From the desired capital stock to investment

  1.   The capital stock changes from two opposing channels

    a.   New capital increases the capital stock; this is gross investment

    b.   The capital stock depreciates, which reduces the capital stock

    c.   Net investment = gross investment ($I$) minus depreciation:

$K_{t+1} - K_t = I_t - dK_t$    (4.5)

where net investment equals the change in the capital stock

    d.   Text Fig. 4.6 shows gross and net investment for Canada

  2.   Rewriting (4.5) gives It = $K_{t+1} - K_t + dK_t$

    a.   If firms can change their capital stocks in one period, then the desired capital stock ($K^*$) = K$_{t+1}$

    b.   So $I_t = K^* - K_t + dK_t$    (4.6)

    c.   Thus investment has two parts

      (1)   Desired net increase in the capital stock over the year ($K^* - K_t$)

      (2)   Investment needed to replace depreciated capital ($dK_t$)

  3.   Lags and investment

    a.   Some capital can be constructed easily, but other capital may take years to put in place

    b.   So investment needed to reach the desired capital stock may be spread out over several years

E.   Investment in inventories and housing

  1.   Marginal product of capital and user cost also apply, as with equipment and structures

III. Goods Market Equilibrium (Sec. 4.3)
    A.   The real interest rate adjusts to bring the goods market into equilibrium
        1.   $Y = C^d + I^d + G$  (4.7)
            goods market equilibrium condition
        2.   Differs from income-expenditure identity, as goods market equilibrium condition need not hold; undesired goods may be produced, so goods market won't be in equilibrium
        3.   Alternative representation: since $S^d = Y - C^d - G$,
            $S^d = I^d$   (4.9)

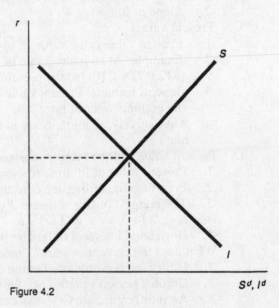

Figure 4.2

    B.   The saving-investment diagram
        1.   Plot $S^d$ vs. $I^d$ (Fig. 4.2; Key Diagram 3; like text Fig. 4.7)
        2.   Equilibrium where $S^d = I^d$
        3.   How to reach equilibrium? Adjustment of $r$
        4.   Shifts of the saving curve
            a.   Saving curve shifts right due to a rise in current output, a fall in expected future output, a fall in wealth, a fall in government purchases, a rise in taxes (unless Ricardian equivalence holds, in which case tax changes have no effect)
            b.   Example: Temporary increase in government purchases shifts $S$ left
            c.   Result of lower savings: higher $r$, causing crowding out of $I$
        5.   Application: the effect of wars on investment and the real interest rate
            a.   Investment generally declines during wars
            b.   But in Canadian history, real interest rates don't always rise during wars
            c.   Barro finds consistent rise in real interest rates in British data during wars
        6.   Shifts of the investment curve
            a.   Investment curve shifts right due to a fall in the effective tax rate or a rise in expected future marginal productivity of capital
            b.   Result of increased investment: higher $r$, higher $S$ and $I$

IV.  Appendix 4.A:  A Formal Model of Consumption and Saving
  A.   How much can the consumer afford? The budget constraint
    1.   Current income $y$; future income $y^f$; initial wealth $a$
    2.   Choice variables: $a^f$ = wealth at beginning of future period; $c$ = current consumption; $c^f$ = future consumption
    3.   $a^f = (y + a - c)(1 + r)$, so $c^f = (y + a - c)(1 + r) + y^f$    (4.A.1)   the budget constraint
  B.   The budget line
    1.   Graph budget line in $(c, c^f)$ space (Fig. 4.A.1)
    2.   Slope of line = $-(1 + r)$
  C.   Present values
    1.   Present value is the value of payments to be made in the future in terms of today's dollars or goods
    2.   Example: At an interest rate of 10%, $12,000 today invested for one year is worth $13,200 ($12,000 x 1.10); so the present value of $13,200 in one year is $12,000
    3.   General formula: Present value = future value / $(1 + i)$, where amounts are in dollar terms and $i$ is the nominal interest rate
    4.   Alternatively, if amounts are in real terms, use the real interest rate $r$ instead of the nominal interest rate $i$
  D.   Present value and the budget constraint
    1.   Present value of lifetime resources: $PVLR = y + y^f/(1+r) + a$    (4.A.2)
    2.   Present value of lifetime consumption: $PVLC = c + c^f/(1+r)$    (4.A.3)
    3.   The budget constraint means $PVLC = PVLR$
    4.   $c + c^f/(1+r) = y + y^f/(1+r) + a$
    5.   Horizontal intercept of budget line is $c = PVLR$, $c^f = 0$
  E.   What does the consumer want? Consumer preferences
    1.   Utility = a person's satisfaction or well-being
    2.   Graph a person's preference for current versus future consumption using indifference curves
    3.   An indifference curve shows combinations of $c$ and $c^f$ that give the same utility (Fig. 4.A.2)
    4.   A person is equally happy at any point on an indifference curve
    5.   Three important properties of indifference curves
      a.   Slope downward from left to right: Less consumption in one period requires more consumption in the other period to keep utility unchanged
      b.   Indifference curves that are farther up and to the right represent higher levels of utility, because more consumption is preferred to less
      c.   Indifference curves are bowed toward the origin, because people have a consumption-smoothing motive, they prefer consuming equal amounts in each period rather than consuming a lot one period and little the other period
  F.   The optimal level of consumption
    1.   Optimal consumption point is where the budget line is tangent to an indifference curve (Fig. 4.A.3)
    2.   That's the highest indifference curve that it's possible to reach
    3.   All other points on the budget line are on lower indifference curves

G.  The Effects of Changes in Income and Wealth on Consumption and Saving
    1.  The effect on consumption of a change in income (current or future) or wealth depends only on how the change affects the *PVLR*
        a.  An increase in current income (Fig. 4.A.4)
            (1)  Increases *PVLR*, so shifts budget line out parallel to old budget line
            (2)  If there is a consumption-smoothing motive, both current and future consumption will increase
            (3)  Then both consumption and saving rise because of the rise in current income
        b.  An increase in future income
            (1)  Same outward shift in budget line as an increase in current income
            (2)  Again, with consumption smoothing, both current and future consumption increase
            (3)  Now saving declines, since current income is unchanged and current consumption increases
        c.  An increase in wealth
            (1)  Same parallel shift in budget line, so both current and future consumption rise
            (2)  Again, saving declines, since c rises and y is unchanged
        d.  The permanent income theory
            (1)  Different types of changes in income
                (a)  Temporary increase in income: $y$ rises and $y^f$ is unchanged
                (b)  Permanent increase in income: Both $y$ and $y^f$ rise
            (2)  Permanent income increase causes bigger increase in *PVLR* than a temporary income increase
                (a)  So current consumption will rise more with a permanent income increase
                (b)  So saving from a permanent increase in income is less than from a temporary increase in income

         (3)    This distinction between permanent and temporary income changes was made by Milton Friedman in the 1950s and is known as the permanent income theory
            (a)  Permanent changes in income lead to much larger changes in consumption
            (b)  Thus permanent income changes are mostly consumed, while temporary income changes are mostly saved

H.   Consumption and Saving Over Many Periods: The Life-Cycle Model
    1.   Life-cycle model was developed by Franco Modigliani and associates in the 1950s
       a.   Looks at patterns of income, consumption, and saving over an individual's lifetime
       b.   Typical consumer's income and saving pattern shown in Fig. 4.A.5
       c.   Real income steadily rises over time until near retirement; at retirement, income drops sharply
       d.   Lifetime pattern of consumption is much smoother than the income pattern
          (1)   In reality, consumption varies somewhat by age
          (2)   For example, when raising children, household consumption is higher than average
          (3)   The model can easily be modified to handle this and other variations
       e.   Saving has the following lifetime pattern
          (1)   Saving is low or negative early in working life
          (2)   Maximum saving occurs when income is highest (ages 50 to 60)
          (3)   Dissaving occurs in retirement
    2.   Bequests and saving
       a.   What effect does a bequest motive (a desire to leave an inheritance) have on saving?
       b.   Simply consume less and save more than without a bequest motive
    3.   Ricardian equivalence
       a.   We can use the two-period model to examine Ricardian equivalence
       b.   The two-period model shows that consumption is changed only if the *PVLR* changes
       c.   Suppose the government reduces taxes by 100 in the current period, the interest rate is 10%, and taxes will be increased by 110 in the future period
       d.   Then the *PVLR* is unchanged, and thus there is no change in consumption
    4.   Excess sensitivity and borrowing constraints
       a.   Generally, theories about consumption, including the permanent income theory, have been supported by looking at real-world data
       *b.*   But some researchers have found that the data show that the impact of an income or wealth change is different than that implied by a change in the *PVLR*
       c.   There seems to be excess sensitivity of consumption to changes in current income
          (1)   This could be due to short-sighted behavior
          (2)   Or it could be due to borrowing constraints
       d.   Borrowing constraints mean people can't borrow as much as they want
          Lenders may worry that a consumer won't pay back the loan, so they won't lend
       e.   If a person wouldn't borrow anyway, the borrowing constraint is said to be nonbinding
       f.   But if a person wants to borrow and can't, the borrowing constraint is binding
       g.   A consumer with a binding borrowing constraint spends all income and wealth
          (1)   So an increase in income or wealth will be entirely spent on consumption as well
          (2)   This causes consumption to be excessively sensitive to current income changes
       h.   How prevalent are borrowing constraints? Perhaps 20% to 50% of the Canadian population faces binding borrowing constraints

I.  The Real Interest Rate and the Consumption-Saving Decision
    1.  The real interest rate and the budget line (Fig. 4.A.6)
        a.  When the real interest rate rises, one point on the old budget line is also on the new budget line: the no-borrowing, no-lending point
        b.  Slope of new budget line is steeper
    2.  The substitution effect
        a.  A higher real interest rate makes future consumption cheaper relative to current consumption
        b.  Increasing future consumption and reducing current consumption increases saving
        c.  Suppose a person is at the no-borrowing, no-lending point when the real interest rate rises (Fig. 4.A.7)
            (1)  An increase in the real interest rate unambiguously leads the person to increase future consumption and decrease current consumption
            (2)  The increase in saving, equal to the decrease in current consumption, represents the substitution effect
    3.  The income effect
        a.  If a person is planning to consume at the no-borrowing, no-lending point, then a rise in the real interest rate leads just to a substitution effect
        b.  But if a person is planning to consume at a different point than the no-borrowing, no-lending point, there is also an income effect
        c.  The intuition of the income effect
            (1)  If the person originally planned to be a lender, the rise in the real interest rate gives the person more income in the future period; the income effect works in the opposite direction of the substitution effect, since more future income increases current consumption
            (2)  If the person originally planned to be a borrower, the rise in the real interest rate gives the person less income in the future period; the income effect works in the same direction as the substitution effect, since less future income reduces current consumption further
    4.  The income and substitution effects together
        a.  Split the change in the budget line into two parts (Fig. 4.A.8)
            (1)  A budget line with the same slope as the new budget line, but going through the original consumption point ($BL^{int}$)
            (2)  The substitution effect is shown by the change from budget line $BL^1$ to budget line $BL^{int}$, with the consumption point changing from point $D$ to point $P$
            (3)  The income effect is shown by the change from budget line $BL^{int}$ to budget line $BL^2$, with consumption point changing from point $P$ to point $Q$
        b.  The substitution effect decreases current consumption, but the income effect increases current consumption; so saving may increase or decrease
        c.  Both effects increase future consumption
        d.  For a borrower, both effects decrease current consumption, so saving definitely increases but the effect on future consumption is ambiguous
        e.  The effect on aggregate saving of a rise in the real interest rate is ambiguous theoretically
            (1)  Empirical research suggests that saving increases, but the effect is small

# MULTIPLE-CHOICE QUESTIONS

1. Historically, national surveys of consumer confidence show that consumers' expectations
   a. are very stable over the business cycle.
   b. are very sensitive indicators of recessions and other macroeconomic shocks.
   c. are unaffected by foreign shocks to the national economy.
   d. are insensitive to important changes in labour market conditions.

2. At full-employment output, desired consumption spending will increase if
   a. income falls.
   b. wealth falls.
   c. government purchases increase.
   d. the expected real interest rate falls.

3. A small increase in the real interest rate will most likely
   a. increase desired saving, but the effect will be relatively small.
   b. increase desired saving substantially.
   c. decrease desired saving substantially.
   d. decrease desired saving, but the effect will be relatively small.

4. An increase in the personal income tax rate on interest income will
   a. increase desired saving because the expected after-tax real interest rate rises.
   b. decrease desired saving because the expected after-tax real interest rate rises.
   c. decrease desired saving because the expected after-tax real interest rate falls.
   d. increase desired saving because the expected after-tax real interest rate falls.

5. The expected real after-tax rate of return on saving is the after-tax nominal rate of return minus expected
   a. future income.
   b. future wealth.
   c. future capital gains.
   d. inflation.

6. With a nominal interest rate of 8%, an expected inflation rate of 3%, and interest income taxed at a 25% rate, what is the expected after-tax real interest rate?
   a. 5%
   b. 3.75%
   c. 3%
   d. 1%

7. The relationship between a bond's maturity and the interest rate it pays is called the
   a. yield curve.
   b. amortization schedule.
   c. federal funds rate.
   d. desired investment curve.

8.  According to the Ricardian equivalence proposition, a temporary government budget deficit created by cutting taxes
    a.  will cause desired consumption to increase.
    b.  will cause future taxes to increase but will have no real economic effects.
    c.  will have the same real economic effects as a budget deficit created by raising government spending.
    d.  would have the same real effects whether or not consumers expect future taxes to change.

9.  The desired level of the capital stock will increase if the
    a.  user cost of capital increases.
    b.  expected future marginal product of capital increases.
    c.  effective tax rate increases.
    d.  price of capital increases.

10. An increase in the price of capital goods will
    a.  increase the expected future marginal product of capital.
    b.  reduce the expected future marginal product of capital.
    c.  increase the interest cost and the depreciation cost of capital.
    d.  increase the interest cost but not affect the depreciation cost of capital.

11. You have just purchased a new VCR to show videos to your customers. The VCR cost $500, and you depreciate the machine at a rate of 25% each year. You can borrow money from the bank at 10%, or receive 6% for depositing money at the bank. The expected inflation rate in the coming year is 5%. You used the company's own funds to purchase the VCR. The firm's user cost of capital for the first year is
    a.  $130.
    b.  $150.
    c.  $155.
    d.  $175.

12. You have just purchased a new VCR to show videos to your customers. The VCR cost $500, and you depreciate the machine at a rate of 25% each year. You can borrow money from the bank at 10%, or receive 6% for depositing money at the bank. The expected inflation rate in the coming year is 5%. You borrowed money from the bank to purchase the VCR. The firm's user cost of capital for the first year is
    a.  $130.
    b.  $150.
    c.  $155.
    d.  $175.

13. Calculate the user cost of capital of a machine that costs $5,000 and depreciates at a 25% rate, when the nominal interest rate is 5% and the expected inflation rate is 10%.
    a.  $100
    b.  $1000
    c.  $1500
    d.  $5000

14. If a firm's expected marginal product of capital exceeds its tax-adjusted user cost of capital, the firm will
    a.  increase its investment spending on capital goods.
    b.  reduce its investment spending on capital goods.
    c.  not change its investment spending on capital goods.
    d.  increase the tax-adjusted user cost of capital.

15. Calculate the after-tax user cost of capital of a machine that costs $5000 and depreciates at a 25% rate, when the interest rate is 5% and the tax rate on revenue is 25%.
    a.   $ 200
    b.   $ 275
    c.   $2000
    d.   $2750

16. A decrease in the expected real interest rate will
    a.   increase the desired capital stock.
    b.   decrease the desired capital stock.
    c.   have no effect on the desired capital stock.
    d.   have the same effect on the desired capital stock as an increase in corporate taxes.

17. Your firm has capital stock of $15 million and a depreciation rate of 10%. Gross investment is $2.5 million. How much is net investment?
    a.   $13.5 million
    b.   $ 2.5 million
    c.   $ 1.5 million
    d.   $ 1.0 million

18. In the goods market equilibrium condition for a closed economy, the total demand for goods equals
    a.   $C^d + I^d$.
    b.   $C^d + I^d + G$.
    c.   $C + I + G$.
    d.   $C + I + G^d$.

19. One way of writing the goods market equilibrium condition for a closed economy is
    a.   $Y + C + G = S$.
    b.   $Y + C^d + G^d = S$.
    c.   $S^d = I^d$.
    d.   $Y - C^d - G - S^d = I^d$.

20. An economy has government purchases of 2000. Desired national saving and desired investment are given by

    $$S^d = 200 + 5000r + .10Y - .20G$$
    $$I^d = 1000 - 4000r$$

    When the full-employment level of output equals 5000, then the real interest rate that clears the goods market will be
    a.   7.78%.
    b.   10.00%.
    c.   14.44%.
    d.   23.33%.

21. A higher real interest rate will
    a.   increase the profitability of new investment.
    b.   decrease lending of funds from firms to other economic agents.
    c.   reduce the desired investment of all firms.
    d.   reduce the desired investment of only those firms that have to borrow.

22. In the saving-investment diagram, an increase in current output would
    a. shift the saving curve to the left.
    b. shift the investment demand curve to the left.
    c. not shift the curves.
    d. shift the saving curve to the right.

23. A reduction in government spending will shift the
    a. investment curve to the left.
    b. investment curve to the right.
    c. saving curve to the right.
    d. saving curve to the left.

24. A temporary decrease in government purchases would cause
    a. an increase in the real interest rate and a decrease in desired investment.
    b. a decrease in the real interest rate and an increase in desired investment.
    c. a decrease in the real interest rate and an uncertain effect on desired investment.
    d. an uncertain effect on the real interest rate and an increase in the

## REVIEW QUESTIONS

1. What is the marginal propensity to consume, and why is it always less than one?

2. At a given output level, how are desired saving and desired consumption related? Briefly explain. What role do expectations have in determining desired consumption and saving? Briefly explain.

3. Does an increase in the tax rate on interest earnings reduce desired saving? Briefly explain.

4. How would the expected real after-tax rate of return be affected by each of the following events?
   (1) the tax rate on interest income increases
   (2) expected inflation declines

5. What is the effect on the real interest rate of a government budget deficit caused by a temporary increase in government purchases? What does the Ricardian equivalence proposition tell us about the expected real economic effects of a temporary government budget deficit caused by a temporary tax cut? Briefly explain.

6. Identify two variables that shift the desired saving curve. Is desired saving negatively related or positively related to each of these variables?

7. Identify two variables that shift the desired investment curve. Is desired investment negatively related or positively related to each of these variables?

## NUMERICAL PROBLEMS

1. The one-year T-bill rate was 8% on 1/1/91, 7% on 1/1/92, and 6% on 1/1/93. The GDP deflator (1982 = 100) was 150 on 1/1/91, 159 on 1/1/92, 165.4 on 1/1/93, and 173.6 on 1/1/94. The tax rate on interest income is 30%.

a.    Calculate the after-tax nominal rate of return for 1991, 1992, and 1993.

b.    If you began with $1000 on 1/1/91 and invested in T-bills each year (paying taxes at the end of each year), how much would you have in nominal terms on 1/1/94? How much would you have in real terms (1982 dollars)?

c.    How much was your nominal after-tax interest earned in part b over the three years? How much did you earn in real after-tax dollars?

2.    Suppose the nominal interest rate is 6%, the tax rate on interest income is 30%, and expected inflation is 3%.

a.    Calculate the expected after-tax real interest rate.

b.    Calculate the expected after-tax real interest rate if the nominal interest rate falls to 4%.

c.    Calculate the expected after-tax real interest rate if the tax rate increases to 50% (with the nominal interest rate at its original value of 6%).

d.    Calculate the expected after-tax real interest rate if expected inflation increases to 5% (with the nominal interest rate at its original value of 6% and the tax rate at its original value of 30%).

3.    Calculate the value of net investment for each of the following values for gross investment ($I_t$) and depreciation ($d$), assuming that $K_t$ = $5000 billion.
      (a) $I_t$ = $1250 billion and $d$ = 10%
      (b) $I_t$ = $750 billion and $d$ = 5%.

4.    Suppose desired consumption equals 0.9 $Y$, where $Y$ is income. Government purchases are $1000, net exports are zero, and desired investment varies with the real interest rate according to the following schedule:

| $r$ | $I^d$ |
|---|---|
| 5% | $3000 |
| 4% | 3500 |
| 3% | 4000 |
| 2% | 4500 |

Assume the interest rate adjusts so that the economy gets to equilibrium. Equilibrium output at full employment is $50,000. Find the values of consumption, investment, and the real interest rate at full-employment equilibrium.

## ANALYTICAL QUESTIONS

1.  How would each of the following changes affect the user cost of capital?
    (1) an increase in the price of capital goods
    (2) a decrease in the real interest rate

2.  How would the desired capital stock be affected by a decline in the user cost of capital?

3.  What would be the effect on a firm's desired capital stock of a technological advance?

4.  How would each of the following changes affect the level of desired capital stock?
    (1) an increase in the effective tax rate on capital
    (2) a decrease in the depreciation rate

5.  What are the economic consequences of reductions in defense spending by the government? What happens to national saving, the interest rate, and investment?

## ANSWERS TO MULTIPLE-CHOICE QUESTIONS

| Number | Answer | | Number | Answer | | Number | Answer |
|--------|--------|---|--------|--------|---|--------|--------|
| 1 | b | | 11 | a | | 21 | c |
| 2 | d | | 12 | b | | 22 | d |
| 3 | a | | 13 | b | | 23 | c |
| 4 | c | | 14 | a | | 24 | b |
| 5 | d | | 15 | c | | | |
| 6 | c | | 16 | a | | | |
| 7 | a | | 17 | d | | | |
| 8 | b | | 18 | b | | | |
| 9 | b | | 19 | c | | | |
| 10 | c | | 20 | a | | | |

## ANSWERS TO REVIEW QUESTIONS

1.  The marginal propensity to consume (*MPC*) is the amount by which desired consumption rises when current income rises by one unit. The marginal propensity to consume is less than one because a part of any increase in current income is saved.

2.  At a given output level, desired consumption is negatively related to desired saving. Any increase in desired consumption is a decrease in desired saving, and vice-versa. Expectations play a major role in determining desired consumption and desired saving. Expected future income and expected inflation are two examples of expectations variables that partly determine desired consumption and desired saving.

3.  An increase in the tax rate on interest earnings has the same effect on desired saving as a decline in the interest rate, since both reduce the after-tax real interest rate. But empirical researchers have not been able to agree on the strength of the effect of a change in the real interest rate on desired saving. Most researchers believe that desired saving is positively related to the interest rate, but that the interest rate is a relatively weak determinant of saving. This is because there's an incentive to save more at a higher rate of return on saving because of the higher payoff, but there's also an incentive to save less, since a saver doesn't need to save as much to reach a target level of accumulated wealth, since the interest rate is higher.

4.  The expected real after-tax rate of return is
    $$r_{a\text{-}t} = (1 - t)\, i - \pi^e.$$
    (1)  Clearly $r_{a\text{-}t}$ would decline if the tax rate on interest income increases.
    (2)  From the formula, $r_{a\text{-}t}$ would increase if expected inflation declines.

5.  A government budget deficit created by a temporary increase in government purchases causes the saving curve to shift to the left. With no shift in the desired investment curve, the result is an increase in the real interest rate, as Figure 4.3 shows.

Figure 4.3

    According to the Ricardian equivalence proposition, a temporary government budget deficit created by a tax cut will not have any real economic effect, because it will not change national saving, so it will not shift the saving curve. The proposition assumes that households realize they will have to save all the income received from the tax cut in order to pay off the future tax increase needed to pay off the government debt created by the temporary tax cut.

6.  Variables that shift the desired saving curve are current output, expected future output, wealth, the expected real interest rate, government purchases, and taxes. Of these, current output, the expected real interest rate (probably), and taxes (possibly) are positively related to saving; the rest are negatively related.

7.  Variables that shift the desired investment curve are the real interest rate, the expected future marginal product of capital, and the effective tax rate. Desired investment is positively related to the future marginal product of capital, but negatively related to the real interest rate and the effective tax rate.

## ANSWERS TO NUMERICAL PROBLEMS

1. a.  1991: 5.6% = .08 x .7; 1992: 4.9% = .07 x .7; 1993: 4.2% = .06 x .7

   b.  Nominal: $1154.27 = $1000 x 1.056 x 1.049 x 1.042; Real: $664.90 = $1154.27/(173.6/100)

   c.  Nominal: $154.27 = $1154.27 - $1000; Real: -$1.77 = $664.90 - $1000/(150/100) = $664.90 - $666.67

2. The expected after-tax real interest rate is $r_{a-t} = (1-t)i - \pi^e$.

   a.  Given the initial values, $r_{a-t} = (1 - .30).06 - .03 = 0.012 = 1.2\%$.

   b.  When $i = 4\%$, $r_{a-t} = (1 - .30).04 - .03 = -0.002 = -0.2\%$.

   c.  When $t = 50\%$, $r_{a-t} = (1 - .50).06 - .03 = 0.0 = 0.0\%$.

   d.  When $\pi^e = 5\%$, $r_{a-t} = (1 - .30).06 - .05 = -0.008 = -0.8\%$.

3. Net investment $= I_t - dK_t$.

   (a)  Net investment = $1250 billion - (.10 x $5000 billion) = $750 billion.

   (b)  Net investment = $750 billion - (.05 x $5000 billion) = $500 billion.

4. Since $Y = C^d + I^d + G$, $Y = 0.9Y + I^d + G$, so $0.1 Y = I^d + G$. Then you can calculate the following table:

| $r$ | $I^d$ | $G$ | $Y$ | $C^d$ |
|---|---|---|---|---|
| 5% | $3000 | $1000 | $40,000 | $36,000 |
| 4% | 3500 | 1000 | 45,000 | 40,500 |
| 3% | 4000 | 1000 | 50,000 | 45,000 |
| 2% | 4500 | 1000 | 55,000 | 49,500 |

At equilibrium, $Y = $50,000$, so $r = 3\%$, $I^d = $4000$, and $C = $45,000$.

## ANSWERS TO ANALYTICAL QUESTIONS

1.  The user cost of capital is $uc = rp_K + dp_K = (r + d)p_K$, where $r$ = the expected real interest rate, $d$ = the depreciation rate for capital, and $p_k$ = the real price of capital goods.

    (1)  From the equation, the user cost of capital increases if the price of capital goods increases.
    (2)  From the equation, the user cost of capital decreases if the real interest rate decreases.

2.  A firm sets its capital stock such that the future marginal product of capital equals the user cost, where the future marginal product of capital declines as the amount of capital increases. A decline in the user cost requires that the future marginal product of capital also decline to maintain the equality. So the desired capital stock increases.

Figure 4.4

3.  A technological advance causes the future marginal product of capital to increase. This increases the equilibrium level of the capital stock, as Figure 4.4 shows.

4.  A firm's desired capital stock is the level at which $MPK^f = uc/(1-\tau) = (r+d)p_K/(1-\tau)$.

    (1)  An increase in the effective tax rate on capital reduces the desired capital stock, since it increases the tax-adjusted user cost of capital.
    (2)  A decrease in the depreciation rate reduces the user cost of capital, thus increasing the desired capital stock.

5.  The reduction in defense spending increases national saving, so that the desired saving curve shifts to the right. As a result, the real interest rate declines, and investment increases, as shown in Figure 4.5.

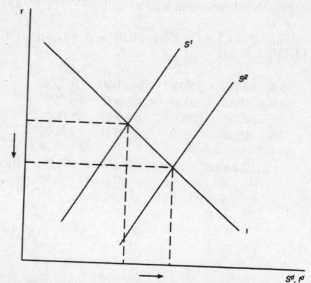

Figure 4.5

# CHAPTER 5: SAVING AND INVESTMENT IN THE OPEN ECONOMY

## INTRODUCTION

Chapter 4 introduced equilibrium in the goods market, but to keep things simple it assumed that the economy was closed. In this chapter, we allow for the economy to trade with other countries to see how that changes things. In such an open economy, we find that a country's spending need not equal its production every period—it can borrow or lend to other countries. As in a closed economy, though, what's most important are the country's decisions about how much to save and invest. The chapter begins with some basic balance of payments accounting in Section 5.1, explaining the trade balance and current-account balance, among other things. Then Section 5.2 shows how the condition for equilibrium in the goods market is changed by allowing for international trade. When an open economy is small, it has no effect on the world real interest rate, as discussed in Section 5.3. But when an open economy is large enough to affect the world real interest rate, the analysis is different, as Section 5.4 shows. Finally, Section 5.5 looks at the relationship between government budget deficits and current account deficits.

This is a pretty tough chapter. First, the nuances of balance of payments accounting are a bit difficult to understand. You need to be sure to figure out what's a debit and what's a credit. Then, there are two different models to follow—one for a small economy and the other for a large economy. So the first thing to ask yourself in analyzing any economy is: is the economy small or large? If it's small, then the world real interest rate isn't affected by shifts in saving or investment in the economy. But if the economy is large, then it affects the rest of the world whenever there's a shift in its saving or investment.

## CHAPTER OUTLINE

I.   Balance of Payments Accounting (Sec. 5.1)
    A.   Balance of payments accounts
        1.   The record of a country's international transactions
        2.   Text Table 5.1 shows recent Canadian data
        3.   Any transaction that involves a flow of money into Canada is a credit (+) item (enters with a plus sign); for example, exports
        4.   Any transaction involving a flow of money out of Canada is a debit (-) item (enters with a minus sign); for example, imports
        5.   In touch with the macroeconomy: the balance of payments accounts
            Data released quarterly in *Canaidan Economic Observer*
    B.   The current account
        1.   Net exports of goods and services
          a.   Merchandise trade: Exports of goods minus imports of goods = merchandise trade balance
          b.   Internationally traded services (transportation, tourism, insurance, education, financial services) are also important
        2.   Net income from abroad
          a.   Income received from abroad is a credit item, since it causes funds to flow into Canada
          b.   Payment of income to foreigners is a debit item
          c.   Net income from abroad is part of the current account, and is about equal to NFP, net factor payments

3. Net unilateral transfers
    a. Payments made from one country to another
    b. Negative net unilateral transfers for Canada, since Canada is a net donor to other countries
4. Sum of net exports of goods and services, net income from abroad, and net unilateral transfers is the current account balance
    a. Positive current account balance implies current account surplus
    b. Negative current account balance implies current account deficit

C. The capital and financial account
  1. The capital and financial account records trades in existing assets, either real (for example, houses) or financial (for example, stocks and bonds)
  2. The capital account records the net flow of unilateral transfers of assets into the country
  3. Most transactions appear in the financial account part of the capital and financial account
    a. When home country sells assets to foreign country, that is a capital inflow for the home country and a credit (+) item in the capital and financial account
    b. When assets are purchased from a foreign country, there is a capital outflow from the home country and a debit (-) item in the capital and financial account
  4. The official settlements balance
    a. Transactions in official reserve assets are conducted by central banks of countries
    b. Official reserve assets are assets (foreign government securities, bank deposits, and SDRs of the IMF, gold) used in making international payments
    c. Central banks buy (or sell) official reserve assets with (or to obtain) their own currencies
    d. Official settlements balance
      (1) Also called the balance of payments, it equals the net increase in a country's official reserve assets
      (2) For Canada, the net increase in official reserve assets is the rise in Canadian government reserve assets minus foreign central bank holdings of Canadian dollar assets
    e. Having a balance of payments surplus means a country is increasing its official reserve assets; a balance of payments deficit is a reduction in official reserve assets

D. The relationship between the current account and the capital account
  1. Current account balance ($CA$) + capital and financial account balance ($KFA$) = 0   (5.1)
  2. $CA + KFA = 0$ by accounting; every transaction involves offsetting effects
  3. Examples given of offsetting transactions (text Table 5.2)
  4. In practice, measurement problems, recorded as a statistical discrepancy, prevent $CA + KFA = 0$ from holding exactly.

E. Net foreign assets and the balance of payments accounts
  1. Net foreign assets are a country's foreign assets minus its foreign liabilities
    a. Net foreign assets may change in value (example: change in stock prices)
    b. Net foreign assets may change through acquisition of new assets or liabilities
  2. The net increase in foreign assets equals a country's current account surplus
  3. A current account surplus implies a capital and financial account deficit, and thus a net increase in holdings of foreign assets (a financial outflow)
  4. A current account deficit implies a capital and financial account surplus, and thus a net decline in holdings of foreign assets (a financial inflow)
  5. Summary: Equivalent measures of a country's international trade and lending
  6. Current account surplus = capital and financial account deficit = net acquisition of foreign assets = net foreign lending = (if $NFP$ and net unilateral transfers are zero) net exports

F. Box 5.1: Does Mars have a current account surplus?

1. Adding together all countries' current account balances gives a current account deficit for the world
2. The statistical problem is primarily a misreporting of income from assets held abroad

II. Goods Market Equilibrium in an Open Economy (Sec. 5.2)
   A. From Ch. 2, $S = I + CA = I + (NX + NFP)$  (5.2)
      1. So national saving has two uses:
         a. Increase the capital stock by domestic investment
         b. Increase the stock of net foreign assets by lending to foreigners
      2. To get goods market equilibrium, national saving and investment must equal their desired levels:
         a. $S^d = I^d + CA = I^d + (NX + NFP)$  (5.3)
         b. Goods market equilibrium in an open economy
         c. Assuming net factor payments are zero, then $S^d = I^d + NX$  (5.4)
      3. Alternative method:
         a. $Y = C^d + I^d + G + NX$  (5.5)
         b. $NX = Y - (C^d + I^d + G)$  (5.6)
            Net exports equal output ($Y$) minus absorption ($C^d + I^d + G$)

III. Saving and Investment in a Small Open Economy
   (Sec. 5.3)
   A. Small open economy: an economy too small to affect the world real interest rate
      1. World real interest rate ($r^w$): the real interest rate in the international capital market
      2. Key assumption: Residents of the small open economy can borrow or lend at the expected world real interest rate (Fig. 5.1; Key diagram 4; like text Figs. 5.1 and 5.2)
      3. Result: $r^w$ may be such that $S^d > I^d$, $S^d = I^d$, or $S^d < I^d$
         a. If $r^w = r_1$, then $S^d > I^d$, so the excess of desired saving over desired investment is lent internationally (net foreign lending is positive) and $NX > 0$
         b. If $r^w = r_2$, then $S^d = I^d$, so there is no net foreign lending and $NX = 0$
         c. If $r^w = r_3$, then $S^d < I^d$, so the excess of desired investment over desired saving is financed by borrowing internationally (net foreign lending is negative) and $NX < 0$
      4. Alternative interpretation: in terms of output and absorption

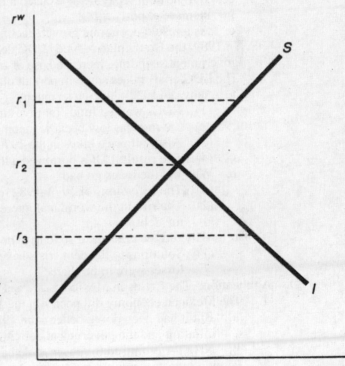

Figure 5.1

5.  Net exports equals net foreign lending equals the current account balance (assuming net factor payments and net unilateral transfers are zero)

B.  The effects of economic shocks in a small open economy
1.  Anything that increases desired national saving (Y rises, future output falls, or G falls) relative to desired investment ($MPK^f$ falls, $\tau$ rises) at a given world interest rate increases net foreign lending, and vice versa
2.  A temporary adverse supply shock
Temporary drop in income leads to a drop in saving, so net foreign lending declines; shown in text Fig. 5.3
3.  An increase in the expected future marginal product of capital
Desired investment rises, so net foreign lending falls; shown in text Fig. 5.4

C.  Application: The LDC debt crisis
1.  Less developed countries (LDCs) borrowed heavily from abroad in the 1970s
    a.  By 1986 their debt exceeded 60% of their GDP
2.  In 1982, bankers lost confidence in LDCs' ability to repay the loans
    a.  Despite the loss of credit, LDCs were mostly able to repay interest and principal as promised
    b.  But the debt repayments exacted a heavy toll, since the LDC's had to reduce imports and increase exports
    c.  As a result, economic growth declined and living standards fell
3.  In 1989, the Brady plan reduced LDC debt in exchange for economic reforms in LDCs (lower government spending, increased use of free markets)
4.  The LDC crisis raises some important questions:
    a.  Why did LDCs borrow so much?
        (1)  LDCs wanted funds for investment
        (2)  Saving was low because income was low
        (3)  Also, oil price hikes in the 1970s further reduced income and saving
        (4)  The result: LDCs borrowed a lot from other countries
    b.  Why did the loans go bad?
        (1)  The recessions of 1979–1982 reduced demand for LDC exports
        (2)  The rise in the world real interest rate in the early 1980s greatly increased the burden of the debt
    c.  Why did the crisis take so long to be resolved?
        (1)  Solutions to the debt crisis have developed slowly because of disagreement over how the losses were to be shared

D.  Application:  The Crises in Mexico, East Asia and Russia
1.  The Mexican economy did poorly in the 1980s
    a.  But it had been doing better from 1987 into the 1990s by reducing foreign debt, reducing inflation and the government deficit, and relying more on free markets
    b.  NAFTA promised to reduce trade barriers with Canada in 1993
2.  Foreign investors poured money into Mexico in 1992 and 1993
    a.  But the capital account surplus necessitated a current account deficit
3.  In 1994, doubts about Mexico's political stability and questions about the government's willingness to stick to its reform policies made foreign investors uneasy
    a.  Investors began selling off Mexican assets and not renewing loans
    b.  The loss of capital inflows forced Mexico to reduce its current account deficit
    c.  Mexico increased its saving (by cutting consumption) and reduced investment to reduce the current account deficit
    d.  The result was a severe recession
4.  Large capital inflows are a two-edged sword

a.  They help an economy grow more quickly
b.  But sudden withdrawal of foreign funds can be disastrous

E.  The political environment: default and sovereign debt
1.  There is no international agency that can enforce international debt contracts
2.  But sovereign governments don't often default on loans, since doing so might disrupt trade and prevent them from borrowing in the future

IV. Saving and Investment in Large Open Economies (Sec. 5.4)
F.  Large open economy: an economy large enough to affect the world real interest rate
1.  Suppose there are just two economies in the world
a.  The home or domestic economy (saving $S$, investment $I$)
b.  The foreign economy, representing the rest of the world (saving $S_{For}$, investment $I_{For}$)
2.  The world real interest rate moves to equilibrate desired international lending by one country with desired international borrowing by the other (Fig. 5.2; Key diagram 5; text Fig. 5.6)

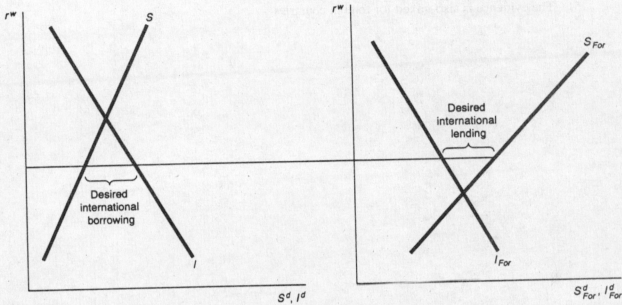

Figure 5.2

3.  Equivalent statement: The equilibrium world real interest rate is determined such that a current account surplus in one country is equal in magnitude to the current account deficit in the other
4.  Changes in the equilibrium world real interest rate: Any factor that increases desired international lending of a country relative to desired international borrowing causes the world real interest rate to fall

V.  Fiscal Policy and the Current Account (Sec. 5.5)
Are government budget deficits necessarily accompanied by current account deficits?  That is, are there "twin deficits"?
A.  The critical factor: the response of national saving
1.  An increase in the government budget deficit raises the current account deficit only if the increase in the budget deficit reduces desired national saving
2.  In a small open economy, if an increase in the government budget deficit reduces desired national saving, the saving curve shifts left, thus reducing the current account balance
B.  The government budget deficit and national saving
1.  A deficit caused by increased government purchases

      a.    No question here: The deficit definitely reduces national saving

      b.    Result: The current account balance declines

  2.    A deficit resulting from a tax cut

      a.    $S^d$ falls only if $C^d$ rises

      b.    So $S^d$ won't change if Ricardian equivalence holds, since then a tax cut won't affect consumption

      c.    But if people don't foresee the future taxes implied by a tax cut today, they will consume more, desired saving will decline, and so will the current account balance

C.   Application: the twin deficits

  1.    Relationship between the Canadian government budget deficit and Canadian current account deficit

  2.    Text Fig. 5.9 shows data from 1961 to 2001

  3.    The deficits appear to be twins in the 1980s and early 1990s, moving closely together

  4.    But at other times (during World War II, and during 1997 and 1998) government budget deficits grew, yet the current account balance increased

  5.    The evidence is also mixed for foreign countries

# MULTIPLE-CHOICE QUESTIONS

1. Which of the following transactions would not be included in the current account of the home country?
   a. A consumer good is imported into the home country.
   b. A home country resident makes a deposit in a foreign bank.
   c. A foreign student pays tuition to a university in the home country.
   d. A home country resident receives income on his or her foreign assets.

2. If Canada donates footballs to Japan, how is the transaction recorded on the Canadian balance of payments accounts?
   a. debit: merchandise trade; credit: capital and financial account
   b. debit: capital and financial account; credit: merchandise trade
   c. debit: net unilateral transfers; credit: merchandise trade
   d. debit: merchandise trade; credit: net unilateral transfers

3. If a Canadian firm buys stereos from a Japanese firm and the Japanese firm uses the dollars it gets to buy Canadian Treasury bonds, what items are recorded in the Canadian balance of payments accounts?
   a. credit the trade account; credit the capital and financial account
   b. credit the trade account; debit the capital and financial account
   c. debit the trade account; debit the capital and financial account
   d. debit the trade account; credit the capital and financial account

4. If a Canadian company imports 10 Toyotas from Japan at $15,000 each, and the Japanese company buys airline tickets on a Canadian airline with the money, how does this affect the Canadian balance of payments accounts?
   a. debit: merchandise trade; credit: capital and financial account
   b. debit: capital and financial account; credit: merchandise trade
   c. debit: merchandise trade; credit: services
   d. debit: services; credit: merchandise trade

5. If a French company sells 1000 gallons of Perrier to a Canadian company at 25 francs per gallon, and uses the money to buy stock in a Spanish cork company, how does this affect the French balance of payments accounts?
   a. debit: capital and financial account; credit: merchandise trade
   b. debit: merchandise trade; credit: capital and financial account
   c. debit: net investment income from abroad; credit: capital and financial account
   d. debit: merchandise trade; credit: net investment income from abroad

6. The difference between the current account balance and net exports is
   a. the capital account.
   b. net unilateral transfers plus net factor payments from abroad.
   c. adjustments in net foreign assets.
   d. income receipts from foreign assets.

7. A country has a current account surplus if
   a. the value of its exports exceeds the value of its imports, assuming net income from foreign assets and net unilateral transfers have a value of zero.
   b. the value of its net exports of services exceeds the value of its net exports of goods.
   c. it receives more income from foreign assets than it pays to foreigners for foreign-owned domestic assets.
   d. its capital inflows exceed its capital outflows.

8. If the Bank of Canada buys $3 billion worth of Japanese yen, $4 billion of German marks, and $2 billion of French francs, and sells $5 billion of British pounds, how does this affect the official settlements balance?
   a. Falls by $4 billion
   b. Rises by $4 billion
   c. Rises by $9 billion
   d. Falls by $5 billion

9. An economic benefit of capital outflows is that they
   a. reduce domestic unemployment.
   b. reduce domestic saving.
   c. increase domestic investment.
   d. create future income payment inflows.

10. A negative value for the Canadian official reserve assets line in the balance of payments accounts means that
    a. Canadian residents have sold more gold to foreigners than they bought.
    b. Canadian residents bought more gold from foreigners than they sold.
    c. the Canadian central bank has increased its holdings of foreign reserve assets.
    d. the Canadian central bank has decreased its holdings of foreign reserve assets.

11. The official settlements balance
    a. is always negative when there is a current account deficit.
    b. always equals zero.
    c. declines when Canadian official reserves increase.
    d. is also called the balance of payments.

12. If a country has a balance of payments deficit, then
    a. its capital outflows exceed its capital inflows.
    b. it cannot compete in international markets.
    c. it is reducing its holdings of official reserve assets.
    d. it has a current account deficit.

13. A country's capital and financial account balance decreases if
    a. its current account balance increases.
    b. its income payment inflows on foreign assets decrease.
    c. its domestic residents working abroad reduce the income they send home to their families.
    d. foreigners increase their purchases of its existing assets.

14. If Canada acquired net foreign assets of $50 billion in one year, this would be the equivalent of
    a.  net imports of $50 billion.
    b.  net foreign borrowing of $50 billion.
    c.  a capital account deficit of $50 billion.
    d.  a current account deficit of $50 billion.

15. You just read that forecasters predict Canada will run a current account deficit in 2001. From this you would infer that Canada will also
    a.  run a capital and financial account deficit in 2001.
    b.  decrease its official reserve assets.
    c.  run a balance of payments surplus.
    d.  decrease its holding of net foreign assets.

16. A friend claims that Canada is a net international debtor. The best way of testing this claim is to
    a.  see whether Canadian foreign liabilities exceeded Canadian foreign income.
    b.  see whether Canadian receipts from foreign assets exceeded Canadian payments to foreign owners of Canadian assets.
    c.  see whether Canadian official reserve assets were positive or negative.
    d.  see whether Canada ran a balance of payments surplus or deficit last year.

17. Absorption refers to
    a.  the total amount of imports purchased by a country.
    b.  the net amount of imports purchased by a country.
    c.  total spending by domestic residents, businesses, and governments.
    d.  GDP less desired consumption, desired investment, and government purchases.

18. The goods market equilibrium condition in an open economy shows that
    a.  $NX = S^d - I^d$
    b.  $S^d + NX = I^d$
    c.  $S^d + I^d = NX$
    d.  $S^d = I^d$

19. In a saving-investment diagram for a small open economy
    a.  the saving curve is vertical at some fixed level of output.
    b.  the saving curve is horizontal at some fixed interest rate.
    c.  the interest rate is fixed at the world real interest rate.
    d.  equilibrium requires that $S^d = I^d$.

20. Suppose output is $35 billion, government purchases are $10 billion, desired consumption is $15 billion, and desired investment is $6 billion. Desired savings is equal to
    a.  $ 2 billion.
    b.  $10 billion.
    c.  $14 billion.
    d.  $16 billion.

21. You have just read in the newspaper that a hurricane has destroyed Guatemala's coffee crop for this year. Guatemala is a small open economy. Based on this information alone, you would expect that
    a. desired investment would fall in Guatemala.
    b. desired investment would increase in Guatemala.
    c. net foreign lending by Guatemala would increase.
    d. net foreign lending by Guatemala would decrease.

22. For a small open economy, an increase in the world real interest rate would necessarily
    a. increase net foreign lending.
    b. decrease net exports.
    c. decrease the current account balance.
    d. worsen the balance of payments.

23. When a temporary adverse supply shock hits a small open economy, it causes the current account to _____ and investment to _____.
    a. fall; fall
    b. rise; remain unchanged
    c. fall; remain unchanged
    d. rise; fall

24. Which of the statements below is *not* a reason for the high level of lending to less developed countries in the 1970s?
    a. Most countries borrow large amounts of money in the initial stages of development.
    b. The world real interest rate was high in the 1970s.
    c. In a growing developing economy, investment opportunities exceed the domestic population's capacity to save.
    d. The OPEC price increases caused consumers in non-oil exporting LDCs to reduce their savings.

25. One important reason why the loans to less developed countries went bad was
    a. lower inflation rates in developed countries.
    b. higher oil prices after 1982.
    c. larger government deficits among developing countries.
    d. higher interest rates in the early 1980s.

26. A country's real interest rate would increase if
    a. the government imposed capital controls in a large open economy and the capital and financial account had been in surplus.
    b. the government imposed capital controls in a large open economy and the capital and financial account had been in deficit.
    c. there were a temporary positive supply shock in a small open economy.
    d. there were a temporary negative supply shock in a small open economy.

27. A large open economy
    a. dominates world trade in one or more products.
    b. is physically larger than all small open economies.
    c. has a larger population than all small open economies.
    d. lends or borrows enough in the international capital market to influence the world real interest rate.

28. In a two-economy model of Canada and another large economy made up of the rest of the world, if desired saving by the rest of the world declined,
    a. Canadian investment would increase.
    b. Canadian saving would decrease.
    c. the world real interest rate would increase.
    d. the world real interest rate would decrease.

29. When future labour income falls in a large open economy, it causes the current account to _____ and investment to _____.
    a. fall; rise
    b. rise; remain unchanged
    c. fall; remain unchanged
    d. rise; rise

30. Assume that Costa Rica, a small open economy, has increased the government budget deficit by 10 million colon, reducing the current account balance in the process. All else being equal, you would expect this action to cause
    a. an increase in desired saving in Costa Rica.
    b. an increase in the real world interest rate.
    c. an increase in exports by Costa Rica.
    d. an increase in Costa Rica's absorption.


## REVIEW QUESTIONS

1. Briefly define the current account and the capital and financial account. Why is the sum of these two accounts equal to zero?

2. What determines the interest rate in a small open economy?

3. How did the LDC debt problem become a crisis? Identify and briefly explain two causes of the LDC debt crisis.

4. Is Canada a large open economy? Briefly explain.

5. What were the principal causes of the Canadian government budget deficits of the 1980s? How did these budget deficits lead to the twin deficits? According to the Ricardian equivalence proposition, should twin deficits arise as a result of tax cuts?

## NUMERICAL PROBLEMS

1.  Show where each of the following transactions belongs on the Canadian balance of payments table, using an exchange rate of 100 Japanese yen per Canadian dollar.
    a.  A Japanese firm spends 5 billion yen to buy personal computers from a Canadian firm
    b.  A wealthy Japanese businessman gives $100 thousand to the San Diego Zoo.
    c.  A Canadian firm buys 1 million Sony Walkmans at 6000 yen each (Sony is a Japanese firm).
    d.  A Japanese investment banking firm buys 500 million dollars worth of newly issued Canadian government Treasury bills.
    e.  Canadian steel firms send 2000 executives to Japan to take courses in the Japanese method of steel production and Japanese management techniques, paying 2 million yen per executive.
    f.  Repeat parts a. - e. for the balance of payments table of Japan.

2.  Use the following data to calculate net exports ($NX$), the current account balance ($CA$), and the capital and financial account balance ($KFA$):  Exports = $800 billion, imports = $900 billion, net income from foreign assets = $25 billion, net unilateral transfers = - $25 billion, net increase in Canadian-owned assets abroad other than official reserve assets = $90 billion, and official settlements balance = - $10 billion.

3.  In a small open economy,
    $S^d$ = $20 billion + ($100 billion) $r^w$,
    $I^d$ = $30 billion - ($100 billion) $r^w$,
    $Y$ = $70 billion,
    $G$ = $20 billion,
    $r^w$ = .04.

    a.  Calculate the current account balance.
    b.  Calculate net exports.
    c.  Calculate desired consumption.
    d.  Calculate absorption.

4.  Assume that net exports equal the current account balance ($NX = CA$), and that initially $NX$ = $50 billion. Use the goods market equilibrium condition for a small open economy to calculate the effect of a temporary tax cut of $200 billion on net exports under each of the following conditions:
    (a)  $S^d$ and $I^d$ remain unchanged
    (b)  $S^d$ declines by $50 billion and $I^d$ declines by $50 billion
    (c)  $S^d$ declines by $200 billion and $I^d$ remains unchanged

## ANALYTICAL QUESTIONS

1.  Suppose the government of a large open economy announces a major expansion of government spending to dig a tunnel to the earth's core, to be financed entirely by borrowing. What effect does this have on the world real interest rate, national saving, investment, and the current account balance in equilibrium?

## ANSWERS TO MULTIPLE-CHOICE QUESTIONS

| Number | Answer | Number | Answer | Number | Answer |
|--------|--------|--------|--------|--------|--------|
| 1 | b | 11 | d | 21 | d |
| 2 | c | 12 | c | 22 | a |
| 3 | d | 13 | a | 23 | c |
| 4 | c | 14 | c | 24 | b |
| 5 | a | 15 | d | 25 | d |
| 6 | b | 16 | b | 26 | a |
| 7 | a | 17 | c | 27 | d |
| 8 | b | 18 | a | 28 | c |
| 9 | d | 19 | c | 29 | d |
| 10 | c | 20 | b | 30 | d |

## ANSWERS TO REVIEW QUESTIONS

1.  The current account measures the value of net exports of currently produced goods and services, plus net factor payments from abroad, and net unilateral transfers into a country.  The capital and financial account measures the value of net capital inflows into a country from trade in existing real and financial assets.

    The current account plus the capital and financial account equals zero because every international transaction is a trade of goods, services, or assets, and the two sides to any transaction always have offsetting effects on the current account and the capital and financial account.

2.  The world real interest rate is determined by the aggregate supply of saving and demand for investment in the international capital market.  Changes in domestic saving or investment in a small open economy do not affect the interest rate.

3.  The LDC debt problem became a crisis because developed country lenders incurred extraordinarily    large losses on these loans in the 1980s.  Some debtor countries threatened to default on the remainder of their huge foreign debts, and such large defaults could have threatened the health of some large bank lenders.

    Two causes of the LDC debt crisis were:  (1) unexpected global macroeconomic events, including the oil shocks in the 1970s followed by worldwide recession in the 1979–1982 period, both of which reduced non-oil exporting LDCs' net exports; and (2) careless lending and poor investment decisions, as banks loaned these countries too much, partly because they were lending recycled petrodollars, and because the LDC borrowers did not efficiently invest all the funds in projects that would produce enough investment income to repay the loans.

4.  Yes, Canada is a large open economy.  It is an open economy because it engages in international transactions; it is a large economy because it lends and borrows enough in international capital markets to affect the world real interest rate.

5.   The principal causes of the Canadian federal government budget deficits of the 1980s were a reduction in government revenue The twin deficits arose because the increased government budget deficit reduced national saving, leading to a current account deficit.  According to the Ricardian equivalence proposition, a government budget deficit created by a tax cut will have no real economic effects because it will not affect saving.  According to this theory the government budget deficit and the trade deficit are independent events.

## ANSWERS TO NUMERICAL PROBLEMS

1.   a.   Credit: $50 million exports of merchandise
     b.   Credit: $100 thousand net unilateral transfers
     c.   Debit: $60 million imports of merchandise
     d.   Credit: $500 million increase in foreign-owned assets in Canada
     e.   Debit: $40 million imports of services
     f.   Debit: 5 billion yen imports of merchandise
          Debit: 10 million yen net unilateral transfers
          Credit: 6 billion yen exports of merchandise
          Debit: 50 billion yen increase in Japanese-owned assets abroad
          Credit: 4 billion yen exports of services

2.   $NX$ = exports - imports
          = $800 billion - $900 billion
          = - $100 billion.

     $CA$ = $NX$ + net income from foreign assets + net unilateral transfers
          = - $100 billion + $25 billion - $25 billion
          = - $100 billion.

     $KFA$ = net increase in CANADA-owned assets abroad - official settlements balance
           = $90 billion + $10 billion
           = $100 billion.

3.   a.   - $ 2 billion
     b.   - $ 2 billion
     c.   $26 billion
     d.   $72 billion

4.   Use the formula $NX = S^d - I^d$.

     (a)  With no change in $S^d$ and $I^d$, $NX$ remains unchanged.

     (b)  When $S^d$ declines by $50 billion and $I^d$ declines by $50 billion, then $NX$ remains unchanged.

     (c)  When $S^d$ declines by $200 billion and $I^d$ remains unchanged, $NX$ declines by $200 billion.

**ANSWERS TO ANALYTICAL QUESTIONS**

1.  Desired national saving shifts left as shown in Figure 5.3, causing the equilibrium world real interest rate to rise, investment to fall, desired national saving to fall, and the current account balance to fall.

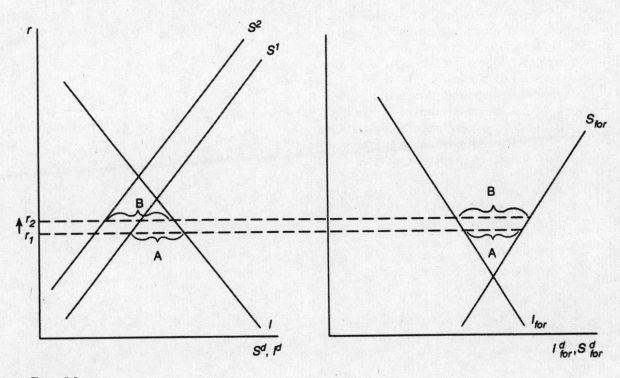

Figure 5.3

# CHAPTER 6: LONG-RUN ECONOMIC GROWTH

## INTRODUCTION

The purpose of this chapter is to identify forces that determine the growth rate of an economy. You'll see that changes in productivity are the key element in determining growth, but that saving and investment decisions are also important. You'll also see the types of policies that governments may use to influence the rate of growth.

Section 6.1 begins by examining the sources of economic growth, starting with a production function for the economy and breaking it down to account for growth in each element. Then, Section 6.2 covers growth dynamics in the Solow model, looks at how in the long run, equilibrium is reached when the economy is at a steady state. This leads to a discussion of what determines long-run living standards. Then, there's a description of endogenous growth theory and how human capital and technological innovation can lead to growth. Finally, Section 6.3 discusses government policies that can be used (potentially) to raise long-run living standards, including policies that increase saving, other policies that increase productivity, and industrial policy.

Many students find the Solow model (also known as the neoclassical growth model) of Section 6.2 quite challenging. There are both equations [especially Equations (6.7) and (6.10)] and figures (Figures 6.2 and 6.3) that you must comprehend well to fully understand how the model works. You should work on a lot of problems that relate to the Solow model in both this study guide and in the textbook to ensure that you understand the model completely.

## CHAPTER OUTLINE

I.  The Sources of Economic Growth (Sec. 6.1)
    A.  Production function   $Y = AF(K,N)$   (6.1)
        1.  Decompose into growth rate form: the growth accounting equation
            $\Delta Y/Y = \Delta A/A + a_K\, \Delta K/K + a_N\, \Delta N/N$   (6.2)
        2.  The $a$ terms are the elasticities of output with respect to the inputs (capital and labour)
        3.  Interpretation
            a.  A rise of 10% in $A$ raises output by 10%
            b.  A rise of 10% in $K$ raises output by $a_K$ times 10%
            c.  A rise of 10% in $N$ raises output by $a_N$ times 10%
        4.  Both $a_K$ and $a_N$ are less than 1 due to diminishing marginal productivity
    B.  Growth accounting
        1.  Four steps in breaking output growth into its causes (productivity growth, capital input growth, labour input growth)
            a.  Get data on $\Delta Y/Y$, $\Delta K/K$, and $\Delta N/N$, adjusting for quality changes
            b.  Estimate $a_K$ and $a_N$ from historical data
            c.  Calculate the contributions of $K$ and $N$ as $a_K \Delta K/K$ and $a_N\, \Delta N/N$, respectively
            d.  Calculate productivity growth as the residual: $\Delta A/A = \Delta Y/Y - a_K\, \Delta K/K - a_N\, \Delta N/N$
        2.  Application: growth accounting and the east Asian "miracle"
            a.  The east Asian "tigers" (Hong Kong, Singapore, South Korea, and Taiwan) grew over 7% per year for 25 years
            b.  Alwyn Young's research found that their rapid growth resulted from capital and labour growth, not productivity growth

c.   The implication is that such rapid growth can't be sustained, since growth in inputs is hard to maintain permanently

3.   Growth accounting and the productivity slowdown

a.   Lithwicks results for 1926–1956 (text Table 6.3)

(1)   Entire period output growth 3.9%; due to labour 0.6%; due to capital 0.6%; due to productivity 2.7%

(2)   Productivity growth is major difference

(a)   1926–1956: 2.7%

(b)   1963–1973: 2.0%

(c)   1974–1986: 0.7%

b.   Productivity growth slowdown occurred in all major developed countries

4.   Application: the post-1973 slowdown in productivity growth
What caused the decline in productivity?

a.   Measurement—inadequate accounting for quality improvements

b.   Technological depletion and slow commercial adaptation—Nordhaus suggests that technological innovation has temporarily dried up; also, companies may be slow to adapt new technology

c.   Oil prices—huge increase in oil prices reduced productivity of capital and labour, especially in basic industries

d.   New industrial revolution—learning process for information technology from 1973 to 1990 meant slower growth

Figure 6.1

II. Growth Dynamics: The Solow Model (also known as the neoclassical growth model) (Sec. 6.2)
  A. Three basic questions about growth
    1. What's the relationship between the long-run standard of living and the saving rate, population growth rate, and rate of technical progress?
    2. How does economic growth change over time? Will it speed up, slow down, or stabilize?
    3. Are there economic forces that will allow poorer countries to catch up to richer countries?
  B. Setup of the Solow model
    1. Basic assumptions and variables
      a. Population and work force grow at same rate $n$
      b. Economy is closed and $G = 0$
      c. $C_t = Y_t - I_t$    (6.3)
      d. Rewrite everything in per-worker terms: $y_t = Y_t/N_t$; $c_t = C_t/N_t$; $k_t = K_t/N_t$
      e. $k_t$ is also called the capital-labour ratio
    2. The per-worker production function
      a. $y_t = f(k_t)$    (6.4)
      b. Assume no productivity growth for now (add it later)
      c. Plot of per-worker production function—text Fig. 6.1
      d. Same shape as aggregate production function
    3. Steady states
      a. Steady state: $y_t$, $c_t$, and $k_t$ are constant over time
      b. Gross investment must
        (1) Replace worn out capital, $dK_t$
        (2) Expand so the capital stock grows as the economy grows, $nK_t$
      c. $I_t = (n + d)K_t$    (6.5)
      d. From Eq. (6.3), $C_t = Y_t - I_t = Y_t - (n + d)K_t$    (6.6)
      e. In per-worker terms, in steady state $c = f(k) - (n + d)k$    (6.7)
      f. Plot of $c$, $f(k)$, and $(n + d)k$ (Fig. 6.1; identical to text Fig. 6.2)
      g. Increasing k will increase c up to a point
        (1) This is $k_1$ in the figure, the Golden Rule capital stock
        (2) For $k$ beyond this point, $c$ will decline
        (3) But we assume henceforth that k is less than $k_1$, so c always rises as $k$ rises
    4. Reaching the steady state
      a. Suppose saving is proportional to current income: $S_t = sY_t$    (6.8), where s is the saving rate, which is between 0 and 1
      b. Equating saving to investment gives $sY_t = (n + d)K_t$    (6.9)
      c. Putting this in per-worker terms gives $sf(k) = (n + d)k$    (6.10)
      d. Plot of $sf(k)$ and $(n + d)k$ (Fig. 6.2; identical to text Fig. 6.3)
      e. The only possible steady-state capital-labour ratio is $k^*$. Output at that point is $y^* = f(k^*)$; consumption is $c^* = f(k^*) - (n + d)k^*$
      f. If $k$ begins at some level other than $k^*$, it will move toward $k^*$
        (1) For $k$ below $k^*$, saving > the amount of investment needed to keep $k$ constant, so $k$ rises
        (2) For $k$ above $k^*$, saving < the amount of investment needed to keep $k$ constant, so $k$ falls
      g. To summarize, with no productivity growth, the economy reaches a steady state, with constant capital-labour ratio, output per worker, and consumption per worker

Figure 6.2

C.    The fundamental determinants of long-run living standards
    1.    The saving rate
        a.    Higher saving rate means higher capital-labour ratio, higher output per worker, and higher consumption per worker (shown in text Fig. 6.4)
        b.    Should a policy goal be to raise the saving rate?
            (1)    Not necessarily, since the cost is lower consumption in the short run
            (2)    There is a trade-off between present and future consumption
    2.    Population growth
        a.    Higher population growth means a lower capital-labour ratio, lower output per worker, and lower consumption per worker (shown in text Fig. 6.5)
        b.    Should a policy goal be to reduce population growth?
            (1)    Doing so will raise consumption per worker
            (2)    But it will reduce total output and consumption, affecting a nation's ability to defend itself or influence world events
        c.    The Solow model also assumes that the proportion of the population of working age is fixed
            (1)    But when population growth changes dramatically this may not be true
            (2)    Changes in cohort sizes may cause problems for social security systems and areas like health care
    3.    Productivity growth
        a.    The key factor in economic growth is productivity improvement
        b.    Productivity improvement raises output per worker for a given level of the capital-labour ratio
        c.    In equilibrium, productivity improvement increases the capital-labour ratio, output per worker, and consumption per worker
            (1)    Productivity improvement directly improves the amount that can be produced at any capital-labour ratio
            (2)    The increase in output per worker increases the supply of saving, causing the long-run capital-labour ratio to rise
        d.    Can consumption per worker grow indefinitely?
            (1)    The saving rate can't rise forever (it peaks at 100%) and the population growth rate can't fall forever
            (2)    But productivity and innovation can always occur, so living standards can rise continuously
        e.    Summary: The rate of productivity improvement is the dominant factor determining how quickly living standards rise
    4.    Application: Do economies converge?
        a.    Unconditional convergence: Poor countries eventually catch up to rich countries
            (1)    This should occur if saving rates, population growth rates, and production functions are the same worldwide
            (2)    Then, even though they start with different capital-labour ratios, all countries should converge with the same capital-labour ratio, output per worker, and consumption per worker
            (3)    If there is international borrowing and lending, there is more support for unconditional convergence
                (a)    Capital should flow from rich to poor countries, as it will have a higher marginal product there
                (b)    So investment wouldn't be limited by domestic saving

  b. Conditional convergence: Living standards will converge in countries with similar characteristics [*s, n, d, f(k)*]

    (1) Countries with different fundamental characteristics will not converge

    (2) So a poor country can catch up to a rich country if both have the same saving rate, but not to a rich country with a higher saving rate

  c. No convergence: Poor countries don't catch up over time; this is inconsistent with the Solow model

  d. What is the evidence?

    (1) Little support for unconditional convergence

    (2) Some support for conditional convergence after correcting for differences in saving rates and population growth (Mankiw, Romer, and Weil, 1992)

    (3) Support for conditional convergence among provinces in Canada (Serge Coulombe, Frank Lee, 1991

    (4) Since there's little support for unconditional convergence, international financial markets must be imperfect (due to limits on foreign investment by governments, tariff barriers, and information costs)

D. Endogenous growth theory—explaining the sources of productivity growth

 1. Aggregate production function $Y = AK$ (6.11)

  a. Constant *MPK*

    (1) Human capital

      (a) Knowledge, skills, and training of individuals

      (b) Human capital tends to increase in same proportion as physical capital

    (2) Research and development programs

    (3) Increases in capital and output generate increased technical knowledge, which offsets decline in *MPK* from having more capital

 2. Implications of endogenous growth

  a. Suppose saving is a constant fraction of output: $S = sAK$

  b. Since investment = net investment + depreciation, $I = \Delta K + dK$

  c. Setting investment equal to saving implies: $\Delta K + dK = sAK$ (6.12)

  d. Rearrange (6.12): $\Delta K/K = sA - d$ (6.13)

  e. Since output is proportional to capital, $)\Delta Y/Y = )\Delta K/K$, so $\Delta)Y/Y = sA - d$ (6.14)

  f. Thus the saving rate affects the long-run growth rate (not true in Solow model)

 3. Summary

  a. Endogenous growth theory attempts to explain, rather than assume, the economy's growth rate

  b. The growth rate depends on many things, such as the saving rate, that can be affected by government policies

III.  Government Policies to Raise Long-Run Living Standards (Sec. 6.3)
    A.  Policies to affect the saving rate
        1.  If the private market is efficient, the government shouldn't try to change the saving rate
            a.  The private market's saving rate represents its trade-off of present for future consumption
            b.  But if tax laws or myopia cause an inefficiently low level of saving, government policy to raise the saving rate may be justified
        2.  How can saving be increased?
            a.  One way is to raise the real interest rate to encourage saving; but the response of saving to changes in the real interest rate seems to be small
            b.  Another way is to increase government saving
                (1)  The government could reduce the deficit or run a surplus
                (2)  But under Ricardian equivalence, tax increases to reduce the deficit won't affect national saving
        3.  The political environment:  economic growth and democracy
            a.  Does democracy conflict with or support economic growth?
            b.  Democracy may promote growth by providing stability, being less likely to start wars, and having good relations with the advanced industrial nations, which are democracies
                (1)  But it may be hard for democracies to make tough choices or undergo unpopular reforms
            c.  Empirical evidence shows that most rich countries are democratic, but many became rich when they weren't democratic
                (1)  However, one study found that growth rates of democratic countries average three times growth rates of nondemocratic countries
                (2)  But other studies didn't find much difference
                (3)  There's certainly no evidence that democracy imposes costs in terms of lost economic growth
    B.  Policies to raise the rate of productivity growth
        1.  Improving infrastructure
            a.  Infrastructure: highways, bridges, utilities, dams, airports
            b.  Empirical studies suggest a link between infrastructure and productivity
            c.  Canadian infrastructure spending has declined in the last two decades
            d.  Would increased infrastructure spending increase productivity?
                (1)  There might be reverse causation: Richer countries with higher productivity spend more on infrastructure, rather than vice versa
                (2)  Infrastructure investments by government may be inefficient, since politics, not economic efficiency, is often the main determinant
        2.  Building human capital
            a.  There's a strong connection between productivity and human capital
            b.  Government can encourage human capital formation through educational policies, worker training and relocation programs, and health programs
            c.  Another form of human capital is entrepreneurial skill
                Government could help by removing barriers like red tape
        3.  Encouraging research and development
            Government can encourage R and D through direct aid to research

C.  Industrial policy

A growth strategy in which government uses taxes, subsidies, or regulation to influence economic development

1.  Some argue that government should promote high-tech industry
2.  But others think the free market allocates resources well without government interference
3.  Why might government interference be desirable?
    a.  Borrowing constraints on small firms or individuals may prevent them from undertaking research and development
    b.  Spillovers of one firm's innovation may help other firms
    c.  Prestige or military advantage may make it important that a nation have a presence in an industry with few worldwide firms
4.  But the government may be bad at picking winning ideas to fund; further, politics, not innovation, may determine what firms get government funding
5.  Empirical evidence (Gene Grossman): Governments frequently pick losing ideas to fund, though sometimes they pick big winners

## MULTIPLE-CHOICE QUESTIONS

1.  From 1970 to 1980 North Samaria's economy grew at an annual rate of 3.5%, but from 1980 to 1990 it grew by only 1% per year.  In 1980 per capita income was $8000.  How much higher would per capita income have been in 1990 if growth from 1980 to 1990 had been 3.5% rather than 1%?
    a.  $2241
    b.  $2448
    c.  $2508
    d.  $3285

2.  Suppose the current level of output is 5000 and the elasticity of output with respect to labour is 0.7.  A 10% increase in labour would increase the current level of output to
    a.  5035.
    b.  5070.
    c.  5350.
    d.  5700.

3.  Suppose the current level of output is 5000. A 10% increase in productivity would increase the current level of output to
    a.  5050.
    b.  5100.
    c.  5500.
    d.  6000.

4.  Suppose the current level of output is 5000. If the elasticities of output with respect to capital and labour are 0.3 and 0.7, respectively, a 10% increase in capital combined with a 5% increase in labour would increase the current level of output to
    a.  5015.
    b.  5325.
    c.  5600.
    d.  5650.

5.  The equation:
    $$\Delta Y/Y = \Delta A/A + a_K \, \Delta K/K + a_N \, \Delta N/N$$
    is known as
    a.  the production function.
    b.  the Solow model.
    c.  the productivity formula.
    d.  the growth accounting equation.

6.  In the growth accounting equation, productivity growth is
    a.  the difference between output growth and labour growth.
    b.  the difference between output per worker growth and labour per worker growth.
    c.  the difference between labour growth and capital growth.
    d.  output growth minus the sum of labour growth and capital growth, weighted by the elasticities of output with respect to labour and capital.

7. Over the past year, output grew 4%, capital grew 0%, and labour grew 5%. If the elasticities of output with respect to capital and labour are 0.4 and 0.6, respectively, how much did productivity grow?
   a. 0.5%
   b. 1.0%
   c. 1.5%
   d. 2.0%

8. According to Rao and Lemprier, during the period from 1974 to 1986 productivity growth was
   a. positive and greater than productivity growth between 1962 and 1973.
   b. positive but less than productivity growth between 1962 and 1973.
   c. positive but less than input growth.
   d. negative.

9. Harvey Lithwick's analysis of the Canadian economy found that
   a. total factor productivity was the largest source of economic growth since 1926.
   b. the contribution of labour growth has been more variable than the contribution of capital growth.
   c. productivity growth has been positive over any period of more than five years since World War II.
   d. the contribution of labour growth has been greater than the contribution of capital growth.

10. The oil price explanation of the slowdown in economic growth after 1973 is inconsistent with which of the following facts?
   a. Prices of used capital goods that were dependent on oil did not drop sharply when oil prices increased.
   b. The productivity slowdown began just as oil prices were quadrupled in 1973.
   c. The productivity slowdown occurred in all industrial countries.
   d. Industry-by-industry analysis of the impact on oil prices bears out the damage done by the oil price increases.

11. A striking conclusion of the Solow model is that in the absence of productivity growth, in the long run
   a. the economy reaches a steady state.
   b. consumption per worker equals the capital stock per worker.
   c. consumption per worker equals output per worker.
   d. consumption per worker equals investment per worker.

12. Which of the following best describes a steady state?
   a. Political stability is maintained by the state.
   b. People's standard of living is increasing at a stable rate.
   c. Each firm in the economy receives a steady stream of income.
   d. Output per worker, consumption per worker, and capital per worker are constant.

13. Steady state consumption per worker is
   a. larger in the short run than in the long run.
   b. less than steady state investment per worker.
   c. less than steady state saving per worker.
   d. steady state production per worker minus steady state investment per worker.

14. According to the Solow model, an increase in the capital-labour ratio will
    a.   always reduce steady state consumption per worker.
    b.   always increase steady state consumption per worker.
    c.   reduce steady state consumption per worker if starting from a low capital-labour ratio.
    d.   increase steady state consumption per worker if starting from low capital-labour ratio.

15. If the steady-state capital-labour ratio is equal to the Golden Rule capital-labour ratio, then in the steady state
    a.   output per worker equals investment per worker.
    b.   output per worker equals depreciation per worker.
    c.   investment per worker is as large as possible.
    d.   consumption per worker is as large as possible.

16. If $f(k) = 6k^{0.5}$, $s = 0.1$, $n = 0.1$, and $d = 0.2$, what is the value of $k$ at equilibrium?
    a.   1
    b.   2
    c.   3
    d.   4

17. If $f(k) = 2k^{0.5}$, $s = 0.25$, $n = 0.05$, and $d = 0.2$, what is the value of $f(k)$ at equilibrium?
    a.   2
    b.   4
    c.   6
    d.   8

18. If $k = 10$, $y = 30$, and $s = 0.2$, what is $c$?
    a.   24
    b.   20
    c.   18
    d.   12

19. According to the Solow model
    a.   there are constant returns to capital in the long run.
    b.   there are increasing returns to labour in the long run.
    c.   an increase in saving per worker will produce continuing increases in a country's standard of living in the long run.
    d.   the steady state capital-labour ratio will be such that steady state saving per worker equals steady state investment per worker.

20. In the Solow model, if saving per worker initially exceeds investment per worker
    a.   the economy will experience inflation.
    b.   the capital-labour ratio will increase.
    c.   investment per worker will decline.
    d.   saving per worker will decline.

21. In the Solow model, the steady state capital-labour ratio will decline if
    a.   the saving rate per worker increases.
    b.   the consumption rate per worker declines.
    c.   population growth increases.
    d.   productivity increases.

22. In the steady state diagram of the Solow model, an increase in saving per worker is shown by
    a.    shifting the saving-per-worker curve down, resulting in a lower steady state capital-labour ratio.
    b.    shifting the saving-per-worker curve up, resulting in a higher steady state capital-labour ratio.
    c.    shifting the saving-per-worker curve up, resulting in a lower steady state capital-labour ratio.
    d.    shifting the saving-per-worker curve down, resulting in a higher steady state capital-labour ratio.

23. An increase in pollution has caused a permanent increase in the rate of capital depreciation. This would cause
    a.    capital per worker to increase.
    b.    output per worker to fall.
    c.    consumption per worker to increase.
    d.    the total capital stock to be unaffected.

24  According to the Solow model, a decline in the rate of population growth in Canada would
    a.    increase steady state output per worker.
    b.    not affect steady state consumption per worker.
    c.    reduce steady state consumption per worker.
    d.    reduce the capital-labour ratio.

25. A productivity improvement raises steady-state output and consumption per worker in all the ways given below *except*
    a.    it increases the amount that can be produced at any given capital-labour ratio.
    b.    it decreases the depreciation rate of capital.
    c.    it causes the steady-state capital-labour ratio to rise.
    d.    it causes saving per worker to rise.

26. According to Solow's model of output growth, the standards of living of people in rich and poor countries
    a.    will conditionally converge.
    b.    will converge in the short run but will diverge in the long run.
    c.    are the same today and will continue to be the same in the future.
    d.    will converge for closed economies but not for open economies.

27. If there's a reduction in the gap in the standards of living between rich and poor nations that have similar characteristics (similar saving rates, population growth rates, and access to technology), this is evidence
    a.    that rich nations inevitably decay and poor nations inevitably prosper.
    b.    that rich nations inevitably prosper and poor nations inevitably decay.
    c.    of unconditional convergence.
    d.    of conditional convergence.

28  Which of the following government policies is the least likely to be used to increase a nation's long-run economic growth?
    a.    Industrial policies
    b.    Human capital formation policies
    c.    Research and development policies
    d.    Pollution control, labour market, and product quality regulation policies

29.  Which of the following is *not* an example of human capital formation?
     a.   Increases in the educational achievements of the population
     b.   Increases in job skills of the labour force
     c.   Improvements in the nutrition and health of the labour force
     d.   Increases in the birth rate of the population

## REVIEW QUESTIONS

1.   Identify and briefly describe the three principal sources of economic growth.  Identify and briefly describe one cause of a change in each of these three variables that would increase economic growth.

2.   Identify and briefly explain four potential causes of the post-1973 growth slowdown in Canada.

3.   Briefly explain the shape of the per-worker production curve in the Solow model.  If investment per worker initially exceeds saving per worker, how is the steady state capital-labour ratio achieved?

4.   How would each of the following changes affect the capital-labour ratio?
     a.   a decline in saving per worker
     b.   a decline in population
     c.   a decline in productivity

5.   Why does the Solow growth model predict convergence in the standards of living of people in rich and poor countries, and why does the empirical evidence appear to reject the theory?

6.   Describe the main ideas of endogenous growth theory. What does it have to say about the role of government in economic growth?

## NUMERICAL PROBLEMS

1.   Use the growth accounting equation to calculate productivity growth, given output growth of 3.5%, capital stock growth of 5%, labour employment growth of 2%, the output elasticity of capital of 0.3, and the output elasticity of labour of 0.7.

2.   In the past ten years, Patagonia's total output has increased from 2000 to 3000, the capital stock has risen from 4000 to 5200, and the labour force has increased from 400 to 580.  Suppose $a_K = 0.4$ and $a_N = 0.6$.
     a.   How much did capital contribute to economic growth over the decade?
     b.   How much did labour contribute to economic growth over the decade?
     c.   How much did productivity contribute to economic growth over the decade?

3.  A country has the per-worker production function
$$y_t = 3\,k_t^{2/3},$$
where $y_t$ is output per worker and $k_t$ is the capital-labour ratio. The depreciation rate is 0.1 and the population growth rate is 0.05. The saving function is
$$S_t = 0.2Y_t,$$
where $S_t$ is total national saving and $Y_t$ is total output.

a.  What is the steady-state value of capital-labour ratio?

b.  What is the steady-state value of output per worker?

c.  What is the steady-state value of consumption per worker?

4.  Calculate the real GDP per capita after four years of 10% annual economic growth for a country starting with a real GDP per capita of $15,000. Compare this to the real GDP per capita after four years of 1% annual economic growth for a country starting with a real GDP per capita of $20,000. Assume there is no population growth in either country.


## ANALYTICAL QUESTIONS

1.  a.  Draw figures showing the relationship in the Solow model between the capital-labour ratio and (1) output per worker and steady-state investment per worker, (2) consumption per worker, and (3) steady-state investment per worker and saving per worker.

    b.  Suppose the steady state capital stock is less than the Golden Rule capital stock. Show what happens to each of your figures in part (a) when each of the following changes occur, and explain what happens to the capital-labour ratio, output per worker, and consumption per worker.
        (1) Population growth rises.
        (2) The depreciation rate falls.
        (3) The saving rate rises.
        (4) Productivity declines.

## ANSWERS TO MULTIPLE-CHOICE QUESTIONS

| Number | Answer | Number | Answer | Number | Answer |
|--------|--------|--------|--------|--------|--------|
| 1 | b | 11 | a | 21 | c |
| 2 | c | 12 | d | 22 | b |
| 3 | c | 13 | d | 23 | b |
| 4 | b | 14 | d | 24 | a |
| 5 | d | 15 | d | 25 | b |
| 6 | d | 16 | d | 26 | a |
| 7 | b | 17 | b | 27 | d |
| 8 | b | 18 | a | 28 | d |
| 9 | a | 19 | d | 29 | d |
| 10 | a | 20 | b | | |

## ANSWERS TO REVIEW QUESTIONS

1.  The three principal sources of economic growth are: (1) labour growth—increases in the work force; (2) capital growth—increases in the amount of capital employed in the economy; and (3) productivity growth—increases in output for given amounts of labour and capital.

    Causes of positive changes in the sources of economic growth are: (1) labour growth—an increase in the size of the population through immigration or birth and an increase in the share of the population that works (e.g., more women) will increase labour growth; (2) capital growth—an increase in the rate of saving will increase capital growth; and (3) productivity growth—an increase in human capital and a technological advance will increase productivity.

2.  Four of the significant causes of the post-1973 growth slowdown in Canada are:

    (1) Measurement problems. Actual growth may have exceeded measured economic growth during this period; the slowdown may be, at least in part, an illusion. Production of services now dominates production of goods, but increases in the quality and quantity of services (e.g., haircuts and financial consultant services) are harder to measure than increases in the quality and quantity of goods.

    (2) Technological depletion. The technological depletion hypothesis suggests that there were relatively few valuable technological innovations after 1973 and that earlier innovations are no longer producing significant productivity gains. Although significant breakthroughs in electronics (e.g., computers) and in biogenetic engineering (e.g., gene-splicing) have been achieved, they have not as yet produced significant productivity increases.

    (3) Commercial adaptation. Canadian firms have been slow during this period to make commercially profitable use of recent scientific and technological breakthroughs, whereas some foreign firms, including Japanese firms, have benefited greatly from these breakthroughs.

    (4) Oil price increases. The substantial oil price increases in the post-1973 period lowered the amount of output that could be produced from a given amount of capital and labour, thus lowering productivity. Oil price increases caused the prices of all sources of energy and the prices of all intermediate products to increase, thereby significantly increasing final production costs.

3.  The per-worker production curve is positively sloped because adding capital to each unit of labour increases output per worker.  The curve is concave (i.e., increasing at a decreasing rate) because of diminishing marginal productivity of capital; output increases at a slower rate than capital when capital is added to production.

    The steady state capital-labour ratio is the capital-labour ratio at which saving per worker [$s\,f(k)$] equals investment per worker [$(n+d)k$].  If investment per worker initially exceeds saving per worker, then the initial capital-labour ratio exceeds the steady state capital-labour ratio.  The capital-labour ratio will decline because saving is insufficient to provide enough capital to maintain the initial capital-labour ratio.  The capital-labour ratio will continue to decline until it reaches the steady state capital-labour ratio.

4.  a.  A decline in saving per worker causes the steady state capital-labour ratio to decline.

    b.  A decline in population causes the steady state capital-labour ratio to increase.

    c.  A decline in productivity causes the steady state capital-labour ratio to decline.

5.  The Solow model predicts that the standards of living of two closed economies with different capital-labour ratios will eventually converge if they have the same production function, saving rate, and population growth rate.  This is because they will have the same steady state capital-labour ratio toward which both economies move, and the steady state capital-labour ratio determines their long-run standard of living.  If the two countries are open economies, convergence will be faster and will occur even if the two countries have different saving-per-worker functions; in this case, saving will flow out of the rich, high-saving-rate country into the poor country until the investment per worker is the same in each country.  The lack of strong empirical support for unconditional convergence may be explained by inefficiencies in the international capital market and by variables that are missing from the model, including differences in human capital, political stability, and the availability of natural resources.

6.  Endogenous growth theory explains the main sources of productivity growth: human capital (the knowledge, skills, and training of individuals) and technological innovation (caused by research and development programs and learning by doing). Government may play a positive role, because policies that increase the capital-labour ratio may lead to a virtuous circle of growth, raising living standards. Also, the government may foster education and research and development.

## ANSWERS TO NUMERICAL PROBLEMS

1.  The growth accounting equation is $\Delta Y/Y = \Delta A/A + a_K\,\Delta K/K + a_N\,\Delta N/N$.

    Therefore productivity growth is $\Delta A/A = \Delta Y/Y - a_K\,\Delta K/K - a_N\,\Delta N/N$.

    For the given values, productivity growth $= 3.5\% - (0.3)(5\%) - (0.7)(2\%) = 0.6\%$.

2.   a.   $a_K \, \Delta K/K = 0.4 \,(1200 \,/\, 4000) = 12\%$.

     b.   $a_N \, \Delta N/N = 0.6 \,(180 \,/\, 400) = 27\%$.

     c.   $\Delta Y/Y = 50\%$.
          $\Delta A/A = \Delta Y/Y - a_K \, \Delta K/K \; - a_N \, \Delta N/N$
          $\quad\quad\; = 50\% - 12\% - 27\% = 11\%$.

3.   a.   $sf(k) = (n + d)k$, so $0.2 \times 3\, k^{2/3} = 0.15\, k$;
          or $k^{1/3} = 4$, so $k = 64$.

     b.   $y = 3k^{2/3} = 48$.

     c.   $c = (1 - s)y = 0.8y = 38.4$.

4.   One country starts with real GDP per capita =
     $15,000 and achieves 10% economic growth each
     year, with no population growth.  Its real
      GDP per capita at the end of the first year is
     $15,000 x 1.1 = $16,500; at the end of the second
     year it is $16,500 x 1.1 = $18,150; at
     the end of the third year it is $18,150 x 1.1 =
     $19,965; and at the end of the fourth year it is
     $19,965 x 1.1 = $21,962.  Note that the same
     calculation can be done in one step as $15,000 x
     $1.1^4 = $21,962.

     The other country starts with real GDP per
     capita = $20,000 and achieves 1% economic
     growth each year, with no population growth.
     Its real GDP per capita at the end of the first
     year is $20,000 x 1.01 = $20,200; at the end
     of the second year it is $20,200 x 1.01 = $20,402;
     at the end of the third year it is
     $20,402 x 1.01 = $20,606; and at the end of
     the fourth year it s $20,606 x 1.01 = $20,812.   The
     $20,812 real GDP per capita for this
     country is now $1,150 lower than the real GDP per
     capita of the first country, even though it started
     with real GDP per capita that was
     $5,000 lower.  So a country that grows rapidly can
     catch up quickly to a richer country that grows
     more slowly.

Figure 6.3

## ANSWERS TO ANALYTICAL QUESTIONS

1.    a.    See Figures 6.3 and 6.4.

     b.    With the steady state capital stock less than the Golden Rule capital stock, if a change occurs that raises the steady state capital stock, steady state output and consumption will both rise, and vice-versa.

Figure 6.4

        (1)   The rise in population growth shifts the line representing $(n + d)k$ up, as Figure 6.5 shows, so $k$, $y$, and $c$ all fall.

Figure 6.5

        (2)   The fall in the depreciation rate shifts the line representing $(n + d)k$ down, as Figure 6.6 shows, so, $k$, $y$, and $c$ all rise.

Figure 6.6

(3) The rise in the saving rate shifts the line representing *sf(k)* up, as Figure 6.7 shows, so *k*, *y*, and *c* all rise.

(4) The decline in productivity shifts the line representing *sf(k)* down, as Figure 6.8 shows, so *k*, *y*, and *c* all fall.

Figure 6.7

Figure 6.8

# CHAPTER 7: THE ASSET MARKET, MONEY, AND PRICES

## INTRODUCTION

This chapter examines money and prices in great detail. The chapter begins by discussing what money is and why people hold it in Section 7.1. It also discusses the main measures of the money supply. Then, Section 7.2 shows that the decision about money demand is part of a broader portfolio decision, in which people decide on what assets to hold based on expected return, risk, liquidity, and other factors. Section 7.3 covers the demand for money itself, deriving a function that explains money demand and introducing the quantity theory of money. In Section 7.4, equilibrium in the asset market is shown to occur when money supply equals money demand. Finally, Section 7.5 shows how money growth is related to inflation.

## CHAPTER OUTLINE

I. What Is Money? (Sec. 7.1)
   A. The functions of money
      1. Medium of exchange
         a. Barter is inefficient—it requires a double coincidence of wants
         b. Money allows people to trade their labour for money, then use the money to buy goods and services in separate transactions
         c. Money thus permits people to trade with less cost in time and effort
         d. Money also allows specialization, since trading is much easier, so people don't have to produce their own food, clothing, and shelter
      2. Unit of account
         a. Money is the basic unit for measuring economic value
         b. This simplifies comparisons of prices, wages, and incomes
         c. The unit-of-account function is closely linked with the medium-of-exchange function
         d. But countries with very high inflation may use a different unit of account, so they don't have to constantly change prices
      3. Store of value
         a. Money can be used to hold wealth
         b. Most people use money only as a store of value for a short period and for small amounts, because it earns less interest than money in the bank
      4. Box 7.1: money in a prisoner-of-war camp
         a. Radford article on the use of cigarettes as money
         b. Cigarette use as money developed because barter was inefficient
         c. Even nonsmokers used cigarettes as money
         d. Characteristics of cigarettes as money: standardized (so value was easy to ascertain), low in value (so "change" could be made), portable, fairly sturdy
         e. Problem with having a commodity money like cigarettes: can't smoke them and use them as money at the same time
   B. Measuring money—the monetary aggregates
      1. Distinguishing what is money from what isn't money is sometimes difficult
         a. For example, MMMFs allow cheque-writing, but give a higher return than bank chequing accounts: Are they money?
         b. There's no single best measure of the money stock

2. The M1 monetary aggregate
   a. Consists of currency and traveller's cheques held by the public, demand deposits (which pay no interest), and other chequable deposits (which may pay interest)
   b. All components of M1 are used in making payments, so M1 is the closest money measure to our theoretical description of money
3. The M2 monetary aggregate
   a. M2 = M1 + less moneylike assets
   b. Additional assets in M2 include savings deposits, small (< $100,000) time deposits, noninstitutional MMMF balances, money-market deposit accounts (MMDAs)
      (1) Savings deposits include passbook savings accounts
      (2) Time deposits bear interest and have a fixed term (substantial penalty for early withdrawal)
      (3) MMMFs invest in very short-term securities and allow cheque-writing
      (4) MMDAs are offered by banks as a competitor to MMMFs
4. M3 = M2 + less moneylike assets
   a. Large denomination (> $100,000) time deposits
   b. MMMFs held by institutions
   c. Repurchase agreements (repos) are overnight loans made by selling a security and agreeing to repurchase it the next day
   d. Eurodollars are short-term deposits held in foreign branches of Canadian banks
5. Weighted monetary aggregates
   a. The Bank of Canada's money measures add up all the amounts in each category directly
   b. But some assets are more moneylike than others
   c. An alternative approach is to weight each asset by how moneylike it is: Currency has a high weight, Treasury securities have a low weight
   d. This approach seems useful, but is controversial
   e. The Bank of Canada has no official weighted monetary aggregate, just the simple-sum aggregates described above

C. Box 7.2: where have all the U.S. dollars gone?
   1. In 1999, U.S. currency averaged almost $1800 per person, but surveys show people only hold about $100
   2. Some is held by businesses and the underground economy, but most is held abroad
   3. Foreigners hold dollars because of inflation in their local currency and political instability
   4. Since currency is 1/3 of M1 and over half of currency is held abroad, foreigners hold over 1/6 of M1
      a. The data show large fluctuations in M1 when major events occur abroad, like military conflicts
   5. The United States benefits from foreign holdings of our currency, since they essentially get an interest-free loan

D. The money supply
   1. Money supply = money stock = amount of money available in the economy
   2. How does the central bank of a country increase the money supply?
      a. Use newly printed money to buy financial assets from the public—an open-market purchase
      b. To reduce the money supply, sell financial assets to the public to remove money from circulation—an open-market sale
      c. Open-market purchases and sales are called open-market operations
      d. Could also buy newly issued government bonds directly from the government (i.e., the Treasury)
         (1) This is the same as the government financing its expenditures directly by printing money

        (2)   This happens frequently in some countries (though is forbidden by law in Canada)

    3.   Throughout text, use the variable M to represent money supply; this might be M1, M2, or some other aggregate

II.   Portfolio Allocation and the Demand for Assets (Sec. 7.2)

How do people allocate their wealth among various assets? The portfolio allocation decision

   A.   Expected return
      1.   Rate of return = an asset's increase in value per unit of time
         a.   Bank account: Rate of return = interest rate
         b.   Corporate stock: Rate of return = dividend yield + percent increase in stock price
      2.   Investors want assets with the highest expected return (other things equal)
      3.   Returns aren't always known in advance (for example, stock prices fluctuate unexpectedly), so people must estimate their *expected return*

   B.   Risk
      1.   Risk is the degree of uncertainty in an asset's return
      2.   People don't like risk, so prefer assets with low risk (other things equal)

   C.   Liquidity
      1.   Liquidity is the ease and quickness with which an asset can be traded
      2.   Money is very liquid
      3.   Assets like automobiles and houses are very illiquid—it may take a long time and large transaction costs to trade them
      4.   Stocks and bonds are fairly liquid, some more so than others
      5.   Investors prefer liquid assets (other things equal)

   D.   Asset demands
      1.   Trade-off among expected return, risk, and liquidity
      2.   Assets with low risk and high liquidity, like chequing accounts, have low expected returns
      3.   The amount a wealth holder wants of an asset is his or her demand for that asset
      4.   The sum of asset demands equals total wealth

III.   The Demand for Money (Sec. 7.3)
   A.   The demand for money is the quantity of monetary assets people want to hold in their portfolios
      1.   Money demand depends on expected return, risk, and liquidity
      2.   Money is the most liquid asset
      3.   Money pays a low return
      4.   People's money-holding decisions depend on how much they value liquidity against the low return on money

   B.   Key macroeconomic variables that affect money demand
      1.   Price level
         a.   The higher the price level, the more money you need for transactions
         b.   Prices are 10 times as high today as in 1945, so it takes 10 times as much money for equivalent transactions
         c.   Nominal money demand is thus proportional to the price level
      2.   Real income
         a.   The more transactions you conduct, the more money you need
         b.   Real income is a prime determinant of the number of transactions you conduct
         c.   So money demand rises as real income rises
         d.   But money demand isn't proportional to real income, since higher-income individuals use money more efficiently, and since a country's financial sophistication grows as its income rises (use of credit and more sophisticated assets)
         e.   Result:  Money demand rises less than 1-to-1 with a rise in real income

      3.   Interest rates
- a.  An increase in the interest rate or return on nonmonetary assets decreases the demand for money
- b.  An increase in the interest rate on money increases money demand
- c.  This occurs as people trade off liquidity for return
- d.  Though there are many nonmonetary assets with many different interest rates, because they often move together we assume that for nonmonetary assets there's just one nominal interest rate, $i$
- e.  The real interest rate, which affects saving and investment decisions, is $r = i - \pi^e$
- f.  The nominal interest paid on money is $i^m$

C.  The money demand function
1.   $M_d = PL(Y, i)$   (7.1)
- a.  $M^d$ is nominal money demand (aggregate)
- b.  $P$ is the price level
- c.  $L$ is the money demand function
- d.  $Y$ is real income or output
- e.  $i$ is the nominal interest rate on nonmonetary assets
2.   As discussed above, nominal money demand is proportional to the price level
3.   A rise in $Y$ increases money demand; a rise in $i$ reduces money demand
4.   We exclude im from Eq. (7.1) since it doesn't vary much
5.   Alternative expression: $M^d = PL(Y, r + \pi^e)$   (7.2)
    A rise in $r$ or $\pi^e$ reduces money demand
6.   Alternative expression: $M^d/P = L(Y, r + \pi^e)$   (7.3)

D.    Other factors affecting money demand
1.   Wealth: A rise in wealth may increase money demand, but not by much
2.   Risk
- a.  Increased riskiness in the economy may increase money demand
- b.  Times of erratic inflation bring increased risk to money, so money demand declines
3.   Liquidity of alternative assets: Deregulation, competition, and innovation have given other assets more liquidity, reducing the demand for money
4.   Payment technologies: Credit cards, ATMs, and other financial innovations reduce money demand

E.  Elasticities of money demand
1.   How strong are the various effects on money demand?
2.   Statistical studies on the money demand function show results in elasticities
3.   Elasticity: The percent change in money demand caused by a one percent change in some factor
4.   Income elasticity of money demand
- a.  Positive: Higher income increases money demand
- b.  Less than one: Higher income increases money demand less than proportionately
- c.  Goldfeld's results: income elasticity = 2/3
5.   Interest elasticity of money demand
    Small and negative: Higher interest rate on nonmonetary assets reduces money demand slightly
6.   Price elasticity of money demand is unitary, so money demand is proportional to the price level

F.  Application: financial innovation, and a place to stand
1.   Goldfeld (1973) found a stable money (M1) demand function
2.   But late 1974 to early 1976, M1 demand fell relative to that predicted by the model
3.   And in the early 1980s, M1 demand rose relative to that predicted by the model
4.   Why did money demand shift erratically?
    Increased innovation and changes in the financial system

      a.  New assets were invented in the 1970s, liquid assets that paid interest
          People switched wealth from M1 to these assets, reducing M1 demand
          (1)  MMMFs
          (2)  Overnight repurchase agreements
      b.  New assets in the 1980s, interest-bearing chequing accounts; their use brought wealth into M1, raising money demand

  G.  Velocity and the quantity theory of money
    1.  Velocity (V) measures how much money "turns over" each period
    2.  $V$ = nominal GDP / nominal money stock = $PY / M$    (7.4)
    3.  Plot of velocities for M1 and M2 (text Fig. 7.1) shows fairly stable velocity for M2, erratic velocity for M1 beginning in early 1980s
    4.  Quantity theory of money: Real money demand is proportional to real income
      a.  If so, $M^d / P = kY$    (7.5)
      b.  Assumes constant velocity, where velocity isn't affected by income or interest rates
      c.  But velocity of M1 is not constant; it rose steadily from 1960 to 1980 and has been erratic since then
          (1)  Part of the change in velocity is due to changes in interest rates in the 1980s
          (2)  Financial innovations also played a role in velocity's decline in the early 1980s
      b.  M2 velocity is closer to being a constant, but not over short periods

IV.  Asset Market Equilibrium (Sec. 7.4)
  A.  Asset market equilibrium—an aggregation assumption
    1.  Assume that all assets can be grouped into two categories, money and nonmonetary assets
      a.  Money includes currency and chequing accounts
          (1)  Pays interest rate $i^m$
          (2)  Supply is fixed at $M$
      b.  Nonmonetary assets include stocks, bonds, land, etc.
          (1)  Pays interest rate $i = r + \pi^e$
          (2)  Supply is fixed at NM
    2.  Asset market equilibrium occurs when quantity of money supplied equals quantity of money demanded
      a.  $m^d + nm^d$ = total nominal wealth of an individual
      b.  $Md + NMd$ = aggregate nominal wealth (from adding up individual wealth)    (7.6)
      c.  $M + NM$ = aggregate nominal wealth (supply of assets)    (7.7)
      d.  Subtracting (7.7) from (7.6) gives $(M^d - M) + (NM^d - NM) = 0$    (7.8)
      e.  So the excess demand for money $(M^d - M)$ plus the excess demand for nonmonetary assets $(NM^d - NM)$ equals 0.
      f.  So if money supply equals money demand, nonmonetary asset supply must equal nonmonetary asset demand; then the entire asset market is in equilibrium
  B.  The asset market equilibrium condition
    1.  $M / P = L(Y, r + \pi^e)$    (7.9)    real money supply = real money demand
      a.  M is determined by the central bank
      b.  $\pi^e$ is fixed (for now)
      c.  The labour market determines the level of employment; using employment in the production function determines Y
      d.  Given Y, the goods market equilibrium condition determines r
    2.  With all the other variables in Eq. (7.9) determined, the asset market equilibrium condition determines the price level
      a.  $P = M / L(Y, r + \pi^e)$    (7.10)
      b.  The price level is the ratio of nominal money supply to real money demand
      c.  For example, doubling the money supply would double the price level

V.   Money Growth and Inflation (Sec. 7.5)
    A.   The inflation rate is closely related to the growth rate of the money supply
        1.   Rewrite Eq. (7.10) in growth-rate terms:

$$\Delta P / P = \Delta M / M \ - \Delta L(Y, r + \pi^e) \, / \, L(Y, r + \pi^e) \quad (7.11)$$

        2.   If the asset market is in equilibrium, the inflation rate equals the growth rate of the nominal money supply minus the growth rate of real money demand
        3.   To predict inflation we must forecast both money supply growth and real money demand growth
            a.   In long-run equilibrium, we will have $i$ constant, so let's look just at growth in $Y$
            b.   Let $\eta_Y$ be the elasticity of money demand with respect to income
            c.   Then from Eq. (7.11), $\pi = \Delta M / M - \eta_Y \Delta Y / Y$   (7.12)
            d.   Example: If output grows 3% per year, the income elasticity of money demand is 2/3, and the money supply is growing at a 10% rate, then the inflation rate will be 8%
    A.   Application: money growth and inflation in the European countries in transition
        1.   Though the countries of Eastern Europe are becoming more market-oriented, Russia and some others have high inflation because of rapid money growth
        2.   Both the growth rates of money demand and money supply affect inflation, but (in cases of high inflation) usually growth of nominal money supply is the most important factor
            a.   For example, if the income elasticity of money demand were 2/3 and real output grew 15%, real money demand would grow 10% (= 2/3 x 15%); or if income fell 15%, real money demand would fall 10%
            b.   So money demand doesn't vary much, no matter how well or poorly an economy is doing, but nominal money supply growth differs across countries by hundreds of percentage points, so large inflation differences must be due to money supply, not money demand
        3.   Text figure 7.2 shows the link between money growth and inflation in these countries; inflation in clearly positively associated with money growth
        4.   So why do countries allow money supplies to grow quickly, if they know it will cause inflation?
            a.   They sometimes find that printing money is the only way to finance government expenditures
            b.   This is especially true for very poor countries, or countries in political crisis
    C.   The expected inflation rate and the nominal interest rate
        1.   For a given real interest rate ($r$), expected inflation ($\pi^e$) determines the nominal interest rate ($i = r + \pi^e$)
        2.   What factors determine expected inflation?
            a.   People could use Eq. (7.12), relating inflation to the growth rates of the nominal money supply and real income
                (1)   If people expect an increase in money growth, they would then expect a commensurate increase in the inflation rate
                (2)   The expected inflation rate would equal the current inflation rate if money growth and income growth were stable
            b.   Expectations can't be observed directly
                (1)   They can be measured roughly by surveys
                (2)   If real interest rates are stable, expected inflation can be inferred from nominal interest rates

(3)   Policy actions that cause expected inflation to rise should cause nominal interest rates to rise

3.   Text Fig. 7.3 plots Canadian inflation and nominal interest rates
   a.   Inflation and nominal interest rates have tended to move together
   b.   But the real interest rate is clearly not constant
   c.   The real interest rate was negative in the mid-1970s, then became much higher and positive in the late-1970s to early-1980s.

## MULTIPLE-CHOICE QUESTIONS

1. A system in which people trade goods they don't want to consume for goods they do want to consume is called
    a.  an indirect exchange economy.
    b.  a commodity money system.
    c.  a barter system.
    d.  a fiat money system.

2. The following are all functions of money *except*
    a.  medium of exchange.
    b.  store of value.
    c.  source of anxiety.
    d.  unit of account.

3. For something to satisfy the medium of exchange function of money, it must be
    a.  backed by gold.
    b.  readily exchangeable for other goods.
    c.  issued by a central bank.
    d.  an inherently valuable commodity.

4. Which of the following best illustrates the medium of exchange function of money?
    a.  The price of a new car is $25,000.
    b.  A penny saved is a penny earned.
    c.  A person owes $10,000 on his or her credit card.
    d.  You pay $3 to purchase a bag of apples.

5. The number of units of one good that trade for one unit of alternative goods can be determined most easily when
    a.  there is one unit of account.
    b.  the goods all weigh about the same.
    c.  the goods are all new.
    d.  the goods are actively traded through barter.

6. In some countries the Canadian dollar is used as a unit of account rather than the local currency. The primary reason for this is that
    a.  the nation has been running a trade surplus.
    b.  the nation has been running a trade deficit.
    c.  the Canadian inflation rate is higher than the local inflation rate.
    d.  Canadian dollars reduce the need to change prices frequently.

7. One of the criticisms of standard monetary aggregates is that
    a.  they cannot be measured.
    b.  the sum of the assets they contain is not weighted by the frequency of their use in making payments.
    c.  they cannot be controlled by the central bank.
    d.  fluctuations in their size are purely inflationary.

8.  M1 includes
    a.  demand deposits.
    b.  savings deposits.
    c.  time deposits.
    d.  money-market mutual funds.

9.  Which of the following is *not* part of M1?
    a.  Demand deposits
    b.  NOW accounts
    c.  Time deposits
    d.  Traveller's cheques

10. Which of the following statements about M1 and M2 is *not* true?
    a.  Demand deposits are part of M1.
    b.  M2 is more liquid than M1.
    c.  M2 is larger than M1.
    d.  Savings accounts are part of M2.

11. Which of the following is *not* included in M2?
    a.  Money market mutual funds held by individuals
    b.  Money market deposit accounts
    c.  Money market mutual funds held by institutions
    d.  Small-denomination time deposits

12. Compared to M1, the assets in M2
    a.  are more liquid.
    b.  are held more as a store of value.
    c.  are more homogeneous.
    d.  are more stable in value.

13. The stock of Canadian currency per Canadian resident (calculated as the total Canadian currency divided by the Canadian population) in 1999 was about
    a.  $100.
    b.  $500.
    c.  $1000.
    d.  $1800.

14. Suppose you read in the paper that the central bank of Canada plans to expand the money supply.  The central bank is most likely to do this by
    a.  printing more currency and distributing it.
    b.  purchasing government bonds from the public.
    c.  selling government bonds to the public.
    d.  buying newly issued government bonds directly from the government itself.

15. You are putting together a portfolio of assets. The three most important characteristics of the assets you will choose are
    a.   expected return, risk, and liquidity.
    b.   expected return, risk, and collateral.
    c.   expected return, risk, and maturity.
    d.   expected return, liquidity, and maturity.

16. Which of the following portfolio allocation decisions represents the best individual response to an increase in the interest rate on nonmonetary assets?
    a.   Sell some stocks and use the money to buy bonds.
    b.   Sell some bonds and use the money to buy stocks.
    c.   Trade some money for nonmonetary assets.
    d.   Sell some land and use the money to buy nonmonetary assets.

17. A 1% increase in the price level usually leads to _____ in the nominal demand for money.
    a.   a decrease.
    b.   no change.
    c.   an increase of less than 1%.
    d.   an increase of 1%.

18. Between 1980 and 1990, a woman's real income increased from $100,000 to $200,000. All else being equal, her real demand for money probably
    a.   decreased.
    b.   increased, but by less than the increase in real income.
    c.   increased proportionately to the increase in real income.
    d.   increased by more than the increase in real income.

19. During the past year, there was an increase in the price level and an increase in interest rates on financial assets, but a fall in personal incomes. The overall demand for money fell. Which of the following factors was most likely to have contributed to this fall in the demand for money?
    a.   Changes in the price level and in interest rates
    b.   Changes in interest rates and personal incomes
    c.   Changes in the price level and personal incomes
    d.   Changes in personal incomes only

20. Mr. Pierpont has wealth of $200,000. He wants to keep at least $80,000 in bonds at all times, and will shift $10,000 into bonds from his chequing account for each percentage point that the interest rate on bonds exceeds the interest rate on his chequing account. If the interest rate on chequing accounts is 4% and the interest rate on bonds is 9%, how much does Mr. Pierpont keep in his chequing account?
    a.   $ 50,000
    b.   $ 70,000
    c.   $130,000
    d.   $150,000

21. Mr. Pierpont has wealth of $200,000. He wants to keep at least $80,000 in bonds at all times, and will shift $10,000 into bonds from his chequing account for each percentage point that the interest rate on bonds exceeds the interest rate on his chequing account. Currently he keeps $100,000 in bonds, which pay him 7%. What is the current interest rate on chequing accounts?
    a. 5%
    b. 7%
    c. 9%
    d. 10%

22. The money demand function specifies
    a. the variables that determine how much money is held in a given time period.
    b. the uses of money.
    c. the value of money.
    d. how much real income will increase if money demand increases by 5%.

23. If the interest elasticity of money demand is -1/4, by what percent does money demand rise if the nominal interest rate rises from 4% to 5%?
    a. 6.25%
    b. 0.25%
    c. -0.25%
    d. -6.25%

24. If the income elasticity of money demand is 3/4, by what percent does money demand rise if income rises 10%?
    a. 10.00%
    b. 7.50%
    c. 2.50%
    d. 0.75%

25. Instability in M1 money demand in the mid-1970s and since the early 1980s is most closely related to changes in
    a. The directors of the Bank of Canada.
    b. the risks of nonmonetary assets.
    c. real GNP.
    d. deregulation, financial innovations, and payment technologies.

26. According to the quantity theory of money, velocity
    a. increases with nominal income.
    b. is positively related to the real interest rate.
    c. is constant.
    d. is proportional to the price level.

27. If nominal GDP is $7 trillion, the price level is 200, and the nominal money stock is $1 trillion, then velocity is
    a. 1/7.
    b. 2.
    c. 3.5.
    d. 7.

28. Suppose velocity is 6, real output is 6000, and the price level is 200. What is the level of real money demand in this economy?
    a.   1,000
    b.   2,000
    c.   20,000
    d.   200,000

29. If real money demand increases 5%, by about how much does the price level change?
    a.   Falls 5%.
    b.   Falls 50%.
    c.   Rises 50%.
    d.   Rises 5%.

30. If the real interest rate remains constant, an increase in expected inflation from 4% to 8% will cause the nominal interest rate to
    a.   rise to 8%.
    b.   fall to 8%.
    c.   rise by 4 percentage points.
    d.   fall by 4 percentage points.

## REVIEW QUESTIONS

1.   Identify and briefly describe the three principal functions of money.

2.   What are the major components of M1? What are the major components of M2?

3.   Identify and briefly define the three principal characteristics of assets that influence portfolio allocation decisions.

4.   Identify three possible causes of an increase in money demand.

5.   Briefly explain how money demand and velocity are related.

6.   Define asset market equilibrium and state the asset market equilibrium condition.

## NUMERICAL PROBLEMS

1.   Suppose the income elasticity of money demand is 0.75 and the interest elasticity of money demand is -0.2. By what percentage does real money demand change in each of the following circumstances?
    a.   Income rises 2%.
    b.   The interest rate rises from 4% to 5%.
    c.   Income falls 4%.
    d.   The interest rate falls from 6% to 4%.
    e.   Income rises 3% at the same time that the interest rate rises from 2% to 3%.

2.  Calculate the decline in money demand for each of the following changes in the interest rate, given that money demand is $500 billion at an interest rate of 5%.
    a.  The interest rises to 8% and the interest elasticity of money demand is -0.1.
    b.  The interest rate falls to 2% and the interest elasticity of money demand is -0.2.

3.  Calculate the inflation rate for each of the following conditions, assuming that the income elasticity of money demand is 2/3 and that the nominal interest rate is constant.
    a.  Nominal money supply growth is 4% and real income growth is 6%.
    b.  Nominal money supply growth is 12% and real income growth is 6%.
    c.  Nominal money supply growth is -2% and real income growth is -3%.

4.  Calculate the expected rate of inflation for each of the following conditions.
    a.  The nominal interest rate is 10% and the real interest rate is 4%.
    b.  The nominal interest rate is 6% and the real interest rate is 3%.
    c.  The nominal interest rate is 4% and the real interest rate is -1%.

## ANALYTICAL QUESTIONS

1.  In each of the following cases, one factor affecting money demand changes. You must tell how the second factor would have to change if real money demand were to remain unchanged overall.
    a.  Expected inflation rises; real income _____.
    b.  Nominal interest rate on money rises; wealth _____.
    c.  Risk on stocks and bonds rises; efficiency of payments technology _____.
    d.  Risk on money rises; real interest rate on nonmoney assets _____.
    e.  Liquidity of nonmonetary assets rises; expected inflation _____.
    f.  Wealth rises; risk on nonmonetary assets _____.

## ANSWERS TO MULTIPLE-CHOICE QUESTIONS

| Number | Answer | Number | Answer | Number | Answer |
|--------|--------|--------|--------|--------|--------|
| 1 | c | 11 | c | 21 | a |
| 2 | c | 12 | b | 22 | a |
| 3 | b | 13 | d | 23 | d |
| 4 | d | 14 | b | 24 | b |
| 5 | a | 15 | a | 25 | d |
| 6 | d | 16 | c | 26 | c |
| 7 | b | 17 | d | 27 | d |
| 8 | a | 18 | b | 28 | a |
| 9 | c | 19 | b | 29 | a |
| 10 | b | 20 | b | 30 | c |

## ANSWERS TO REVIEW QUESTIONS

1.  The three principal functions of money are the following:

    (1)  Medium of exchange.  Money is used to pay for the factors of production, goods and services, and nonmonetary assets.

    (2)  Unit of account.  Money is the standard used to compare the market values of dissimilar resources, goods, and assets.  For example, the dollar is the monetary standard for Canada; the value of things is measured in dollar units.

    (3)  Store of value.  Money is used as a way of holding wealth.  For example, keeping money in a chequing account represents using money as a store of value.

2.  The principal components of M1 are currency, demand deposits, other chequable deposits, and traveller's cheques.  Currency includes coins and Bank of Canada notes (i.e., paper money).  Other chequable deposits are chequing accounts at banks and thrifts that earn interest (e.g., NOW accounts).

    The principal components of M2 are M1, savings account deposits including money market deposit accounts (MMDAs), small time deposits, and money market mutual funds (MMMFs).  Small time deposits are certificates of deposits (CDs) of less than $100,000 denomination.

3.  The three principal characteristics of assets that determine portfolio allocation decisions are the following:

    (1)  Expected returns:  investor's best guess about the rate of increase in an asset's value over time.

    (2)  Risk:  the likelihood that the actual return will significantly differ from the expected return.

    (3)  Liquidity:  the ease and quickness with which an asset can be exchanged for goods, services, or other assets.

4.  The real quantity of money demanded would increase if real income increased, if the real interest rate on nonmonetary assets declined, if expected inflation declined, if the nominal interest declined, if wealth increased, if the risk on nonmoney assets increased, if the risk on money declined, if the liquidity of alternative assets fell, or if payments technologies became less efficient.

5. Velocity is negatively related to real money demand. Velocity = $PY/M$ = nominal income/nominal money supply = the number of times each dollar is spent in buying final goods and services produced in the current time period. In equilibrium, real money supply = real money demand. By replacing $M/P$ with $L$, we see that velocity equals real output divided by real money demand. Velocity increases when real money demand declines for a given real income. If real demand for money increases relative to real income, velocity declines.

6. Asset market equilibrium exists when the quantity of assets supplied equals the quantity of assets demanded in a national economy in some time period. The aggregate net value of a country's assets is its wealth. The asset market equilibrium equation is $M^d = PL(Y, r + \pi^e)$.

## ANSWERS TO NUMERICAL PROBLEMS

1. Use the formula $\%\Delta m^d = \eta_Y \,\%\Delta Y + \eta_i \,\%\Delta i$.
   a.  1.5%
   b.  -5.0%
   c.  -3.0%
   d.  6.7%
   e.  -7.75%

2. An increase in the interest rate reduces the demand for real money balances. An increase in the interest rate from 5% to 8% is a 60% increase in the interest rate.

   (a) Change in real money demand = -0.1(60%)($500 billion) = (-6%)($500 billion) = -$30 billion.

   (b) Change in real money demand = -0.2(-60%)($500 billion) = (12%)($500 billion) = $60 billion.

3. Use the equation $\pi = \Delta M / M - \eta_Y \Delta Y / Y$.

   a. Inflation rate = 4% - 2/3(6%) = 4% - 4% = 0%.

   b. Inflation rate = 12% - 2/3(6%) = 12% - 4% = 8%.

   c. Inflation rate = -2% - 2/3(-3%) = -2% + 2% = 0%.

4. The expected rate of inflation = the nominal interest rate - the real interest rate.

   a. Expected inflation = 10% - 4% = 6%.

   b. Expected inflation = 6% - 3% = 3%.

   c. Expected inflation = 4% - (-1%) = 5%.

## ANSWERS TO ANALYTICAL QUESTIONS

1.  Money demand is related positively to real income, wealth, the risk on nonmoney assets, and the nominal interest rate on money. Money demand is related negatively to the real interest rate on nonmoney assets, expected inflation, the risk on money, the liquidity of nonmoney assets, and the efficiency of payments technologies.

    a.  The rise in expected inflation reduces money demand, so real income must rise to increase money demand.
    b.  The rise in the nominal interest rate on money rises, so wealth must fall to decrease money demand.
    c.  The increased risk on stocks and bonds raises money demand, so the efficiency of the payments technology must rise to reduce money demand.
    d.  The rise in the risk on money reduces money demand, so the real interest rate on nonmoney assets must fall to increase money demand.
    e.  The rise in the liquidity of nonmonetary assets reduces money demand, so expected inflation must fall to increase money demand.
    f.  The rise in wealth increases money demand, so the risk on nonmonetary assets must fall to decrease money demand.

# CHAPTER 8: BUSINESS CYCLES

## INTRODUCTION

This chapter is the first of four that discuss the business cycle. It discusses the facts about business cycles, Chapter 9 then develops a basic *IS-LM* model of the economy, Chapter 10 looks at the classical approach to analyzing the business cycle, and chapter 11 examines the Keynesian model of the business cycle.

This chapter begins by looking at the basic features of the business cycle in Section 8.1. Section 8.2 then provides a brief history of Canadian business cycles. The relationships between major economic variables are discussed in Section 8.3. Finally, Section 8.4 gives a preview of the economic model that will be used to analyze the business cycle.

## CHAPTER OUTLINE

I.   What Is a Business Cycle? (Sec. 8.1)
    A.   Canadian research on cycles began in 1920 at the National Bureau of Economic Research (NBER)
        1.   NBER maintains the business cycle chronology—a detailed history of business cycles
        2.   NBER sponsors business cycle studies
    B.   Burns and Mitchell (Measuring Business Cycles, 1946) make five main points about business cycles:
        1.   Business cycles arc fluctuations of aggregate economic activity, not a specific variable
        2.   There are expansions and contractions
            a.   Aggregate economic activity declines in a *contraction* or *recession* until it reaches a *trough* (Fig. 8.1)
            b.   Then activity increases in an *expansion* or *boom* until it reaches a *peak*
            c.   A particularly severe recession is called a *depression*
            d.   The sequence from one peak to the next, or from one trough to the next, is a *business cycle*
            e.   Peaks and troughs are *turning points*

Figure 8.1

       f.   Turning points are officially designated by the NBER Business Cycle Dating Committee

   3.  Economic variables show *comovement*—they have regular and predictable patterns of behavior over the course of the business cycle

   4.  The business cycle is recurrent, but not periodic

       a.   Recurrent means the pattern of contraction–trough–expansion–peak occurs again and again

       b.   Not being periodic means that it doesn't occur at regular, predictable intervals

   5.  The business cycle is persistent

       a.   Declines are followed by further declines; growth is followed by more growth

       b.   Because of persistence, forecasting turning points is quite important

  C.  Box 8.1: temporary and permanent components of recessions

   1.  Prior to the 1980s, economists believed that recessions were temporary, and that the economy would return to its prerecession path in the next expansion

   2.  Nelson and Plosser's 1982 article challenged this idea, suggesting that recessions could permanently affect output and other variables

   3.  For example, much of the 1973–1975 drop in output became permanent

   4.  But other recessions show much less permanent effect; Evans's 1989 study suggests on average changes in real output are 30% permanent and 70% temporary

II.  The Canadian Business Cycle: The Historical Record (Sec. 8.2)

  A.  Text Table 8.1 gives the NBER business cycle chronology

  B.  The pre–World War I period

   1.  Recessions were common from 1867 to 1918, with 233 months of contraction and 262 months of expansion [compared to 572 months of expansion and 109 months of contraction from 1945 to 2001]

   2.  The longest contraction on record was 66 months, from November 1873 to May 1879

  C.  The Great Depression and World War II

   1.  The worst economic contraction was the Great Depression of the 1930s

       a.   Real GDP fell nearly 30% from the peak in April 1929 to the trough in March 1933

       b.   The unemployment rate rose from 3% to nearly 25%

       c.   Thousands of banks failed, the stock market collapsed, many farmers went bankrupt, and international trade was halted

       d.   There were really two business cycles in the Great Depression

         (1)  A contraction from April 1929 to March 1933, followed by an expansion that peaked in May 1937

         (2)  A contraction from July 1937 to October 1938

       e.   By July 1937, output had nearly returned to its 1929 peak, but the unemployment rate was high (12%)

       f.   In 1938 the unemployment rate was over 14%

   2.  The Great Depression ended with the start of World War II

       a.   Wartime production brought the unemployment rate below 2%

       b.   Real GDP almost doubled between 1938 and 1944

  D.  Post–World War II business cycles

   1.  From 1945 to 1974 there were six mild contractions

   2.  The longest expansion on record was 160 months, from 1961 to 1974

   3.  Some economists thought the business cycle was dead

   4.  But the OPEC oil shock of 1973 caused a sharp recession, the unemployment rate rising to more than 7%, and inflation rising to double-digit levels

   5.  The 1981–1982 recession was also severe, with the unemployment rate reached 12.8%, but inflation declining from 13% to less than 5%

   6.  The 1990–1991 recession was mild and short, but the recovery was slow and erratic

E.   The "long boom"
1.   From 1982 to the present, only one brief recession, from July 1990 to March 1991
2.   Expansion from 1991 to present is longest in Canadian history
F.   Have Canadian business cycles become less severe?
1.   Economists believed that business cycles weren't as bad after World War II as they were before
2.   The average contraction before 1929 lasted 20 months compared to 12 months after 1945
3.   The average expansion before 1929 lasted 27 months compared to 64 months after 1945
4.   Romer's 1986 article sparked a strong debate, as it argued that pre-1929 data was not measured well, and that business cycles weren't that bad before 1929
5.   Other recent research, though, suggests that in fact business cycles have been much less severe since 1945 than before 1929 and the issue remains unresolved
6.   This result is critical, since policymakers have attempted to smooth the business cycle since 1945; if Romer was right, it would suggest that stabilization policy failed

III.  Business Cycle Facts (Sec. 8.3)
A.   All business cycles have features in common
B.   The cyclical behavior of economic variables—direction and timing
1.   What direction does a variable move relative to aggregate economic activity?
a.   *Procyclical:* in the same direction
b.   *Countercyclical:* in the opposite direction
c.   *Acyclical:* with no clear pattern
2.   What is the timing of a variable's movements relative to aggregate economic activity?
a.   *Leading:* in advance
b.   *Coincident:* at the same time
c.   *Lagging:* after
3.   In touch with the macroeconomy—the index of leading indicators
a.   A weighted average of 10 variables that lead the business cycle and are promptly reported
b.   Developed by Mitchell and Burns in 1938
c.   A decline in the index for two or three months in a row warns of recession danger
d.   Problems with the leading indicators
(1)   Data are available promptly, but often revised later, so the index may give misleading signals
(2)   The index has given a number of false warnings
(3)   The index provides little information on the timing of the recession or its severity
(4)   Structural changes in the economy necessitate periodic revision of the index
C.   Cyclical behavior of key macroeconomic variables, shown in text Figs. 8.2 to 8.8
1.   Procyclical
a.   Coincident: industrial production, consumption, business fixed investment, employment
b.   Leading: residential investment, inventory investment, average labour productivity, money growth, stock prices
c.   Lagging: inflation, nominal interest rates
d.   Timing not designated: government purchases, real wage
2.   Countercyclical: unemployment (timing is unclassified)
3.   Acyclical: real interest rates (timing is not designated)
4.   Volatility: durable goods production is more volatile than nondurable goods and services; investment spending is more volatile than consumption

D.  International aspects of the business cycle
    1.  The cyclical behavior of key economic variables in other countries is similar to that in Canada
    2.  Major industrial countries frequently have recessions and expansions at about the same time
    3.  In addition, each economy faces small fluctuations that aren't shared with other countries
E.  Box 8.2: the seasonal cycle and the business cycle
    1.  Output varies over the seasons: highest in the fourth quarter, lowest in the first quarter

IV.  Business Cycle Analysis:  A Preview (Sec. 8.4)
A.  What explains business cycle fluctuations?
    1.  2 major components of business cycle theories
      a. A description of the shocks
      b.  A model of how the economy responds to shocks
    2.  2 major business cycle theories
      a.  classical theory
      b.  Keynesian theory
    3.  Study both theories in aggregate demand-aggregate supply (*AD-AS*) framework
B.  Aggregate demand and aggregate supply:  a brief introduction
    1.  The model (along with the building block *IS-LM* model) will be developed in chapters 9, 11 and 12
    2.  The model has 3 main components; all plotted in ($P$, $Y$) space
      a.  aggregate demand curve
      b.  short-run aggregate supply curve
      c.  long-run aggregate supply curve
    3.  Aggregate demand curve
      a.  Shows quantity of goods and services demanded ($Y$) for any price level ($P$)
      b.  Higher $P$ means less aggregate demand (lower $Y$), so the aggregate demand curve slopes downward; reasons why discussed in chapter 9
      c.  An increase in aggregate demand for a given $P$ shifts the aggregate demand curve to the right; and vice-versa
        (1)  Example: a rise in the stock market increases consumption, shifting the aggregate demand curve to the right
        (2)  Example: a decline in government purchases shifts the aggregate demand curve to the left

4.  Aggregate supply curve
    a.  The aggregate supply curve shows how much output producers are willing to supply at any given price level
    b.  The short-run aggregate supply curve is horizontal; prices are fixed in the short run
    c.  The long-run aggregate supply curve is vertical at the full-employment level of output
    d.  Equilibrium (Fig. 8.2; like text Fig. 8.14)
        (1)  Short-run equilibrium: the aggregate demand curve intersects the short-run aggregate supply curve
        (2)  Long-run equilibrium: the aggregate demand curve intersects the long-run aggregate supply curve

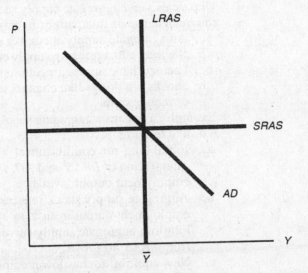

Figure 8.2

C.  Aggregate demand shocks
    1.  An aggregate demand shock is a change that shifts the aggregate demand curve
    2.  Example: a negative aggregate demand shock (Fig. 8.3; like text Fig. 8.15)
        a.  The aggregate demand curve shifts left
        b.  Short-run equilibrium occurs where the aggregate demand curve intersects the short-run aggregate supply curve; output falls, price level is unchanged
        c.  Long-run equilibrium occurs where the aggregate demand curve intersects the long-run aggregate supply curve; output returns to its original level, price level has fallen
    3.  How long does it take to get to the long run?
        a.  Classical theory: prices adjust rapidly
            (1)  So recessions are short-lived
            (2)  No need for government intervention
        b.  Keynesian theory: prices (and wages) adjust slowly
            (1)  Adjustment may take several years
            (2)  So the government can fight recessions by taking action to shift the aggregate demand curve

Figure 8.3

D.  Aggregate supply shocks
    1.  Classicals view aggregate supply shocks as
        the main cause of fluctuations in output
        a.  An aggregate supply shock is a shift of
            the long-run aggregate supply curve
        b.  Factors that cause aggregate supply
            shocks are things like changes in productivity
            or labour supply
    2.  Example: a negative aggregate supply shock (Fig.
        8.4, like text Fig. 8.16)
        a.  Initial long-run equilibrium at
            intersection of $LRAS^1$ and $AD$, with full-
            employment output level $\overline{Y}_1$
        b.  Aggregate supply shock reduces full-
            employment output from $\overline{Y}_1$ to $\overline{Y}_2$, causing
            long-run aggregate supply curve to shift left
            from $LRAS^1$ to $LRAS^2$
        c.  New equilibrium has lower output and higher
            price level
        d.  So recession is accompanied by higher price
            level
    3.  Keynesians also recognize the importance of
        supply shocks; their views are discussed further in
        chapter 11

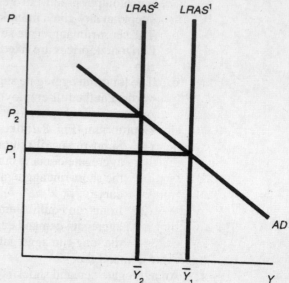

Figure 8.4

## MULTIPLE-CHOICE QUESTIONS

1.  Business cycles all display the following characteristics *except*
    a.   a period of expansion followed by one of contraction.
    b.   comovement of many economic variables.
    c.   rising prices during an expansion and falling prices during the contraction.
    d.   they last a period of one to twelve years.

2.  The fact that business cycles are periodic but not recurrent means that
    a.   business cycles occur at predictable intervals, but do not last a predetermined length of time.
    b.   the business cycle's standard contraction-trough-expansion-peak pattern has been observed to recur over and over again, but not at predictable intervals.
    c.   business cycles occur at predictable intervals, but do not all follow a standard contraction-trough-expansion-peak pattern.
    d.   business cycles last a predetermined length of time, but do not all follow a standard contraction-trough-expansion-peak pattern.

3.  The low point in the business cycle is referred to as the
    a.   contraction.
    b.   recession.
    c.   trough.
    d.   depression.

4.  Turning points in business cycles occur when
    a.   a new business cycle is initiated at the trough.
    b.   the economy hits the peak or trough in the business cycle.
    c.   the business cycle begins to follow a new pattern that differs from previous business cycles.
    d.   a new business cycle is initiated at the peak.

5.  The deepest contraction in Canadian history occurred
    a.   during the 1870s.
    b.   in the years right before World War I.
    c.   during the 1930s.
    d.   during the 1970s.

6.  Christina Romer's estimates of the business cycles prior to World War II showed that
    a.   the business cycle had greater fluctuations before World War II than previous estimates had shown.
    b.   the business cycle had smaller fluctuations before World War II than previously estimated, but still larger fluctuations than after World War II.
    c.   the business cycle had smaller fluctuations before World War II.
    d.   there was no difference in the size of business fluctuations prior to and after World War II.

7.  Which of the following macroeconomic variables is procyclical and leads the business cycle?
    a.   Business fixed investment
    b.   The money supply
    c.   Nominal interest rates
    d.   Unemployment

8. Which of the following macroeconomic variables would you *exclude* from an index of leading economic indicators?
    a. Residential investment
    b. Employment
    c. The money supply
    d. Stock prices

9. Inventory investment displays business cycle patterns that differ from other forms of expenditure, because
    a. inventory investment is countercyclical, but expenditures are generally procyclical.
    b. inventory investment is procyclical, but expenditures are generally coincident with the business cycle.
    c. inventory investment displays large fluctuations that are not associated with business cycle peaks and troughs.
    d. inventory investment lags the business cycle, but expenditures generally lead the business cycle.

10. Some economists contend that the economywide average real wage may not be a good indicator of the real wage, because
    a. when previously unemployed workers enter the work force, the average real wage could decline even if all workers' wages have increased.
    b. it fails to reflect productivity changes.
    c. it fails to reflect qualitative changes in goods.
    d. data used to calculate the average real wage is not collected from all sectors of the economy.

11. Which of the following is not a procyclical variable?
    a. Unemployment rate
    b. Business fixed investment
    c. Average labour productivity
    d. Stock prices

12. Real interest rates are
    a. procyclical, just like nominal interest rates.
    b. acyclical, while nominal interest rates are procyclical.
    c. acyclical, just like nominal interest rates.
    d. countercyclical, while nominal interest rates are procyclical.

13. Which of the following is not a leading variable?
    a. Inflation
    b. Stock prices
    c. Average labour productivity
    d. Residential investment

14. When the values of coincident variables are declining, aggregate economic activity
    a. will begin to decline within six months.
    b. might start to decline in the next year.
    c. has been declining for at least six months.
    d. is declining.

15. Lagging variables are aggregate economic variables that
    a. reach a peak after leading variables but before coincident variables reach a peak.
    b. reach a peak after coincident variables reach a peak.
    c. reach a peak two or more years after aggregate economic activity reaches a peak.
    d. are insensitive to business cycles.

16. Which of the following is *not* a component of the Index of Leading Economic Indicators?
    a. Average weekly initial claims for unemployment insurance
    b. Vender performance
    c. Manufacturers' new orders for nondefense capital goods
    d. Fixed investment by the fifty largest industrial corporations

17. Which of the following macroeconomic variables is countercyclical?
    a. Real interest rates
    b. Unemployment
    c. Money growth
    d. Consumption

18. Which of the following macroeconomic variables would you *exclude* from an index of leading economic indicators?
    a. Residential investment
    b. Employment
    c. Inventory investment
    d. Stock prices

19. Wars, new inventions, harvest failures, and changes in government policy are examples of what economists refer to as
    a. the components of GDP.
    b. propagation mechanisms.
    c. shocks.
    d. demand innovations.

20. When plotted with the aggregate price level on the vertical axis and output on the horizontal axis, the aggregate demand curve
    a. slopes upward.
    b. slopes downward.
    c. is vertical.
    d. is horizontal.

21. When plotted with the aggregate price level on the vertical axis and output on the horizontal axis, the short-run aggregate supply curve (in the absence of misperceptions).
    a. slopes upward.
    b. slopes downward.
    c. is vertical.
    d. is horizontal.

22. In the short run, a decrease in inventory investment by business firms would cause output to _____ and the price level to _____.
    a.   rise; rise
    b.   rise; stay constant
    c.   fall; stay constant
    d.   fall; rise

23. In the long run, a decrease in government purchases of military equipment would cause output to _____ and the aggregate price level to _____.
    a.   stay constant; fall
    b.   fall; fall
    c.   fall; stay constant
    d.   stay constant; stay constant

## REVIEW QUESTIONS

1.   Define the following characteristics of business cycles: recurrence and persistence.

2.   Identify the comovements (i.e., direction and timing) of the following variables over a business cycle:  (a) industrial production;  (b) unemployment;  (c) nominal interest rates; (d) nominal money supply growth;  and (e) investment.

3.   Identify two industries that are particularly sensitive to business cycles.

4.   Briefly describe how the Index of Leading Indicators would forecast a contraction.

5.   Why do Keynesians see an important role for the government in fighting recessions, while classicals do not?

## NUMERICAL PROBLEMS

1.   Use the *NBER* data in Table 8.1 in the textbook on Canadian business cycle turning points to calculate:  a) the shortest business cycle from peak to peak; b) the shortest business cycle from trough to trough; c) the longest business cycle from peak to peak; and d) the longest business cycle from trough to trough.

## ANALYTICAL QUESTIONS

1.   Suppose consumers became more optimistic about the future.  How would this likely change consumption? Would this affect the aggregate-demand curve or aggregate-supply curve?  In the short run, what would be the effect on output and the price level (assuming the *SRAS* curve is horizontal)?

2.   Suppose labour supply declined.  Would this affect the aggregate demand curve or the aggregate supply curve?  What would be the effect on output and the price level?

## ANSWERS TO MULTIPLE-CHOICE QUESTIONS

| Number | Answer | Number | Answer | Number | Answer |
|--------|--------|--------|--------|--------|--------|
| 1 | c | 11 | a | 21 | d |
| 2 | b | 12 | b | 22 | c |
| 3 | c | 13 | a | 23 | a |
| 4 | b | 14 | d |  |  |
| 5 | c | 15 | b |  |  |
| 6 | b | 16 | d |  |  |
| 7 | b | 17 | b |  |  |
| 8 | b | 18 | b |  |  |
| 9 | c | 19 | c |  |  |
| 10 | a | 20 | b |  |  |

## ANSWERS TO REVIEW QUESTIONS

1.  Business cycles exhibit recurrence and persistence:

    1)  Recurrence means that each complete cycle is followed by another complete cycle.

    2)  Persistence means that, once begun, each contraction tends to continue. Likewise, once begun, each expansion tends to continue. For example, the 1981–1982 contraction lasted for 16 months, and the 1982–1990 expansion lasted for 93 months. These are persistent events.

2.  (a)  Industrial production is a procyclical and coincident variable.
    (b)  Unemployment is a countercyclical variable whose timing is unclassified by the Conference Board.
    (c)  Nominal interest rates are procyclical and lagging.
    (d)  Nominal money supply growth is a procyclical and leading variable.
    (e)  Investment includes inventory investment and residential investment, which are procyclical and leading variables; it also includes business fixed investment, which is a procyclical and coincident variable.

3.  Consumer durables, capital investment goods, and housing industries are particularly sensitive to business cycle fluctuations. The auto industry is an example of an industry producing a consumer durable. The drill press industry is an example of an industry producing a capital good.

4.  A decline in the index for three consecutive months during an expansion forecasts that a contraction will begin in the next three to six months.

5.  Keynesians argue that since it takes prices a long time to adjust to restore equilibrium, the government can fight recessions by taking actions like increasing government spending. Classicals, however, think prices adjust quickly, so there's no need for government action.

## ANSWERS TO NUMERICAL PROBLEMS

1.  (a)  The shortest business cycle from peak to peak is 18 months, which extended from February 1980 to July 1981.  This includes 6 months of contraction followed by 12 months of expansion.

    (b)  The shortest business cycle from trough to trough is 28 months, which extended from July 1980 to November 1982.  This includes 12 months of expansion followed by 16 months of contraction.

    (c)  The longest business cycle from peak to peak is 170 months,  which extended from April 1960 to June 1974.  This includes 10 months of contraction followed by 160 months of expansion.

    (d)  The longest business cycle from trough to trough is 170 months, which extended from February 1961 to April 1975.  This includes 160 months of expansion followed by 10 months of contraction.

## ANSWERS TO ANALYTICAL QUESTIONS

1.  Consumption would increase, so the aggregate demand curve would shift to the right, causing output to rise and no change in the price level, as Figure 8.5 shows.

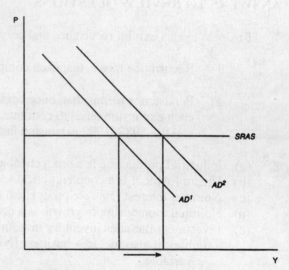

Figure 8.5

2.  The decline in the labour supply shifts the long-run aggregate supply curve to the left, causing the price level to increase and output to decline, as Figure 8.6 shows.

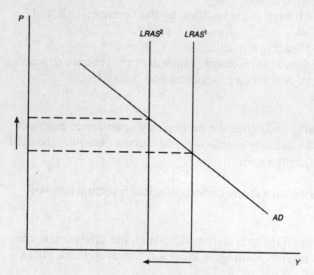

Figure 8.6

# CHAPTER 9: THE *IS-LM/AD-AS* MODEL:
# A GENERAL FRAMEWORK FOR MACROECONOMIC ANALYSIS

## INTRODUCTION

This chapter combines the labour market (Chapter 3), the goods market (Chapter 4), and the asset market (Chapter 7) into a complete macroeconomic model (for a closed economy). Although the *IS-LM* model was originally a Keynesian model because it assumes prices are fixed, by allowing prices to adjust, it's possible to use the *IS-LM* framework to discuss the classical approach. Using one model for both approaches (the classical model in Chapter 10 and the Keynesian model in Chapter 11) avoids the need to learn two different models and helps show clearly both the similarities and the differences of the two approaches.

The chapter is organized along the lines of a section for each piece of the model. Section 9.1 begins by discussing the *FE* line, which represents equilibrium in the labour market. Then, Section 9.2 introduces the *IS* curve, along which there is equilibrium in the goods market. And Section 9.3 covers the *LM* curve, along which the money market is in equilibrium. In all three of these sections, each curve is discussed, followed by an analysis of what shifts each curve. Next, in Section 9.4, the three curves are combined. Their joint intersection is the point of general equilibrium. The way the economy adjusts to reach general equilibrium is by changes in the price level, as Section 9.5 shows. Finally, the *IS, LM,* and *FE* curves are combined in a different way in Section 9.6 to generate the *AD-AS* model.

This chapter is challenging because it introduces the full-blown macro model of the economy. But it really isn't as complicated as it looks. Every time you have to analyze a situation with the model, you just need to think about what curve gets shifted and what direction it shifts. Then look at what happens to the equilibrium point. By working a number of exercises in both the textbook and study guide, you'll find that using the model becomes routine.

## CHAPTER OUTLINE

I.   The *FE* Line: Equilibrium in the Labour Market
     (Sec. 9.1)
     A.   In the discussion of the labour market in Chapter 3, we showed how equilibrium in the labour market leads to employment at its full-employment level $\bar{N}$ and output at $\bar{Y}$
     B.   If we plot output against the real interest rate, we get a vertical line at $Y = \bar{Y}$, since labour market equilibrium is unaffected by changes in the real interest rate (Fig. 9.1)
     C.   Factors that shift the *FE* line
          1.   $\bar{Y}$ is determined by the full-employment level of employment and the current levels of capital and productivity; any change in these variables shifts the *FE* line

Figure 9.1

2.  Summary Table 11 lists the factors that shift the full-employment line
    a.  The full-employment line shifts right because of
        (1) a beneficial supply shock
        (2) an increase in labour supply
        (3) an increase in the capital stock
    b.  The full-employment line shifts left when the opposite happens to the three factors above
II.  The *IS* Curve: Equilibrium in the Goods Market (Sec. 9.2)
    A.  The goods market clears when desired investment equals desired national saving
        1.  Adjustments in the real interest rate bring about equilibrium
        2.  For any level of output $Y$, the *IS* curve shows the real interest rate $r$ for which the goods market is in equilibrium

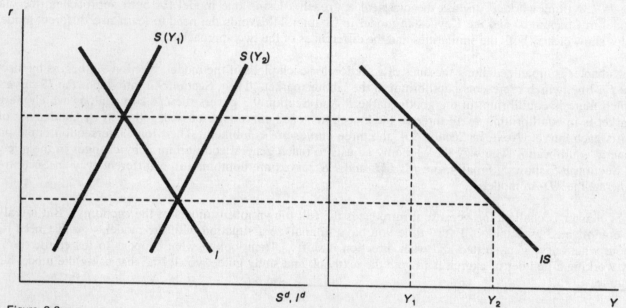

Figure 9.2

3.  Derivation of the *IS* curve from the saving-investment diagram (Fig. 9.2)
    a.  Key features
        (1) The saving curve slopes upward because a higher real interest rate increases saving
        (2) An increase in output shifts the saving curve to the right, because people save more when their income is higher
        (3) The investment curve slopes downward because a higher real interest rate reduces the desired capital stock, thus reducing investment
    b.  Consider two different levels of output
        (1) At the higher level of output, the saving curve is shifted to the right compared to the situation at the lower level of output
        (2) Since the investment curve is downward sloping, equilibrium at the higher level of output has a lower real interest rate
        (3) Thus a higher level of output must lead to a lower real interest rate, so the *IS* curve slopes downward
        (4) The *IS* curve shows the relationship between the real interest rate and output for which investment equals saving
    c.  Alternative interpretation in terms of goods market equilibrium

(1)  Beginning at a point of equilibrium, suppose the real interest rate rises
(2)  The increased real interest rate causes people to increase saving and thus reduce consumption, and causes firms to reduce investment
(4)  So the quantity of goods demanded declines
(5)  To restore equilibrium, the quantity of goods supplied would have to decline
(6)  So higher real interest rates are associated with lower output, that is, the IS curve slopes downward

B.   Factors that shift the *IS* curve
1.  Any change that reduces desired national saving relative to desired investment shifts the *IS* curve up
    a.  Intuitively, imagine constant output, so a reduction in saving means more investment relative to saving; the interest rate must rise to reduce investment and increase saving (Fig. 9.3)

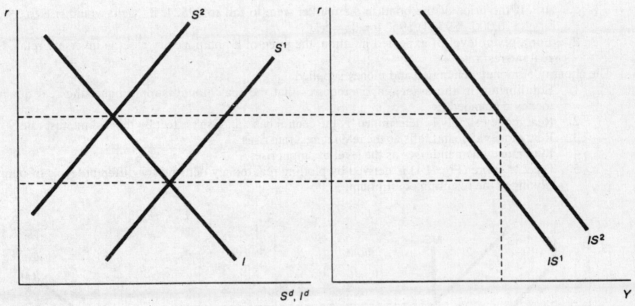

Figure 9.3

2.  Similarly, a change that increases desired national saving relative to desired investment shifts the *IS* curve down
3.  An alternative way of stating this is that a change that increases aggregate demand for goods shifts the *IS* curve up
    a.  In this case, the increase in aggregate demand for goods exceeds the supply
    b.  The real interest rate must rise to reduce desired consumption and investment and restore equilibrium

4.  Summary Table 12 lists the factors that shift the *IS* curve
    a.  The *IS* curve shifts up because of
        (1)  an increase in expected future output
        (2)  an increase in wealth
        (3)  a temporary increase in government purchases
        (4)  a decline in taxes (if Ricardian equivalence doesn't hold)
        (5)  an increase in the expected future marginal product of capital
        (6)  a decrease in the effective tax rate on capital
    b.  The *IS* curve shifts down when the opposite happens to the six factors above

III.  The *LM* Curve: Asset Market Equilibrium (Sec. 9.3)
    A.  The interest rate and the price of a nonmonetary asset
        1.  The price of a nonmonetary asset is inversely related to its interest rate or yield
            a.  Example: A bond pays $10,000 in one year; its current price is $9615, and its interest rate is 4%, since ($10,000 - $9615)/$9615 = .04 = 4%
            b.  If the price of the bond in the market were to fall to $9524, its yield would rise to 5%, since ($10,000 - $9524)/$9524 = .05 = 5%
        2.  For a given level of expected inflation, the price of a nonmonetary asset is inversely related to the real interest rate
    B.  The equality of money demanded and money supplied
        1.  Equilibrium in the asset market requires that the real money supply equal the real quantity of money demanded
        2.  Real money supply is determined by the central bank and isn't affect by the real interest rate
        3.  Real money demand falls as the real interest rate rises
        4.  Real money demand rises as the level of output rises
        5.  The *LM* curve (Fig. 9.4) is derived by plotting real money demand for different levels of output and looking at the resulting equilibrium

Figure 9.4

6. By what mechanism is equilibrium restored?
   a.    Starting at equilibrium, suppose output rises, so real money demand increases
   b.    The rise in people's demand for money makes them sell nonmonetary assets, so the price of those assets falls and the real interest rate rises
   c.    As the interest rate rises, the demand for money declines until equilibrium is reached
7. The *LM* curve shows the combinations of the real interest rate and output that clear the asset market
   a.    Intuitively, for any given level of output, the *LM* curve shows the real interest rate necessary to equate real money demand and supply
   b.    Thus the *LM* curve slopes upward from left to right
C.   Factors that shift the *LM* curve
   1.    Any change that reduces real money supply relative to real money demand shifts the *LM* curve up
      a.    For a given level of output, the reduction in real money supply relative to real money demand causes the equilibrium real interest rate to rise
      b.    The rise in the real interest rate is shown as an upward shift of the *LM* curve
   2.    Similarly, a change that increases real money supply relative to real money demand shifts the *LM* curve down
   3.    Summary Table 13 lists the factors that shift the *LM* curve
      a.    The *LM* curve shifts down because of
         (1)   an increase in the nominal money supply
         (2)   a decrease in the price level
         (3)   an increase in expected inflation
         (4)   a decrease in the nominal interest rate on money
         (5)   a decrease in wealth
         (6)   a decrease in the risk of alternative assets relative to the risk of holding money
         (7)   an increase in the liquidity of alternative assets
         (8)   an increase in the efficiency of payment technologies
      b.    The *LM* curve shifts up when the opposite happens to the eight factors listed above
   4.    Changes in the real money supply
      a.    An increase in the real money supply shifts the *LM* curve down (Fig. 9.5)
      b.    Similarly, a drop in real money supply shifts the *LM* curve up
      c.    The real money supply changes when the nominal money supply changes at a different rate than the price level

Figure 9.5

5.   Changes in real money demand
   a   An increase in real money demand shifts the *LM* curve up (Fig. 9.6)
   b.   Similarly, a drop in real money demand shifts the *LM* curve down

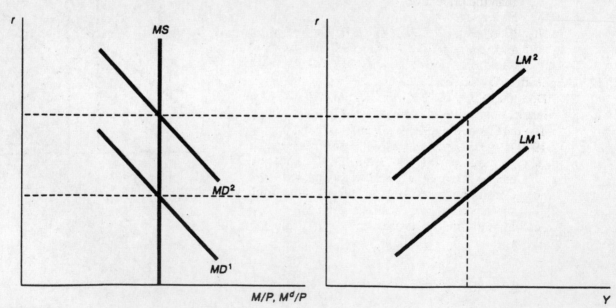

Figure 9.6

IV.  General Equilibrium in the Complete *IS-LM* Model
     (Sec. 9.4)
     A.  When all markets are simultaneously in
         equilibrium there is a *general equilibrium*
         1.  This occurs where the *FE*, *IS*, and *LM*
             curves intersect (Fig. 9.7)
     B.  Applying the *IS-LM* framework: A temporary
         adverse supply shock
         1.  Suppose the productivity parameter in the
             production function falls temporarily
         2.  The supply shock reduces the marginal
             productivity of labour, hence labour demand
             a.  With lower labour demand, the
                 equilibrium real wage and employment fall
             b.  Lower employment and lower
                 productivity both reduce the
                 equilibrium level of output, thus
                 shifting the *FE* line to the left
         3.  There's no effect of a temporary supply shock on
             the *IS* or *LM* curves
         4.  Since the *FE*, *IS*, and *LM* curves don't intersect,
             the price level adjusts, shifting the *LM* curve until
             a general equilibrium is reached
             1.  In this case the price level rises to shift the
                 LM curve up to restore equilibrium (Fig. 9.8)
         5.  The inflation rate rises temporarily, not
             permanently
         6.  Summary: The real wage, employment,
             and output decline, while the real interest
             rate and price level are higher
             a.  There is a temporary burst of
                 inflation as the price level moves to a
                 higher level
             b.  Since the real interest rate is higher
                 and output is lower, consumption and
                 investment must be lower
     C.  Application: Oil price shocks revisited
         1.  Does the *IS-LM* correctly predict the
             results of an adverse supply shock?
         2.  The data from the 1973–1974 and
             1979–1980 oil price shocks shows the following
             a.  As discussed in Chapter 3, output,
                 employment, and the real wage declined
             b.  Consumption fell slightly and investment fell
                 substantially
             c.  Inflation surged temporarily

Figure 9.7

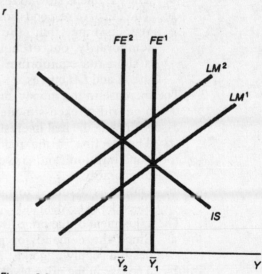

Figure 9.8

        d.   All the above results are consistent with the theory

        e.   But the real interest rate did not rise during the 1973–1974 oil price shock (though it did during the 1979–1980 shock)

           (1)  It could be that people expected the 1973–1974 oil price shock to be permanent

           (2)  In that case the real interest rate would not necessarily rise

           (3)  If so, people's expectations were correct, since the 1973–1974 shock seems to have been permanent, while the 1979–1980 shock was reversed quickly

   D.   Box 9.1: Econometric models and macroeconomic forecasts

       1.   Many models that are used for macroeconomic research and analysis are based on the *IS-LM* model

       2.   There are three major steps in using an economic model for forecasting

          a.   An *econometric model* estimates the parameters of the model (slopes, intercepts, elasticities) through statistical analysis of the data

          b.   Projections are made of *exogenous variables* (variables outside the model), like oil prices and changes in productivity

          c.   The model is solved for the values of *endogenous variables*, such as output, employment, and interest rates

       3.   Large forecasting firms have models that forecast large numbers of variables (examples range from 700 to 1200)

       4.   Forecasters also use time-series methods, current data analysis, and their own judgment in forecasting; they don't rely solely on their econometric models

V.   Price Adjustment and the Attainment of General Equilibrium (Sec. 9.5)

   A.   The effects of a monetary expansion

       1.   An increase in money supply shifts the *LM* curve down

       2.   Because financial markets respond most quickly to changes in economic conditions, the asset market responds to the disequilibrium

          a.   The *FE* line is slow to respond, because job matching and wage renegotiation take time

          b.   The *IS* curve responds somewhat slowly

          c.   We assume that the labour market is temporarily out of equilibrium, so there's a short-run equilibrium at the intersection of the *IS* and *LM* curves

       3.   The increase in the money supply causes people to try to get rid of excess money balances by buying assets, driving the real interest rate down

          a.   The decline in the real interest rate causes consumption and investment to increase temporarily

          b.   Output is assumed to increase temporarily to meet the extra demand

       4.   The adjustment of the price level

          a.   Since the demand for goods exceeds firms' desired supply of goods, firms raise prices

          b.   The rise in the price level causes the *LM* curve to shift up

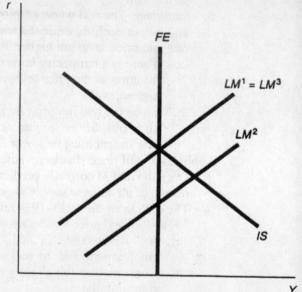

Figure 9.9

    c.   The price level continues to rise until the *LM* curve intersects with the *FE* line and the *IS* curve at general equilibrium (Fig. 9.9)

    d.   The result is no change in employment, output, or the real interest rate

    e.   The price level is higher by the same proportion as the increase in the money supply

    f.   So all real variables (including the real wage) are unchanged, while nominal values (including the nominal wage) have risen proportionately with the change in the money supply

   5.   Trend money growth and inflation

    a.   This analysis also handles the case in which the money supply is growing continuously

    b.   If both the money supply and price level rise by the same proportion, there is no change in the real money supply, and the *LM* curve doesn't shift

    c.   If the money supply grew faster than the price level, the *LM* curve would shift down

    d.   Often, then, we'll discuss things in relative terms

       (1)   The examples can often be thought of as a change in *M* or *P* relative to the expected or trend growth of money and inflation

       (2)   Thus when we talk about "an increase in the money supply," we have in mind an increase in the growth rate relative to the trend

       (3)   Similarly, a result that the price level declines can be interpreted as the price level declining relative to a trend; for example, inflation may fall from 7% to 4%

B.   Classical versus Keynesian versions of the *IS-LM* model

   1.   There are two key questions in the debate between classical and Keynesian approaches

    a.   How rapidly does the economy reach general equilibrium?

    b.   What are the effects of monetary policy on the economy?

   2.   Price adjustment and the self-correcting economy

    a.   The economy is brought into general equilibrium by adjustment of the price level

    b.   The speed at which this adjustment occurs is much debated

    c.   Classical economists see rapid adjustment of the price level

       (1)   So the economy returns quickly to full employment after a shock

       (2)   If firms change prices instead of output in response to a change in demand, the adjustment process is almost immediate

    d.   Keynesian economists see slow adjustment of the price level

       (1)   It may be several years before prices and wages adjust fully

       (2)   When not in general equilibrium output is determined by aggregate demand at the intersection of the *IS* and *LM* curves, and the labour market is not in equilibrium,

   3.   Monetary neutrality

    a.   Money is neutral if a change in the nominal money supply changes the price level proportionately but has no effect on real variables

    b.   The classical view is that a monetary expansion affects prices quickly with at most a transitory effect on real variables

    c.   Keynesians think the economy may spend a long time in disequilibrium, so a monetary expansion increases output and employment and causes the real interest rate to fall

    d.   Keynesians believe in monetary neutrality in the long run but not the short run, while classicals believe it holds even in the relatively short run

VI. Aggregate Demand and Aggregate Supply (Sec. 9.6)
   A.  Use the *IS-LM* model to develop the *AD-AS* model
      1.  The two models are equivalent
      2.  Depending on the issue, one model or the other may prove more useful
         a.  *IS-LM* relates the real interest rate to output
         b.  *AD-AS* relates the price level to output
   B.  The aggregate demand curve
      1.  The *AD* curve shows the relationship between the quantity of goods demanded and the price level when the goods market and asset market are in equilibrium
         a.  So the *AD* curve represents the price level and output level at which the *IS* and *LM* curves intersect (Fig. 9.10)
         b.  The *AD* curve is unlike other demand curves, which relate the quantity demanded of a good to its relative price; the *AD* curve relates the total quantity of goods demanded to the general price level, not a relative price
         c.  The *AD* curve slopes downward because a higher price level is associated with lower real money supply, shifting the *LM* curve up, raising the real interest rate, and decreasing output demanded
      2.  Factors that shift the *AD* curve
         a.  Any factor that causes the intersection of the *IS* and *LM* curves to shift to the left causes the *AD* curve to shift to the left; any factor causing the *IS-LM* intersection to shift to the right causes the *AD* curve to shift to the right
         b.  For example, a temporary increase in government purchases shifts the *IS* curve to the right, so it shifts the *AD* curve to the right as well (Fig. 9.11)

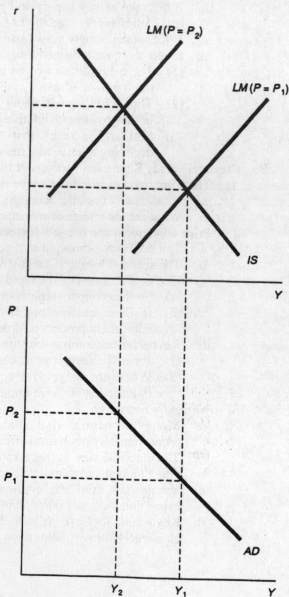

Figure 9.10

c. Summary Table 14: Factors that shift the AD curve
   (1) Factors that shift the *IS* curve up and thus the *AD* curve to the right as well
       (a) Increases in future output ($Y^f$), wealth, government purchases ($G$), or the expected future marginal productivity of capital ($MPK^f$)
       (b) Decreases in taxes ($T$) if Ricardian equivalence doesn't hold, or the effective tax rate on capital ($\tau$)
   (2) Factors that shift the *LM* curve down and thus the *AD* curve to the right as well
       (a) Increases in the nominal money supply (M) or in expected inflation ($\pi^e$)
       (b) Decreases in the nominal interest rate on money ($i^m$) or the real demand for money

C. The aggregate supply curve
   1. The aggregate supply curve shows the relationship between the price level and the aggregate amount of output that firms supply
   2. In the short run, prices remain fixed, so firms supply whatever output is demanded
       a. The short-run aggregate supply curve is horizontal (Fig. 9.12)
   3. Full-employment output isn't affected by the price level, so the long-run aggregate supply curve (*LRAS*) is a vertical line at Y = $\overline{Y}$ in Fig. 9.12
   4. Factors that shift the aggregate supply curves
       a. The *SRAS* curve shifts whenever firms change their prices in the short run
           (1) Factors like increased costs of producing goods lead firms to increase prices, shifting *SRAS* up

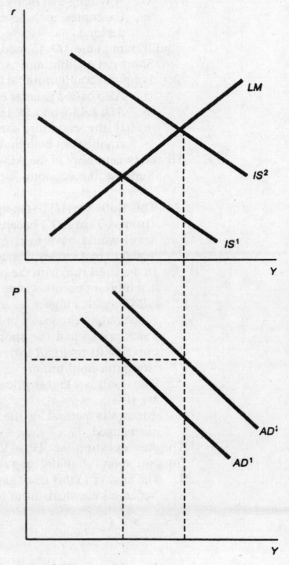

Figure 9.11

(2)   Factors leading to reduced prices shift SRAS down
   b.   Anything that increases  shifts the *LRAS* curve right; anything that decreases  shifts *LRAS* left
   c.   Examples include changes in the labour force or productivity changes that affect labour demand
D.   Equilibrium in the *AD-AS* model
   1.   Short-run equilibrium:  *AD* intersects *SRAS*
   2.   Long-run equilibrium:  *AD* intersects *LRAS*
      a.   Also called general equilibrium
      b.   *AD*, *LRAS*, and *SRAS* all intersect at same point (Fig. 9.13)
      c.   If the economy isn't in general equilibrium, economic forces work to restore general equilibrium both in *AD-AS* diagram and *IS-LM* diagram
E.   Monetary neutrality in the AD-AS model (Fig. 9.14 and key diagram 7)
   1.   Suppose the economy begins in general equilibrium, but then the money supply is increased by 10%
   2.   This shifts the *AD* curve upward by 10% (from $AD^1$ to $AD^2$) because to maintain the aggregate quantity demanded at a given level, the price level would have to rise by 10% so that real money supply wouldn't change and would remain equal to real money demand
   3.   In the short run, with the price level fixed, equilibrium occurs where $AD^2$ intersects $SRAS^1$, with a higher level of output
   4.   Since output exceeds $\overline{Y}$, over time firms raise prices and the short-run aggregate supply curve shifts up to $SRAS^2$, restoring long-run equilibrium
   5.   The result is a higher price level—higher by 10%
   6.   Money is neutral in the long run, as output is unchanged
F.   The key question is:  How long does it take to get from the short run to the long run?
   1.   The answer to this question is what separates classicals from Keynesians

Figure 9.12

Figure 9.13

Figure 9.14

## MULTIPLE-CHOICE QUESTIONS

1.   Which of the following would shift the *FE* line to the left?
     a.   A beneficial supply shock
     b.   A decrease in labour supply
     c.   An increase in the capital stock
     d.   A decrease in the future marginal productivity of capital

2.   A beneficial supply shock would cause the *FE* line to
     a.   shift to the right.
     b.   shift to the left.
     c.   remain unchanged.
     d.   remain unchanged if the shock is temporary; shift to the right if the shock is permanent.

3.   An increase in the effective tax rate on capital would cause the *IS* curve to
     a.   shift up.
     b.   shift down.
     c.   remain unchanged.
     d.   remain unchanged if taxes are fully deductible from income; otherwise, shift up.

4.   An increase in wealth would cause the *IS* curve to
     a.   shift up.
     b.   shift down.
     c.   remain unchanged.
     d.   shift up only if people face borrowing constraints.

5.   The *IS* curve will shift down when
     a.   desired saving declines.
     b.   government purchases increase.
     c.   consumption increases.
     d.   expected future marginal product of capital declines.

6.   A fall in the price of a bond causes the yield of the bond to
     a.   rise.
     b.   fall.
     c.   remain unchanged.
     d.   rise if it's a short-term bond, fall if it's a long-term bond.

7.   The *LM* curve illustrates that when income increases, the
     a.   price level must increase to clear the asset market.
     b.   real interest rate on nonmonetary assets must increase to clear the asset market.
     c.   price level must increase to clear the goods market.
     d.   real interest rate on nonmonetary assets must increase to clear the goods market.

8.   Looking only at the asset market, an increase in output would cause
     a.   the *LM* curve to shift down.
     b.   the *LM* curve to shift up.
     c.   an increase in the real interest rate along the *LM* curve.
     d.   a decrease in the real interest rate along the *LM* curve.

9.  Looking at the macroeconomic statistics for Friedmanland, you discover that at the beginning of the year, the national money supply was equal to $400 million and by the end of the year it was equal to $420 million.  You also found out that the inflation rate in Friedmanland was 7%.  In this case, you would expect the *LM* curve to
    a.  shift up as the real money supply falls.
    b.  shift up as the real money supply rises.
    c.  shift down as the real money supply falls.
    d.  shift down as the real money supply rises.

10. Banks decide to raise the interest rate they pay on NOW accounts from 4.75% to 5.25%.  This action would
    a.  increase money demand, shifting the *LM* curve up.
    b.  increase money demand, shifting the *LM* curve down.
    c.  decrease money demand, shifting the *LM* curve up.
    d.  decrease money demand, shifting the *LM* curve down.

11. A financial innovation, such as money market mutual funds, which increases the liquidity of alternatives to money, would
    a.  increase money demand, shifting the *LM* curve up.
    b.  increase money demand, shifting the *LM* curve down.
    c.  decrease money demand, shifting the *LM* curve up.
    d.  decrease money demand, shifting the *LM* curve down.

12. The probable effect of introducing automatic teller machines is to
    a.  increase money demand, shifting the *LM* curve up.
    b.  increase money demand, shifting the *LM* curve down.
    c.  decrease money demand, shifting the *LM* curve up.
    d.  decrease money demand, shifting the *LM* curve down.

13. People have reduced their expectations of inflation from 5% to 3%, directly causing
    a.  a relative increase in real money demand, shifting the *LM* curve up.
    b.  a relative decrease in real money demand, shifting the *LM* curve down.
    c.  a relative increase in real money demand, shifting the *LM* curve down.
    d.  a relative decrease in real money demand, shifting the *LM* curve up.

14. A decline in wealth that doesn't affect labour supply would cause the *IS* curve to _____ and the *FE* line to _____.
    a.  shift down; be unchanged
    b.  shift down; shift left
    c.  shift up; be unchanged
    d.  shift up; shift left

15. The *IS-LM* model predicts that a temporary adverse supply shock
    a.  reduces output, national saving, and investment, but not the real interest rate.
    b.  reduces output, national saving, and the real interest rate, but not investment.
    c.  reduces the real interest rate, investment, and output, but not national saving.
    d.  reduces output, national saving, investment, and the real interest rate.

16. After a temporary adverse supply shock hits the economy, general equilibrium is restored by
    a.  a downward shift of the *IS* curve.
    b.  a shift to the left of the *FE* line.
    c.  an upward shift of the *LM* curve.
    d.  a downward shift of the *LM* curve.

17. An increase in money supply causes the real interest rate to _____ and output to _____ in the short run, before prices adjust to restore equilibrium.
    a.  rise; rise
    b.  rise; fall
    c.  fall; rise
    d.  fall; fall

18. Suppose the intersection of the *IS* and *LM* curves is to the right of the *FE* line. An increase in the price level would most likely eliminate a disequilibrium among the asset, labour, and goods markets by
    a.  shifting the *LM* curve up.
    b.  shifting the *IS* curve up.
    c.  shifting the *IS* curve down.
    d.  shifting the *FE* curve to the left.

19. A decrease in taxes (when Ricardian equivalence doesn't hold) causes the real interest rate to _____ and the price level to _____ in general equilibrium.
    a.  rise; rise
    b.  rise; fall
    c.  fall; rise
    d.  fall; fall

20. In classical *IS-LM* analysis, the effects of a decline in desired investment include
    a.  a decline in output.
    b.  an increase in the price level.
    c.  a decline in the real interest rate.
    d.  an increase in unemployment.

21. The theory of monetary neutrality suggests that
    a.  a change in the nominal money supply has no effect on real variables.
    b.  changes in the real money supply will not affect the real interest rate.
    c.  money is not an asset.
    d.  a decline in nominal money supply growth could create a recession.

22. Suppose the intersection of the *IS* and *LM* curves is to the right of the *FE* line. What would most likely eliminate a disequilibrium among the asset, labour, and goods markets?
    a.  A rise in the price level, shifting the *LM* curve up
    b.  A fall in the price level, shifting the *LM* curve down
    c.  A rise in the price level, shifting the *IS* curve up
    d.  A fall in the price level, shifting the *IS* curve down

23. Classical economists believe that a market economy will normally
    a.  suffer from extended periods of sustained unemployment.
    b.  achieve full-employment output.
    c.  degenerate into pure monopolies in most industries.
    d.  eliminate the problem of economic scarcity.

24. Keynesians contend that in a recession caused by a decline in aggregate demand, a policy of increasing the nominal money supply would
    a.  raise the level of aggregate demand, which would help return the economy to full-employment output.
    b.  lower the level of aggregate demand, which would help return the economy to full-employment output.
    c.  shift the *LM* curve to left, which would help return the economy to full-employment output.
    d.  not affect the position of the *LM* curve, because the real money supply would not change.

25. At a given output level, a temporary reduction in government purchases will
    a.  increase desired saving, causing the *IS* curve to shift down.
    b.  increase desired saving, causing the *IS* curve to shift up.
    c.  decrease desired saving, causing the *IS* curve to shift down.
    d.  decrease desired saving, causing the *IS* curve to shift up.

26. Which of the following changes shifts the *AD* curve to the right?
    a.    A temporary decrease in government purchases
    b.    A decline in the nominal money supply
    c.    An increase in corporate taxes
    d.    An increase in consumer confidence

27. Which of the following changes shifts the *AD* curve to the left?
    a.    A decline in the nominal money supply
    b.    A decrease in income taxes
    c.    A decrease in the risk on nonmonetary assets
    d.    An increase in the future marginal productivity of capital

28. Which of the following changes shifts the *SRAS* curve down?
    a.    A decrease in the labour force
    b.    A decrease in firms' costs
    c.    An increase in government purchases
    d.    A decrease in the money supply

29. When the money supply declines by 10%, in the short run, output _____ and the price level _____.
    a.    is unchanged; is unchanged
    b.    declines; falls
    c.    is unchanged; falls
    d.    declines; is unchanged

30. An increase in the effective tax rate on capital causes the real interest rate to _____ and the price level to _____ in general equilibrium.
    a.    rise; rise
    b.    rise; fall
    c.    fall; rise
    d.    fall; fall

# REVIEW QUESTIONS

1. Briefly describe the relationship between output and the interest rate on the *FE* line and explain why this relationship exists.

2. Identify changes in three variables that would cause the *FE* line to shift to the right.

3. Identify two variables that change in value as we move down the *IS* curve and state the direction in which they are changing.

4. Can monetary policy be used to offset the real interest rate effects of an adverse supply shock or a decline in desired investment, if prices adjust quickly to restore general equilibrium? Briefly explain.

# NUMERICAL PROBLEMS

1. Calculate the price of a bond that pays no interest but pays its face value of $1000 at maturity in one year for each of the following nominal interest rates: a) 3%; b) 6%; c) 9%.

2. Calculate the real money supply growth rate when the nominal money supply increases by 10% and the price level increases by each of the following percentages: a) 2%; b) 8%; c) 10%; d) 15%.

# ANALYTICAL QUESTIONS

1. Draw a saving-investment diagram to show how each of the following changes shifts the *IS* curve.
   a. Future income declines.
   b. The future marginal productivity of capital declines.
   c. Government purchases increase temporarily.
   d. The effective corporate tax rate declines.

2. Describe the effects, in both the short run and the long run, of a decline in the money supply. Explain what happens to real output and the price level.

3. Suppose monetary policymakers decide they will increase output in the economy by increasing the money supply. Beginning from a position of general equilibrium, what effect does this have in the very short run (before general equilibrium is restored)? What must happen to restore general equilibrium? What would happen if the monetary policymaker persistently increased the money supply to try to increase output?

4. For each of the following changes, what happens to the real interest rate and output in the very short run, before the price level has adjusted to restore general equilibrium?
   a. Wealth declines.
   b. Money supply declines.
   c. The future marginal productivity of capital declines.
   d. Expected inflation rises.
   e. Future income rises.

## ANSWERS TO MULTIPLE-CHOICE QUESTIONS

| Number | Answer | | Number | Answer | | Number | Answer |
|--------|--------|---|--------|--------|---|--------|--------|
| 1 | b | | 11 | d | | 21 | a |
| 2 | a | | 12 | d | | 22 | a |
| 3 | b | | 13 | a | | 23 | b |
| 4 | a | | 14 | a | | 24 | a |
| 5 | d | | 15 | a | | 25 | a |
| 6 | a | | 16 | c | | 26 | d |
| 7 | b | | 17 | c | | 27 | a |
| 8 | c | | 18 | a | | 28 | b |
| 9 | a | | 19 | a | | 29 | d |
| 10 | a | | 20 | c | | 30 | d |

## ANSWERS TO REVIEW QUESTIONS

1.   Along the *FE* line, output is independent of the current interest rate, since the *FE* line is vertical.

2.   An increase in productivity, an increase in the supply of capital, or an increase in the supply of labour would increase the full-employment level of output, as illustrated by a rightward shift in the *FE* line.

3.   As we move down an *IS* curve, output ($Y$) increases and the real interest rate ($r$) declines.

4.   No.  Given flexible prices, monetary policy cannot shift the *LM* curve; therefore, it cannot offset either of these changes.  Although the Bank of Canada can change the nominal money supply, any change in $M$ creates a proportional change in $P$, so that the real money supply, $M/P$, does not change.

## ANSWERS TO NUMERICAL PROBLEMS

1.   If $B$ is the price or present value of the bond, $i$ is the nominal interest rate, and $F$ is the face value of the bond, then $B(1 + i) = F$.  Dividing through by $1+i$ gives $B = F/(1 + i)$.
a)  $i = 3\%$, $B = \$1000/1.03 = \$970.87$.
b)  $i = 6\%$, $B = \$1000/1.06 = \$943.40$.
c)  $i = 9\%$, $B = \$1000/1.09 = \$917.43$.

2.   Real money supply growth rate = nominal money supply growth rate minus the price level growth rate. (The price level growth rate is the inflation rate.)
a)   Real money supply growth rate = 10% - 2% = 8%.
b)   Real money supply growth rate = 10% - 8% = 2%.
c)   Real money supply growth rate = 10% - 10% = 0%.
d)   Real money supply growth rate = 10% - 15% = -5%.

## ANSWERS TO ANALYTICAL QUESTIONS

1.  a.  *IS* shifts down.
    b.  *IS* shifts down.
    c.  *IS* shifts up.
    d.  *IS* shifts up.

2.  In the short run, a decline in the money supply reduces output and has no effect on the price level.  In the long run, a decline in the money supply has no effect on output and reduces the price level.

3.  In the very short run, output increases and the real interest rate declines, as shown in Figure 9.15. But the price level must rise and the *LM* curve must shift up to restore general equilibrium. An attempt to persistently increase the money supply causes persistent inflation.

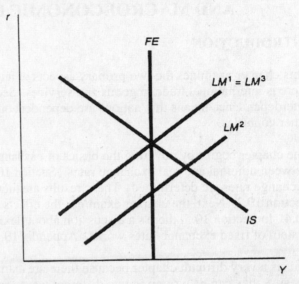

Figure 9.15

4.  a.  The *IS* curve shifts down, so *r* falls and *Y* falls.
    b.  The *LM* curve shifts up, so *r* rises and *Y* falls.
    c.  The *IS* curve shifts down, so *r* falls and *Y* falls.
    d.  The *LM* curve shifts down, so *r* falls and *Y* rises.
    e.  The *IS* curve shifts up, so *r* rises and *Y* rises.

# CHAPTER 10: EXCHANGE RATES, BUSINESS CYCLES, AND MACROECONOMIC POLICY IN THE OPEN ECONOMY

## INTRODUCTION

This chapter examines the two primary aspects of interdependence between economies of different nations. First, there is international trade in goods and services. Second, financial markets are integrated worldwide. Interdependence means that nations are dependent on each other, so policy changes in one country may affect other countries.

The chapter begins by covering the basics of exchange rates in Section 10.1, including a look at the difference between nominal and real exchange rates. Section 10.2 uses supply-and-demand analysis to examine how exchange rates are determined. These results are then used to develop an *IS-LM* model for the open economy in Section 10.3. Next, the chapter examines the effects of macroeconomic policy in the open economy in Section 10.4. In Section 10.5, there's a discussion about flexible exchange rates. Finally, Section 10.6 talks about how a system of fixed exchange rates works. Appendix 10.A presents an algebraic version of the model.

This is a very difficult chapter because there are many new concepts. Exchange rates themselves are confusing because they can be written in two different ways: for example, yen per dollar or dollars per yen. Then there are distinctions between real and nominal exchange rates, between depreciation and devaluation, and between fixed- and flexible-exchange rates. Here are a couple of hints to help you. If an exchange rate (such as yen per dollar) rises, it means the second currency (the dollar in this case) has appreciated (become more valuable) relative to the first currency (the yen). Whenever the demand for a currency rises relative to other currencies, because foreigners increase their demand for either its goods (perhaps because the goods have increased in quality or fallen in price) or its assets (such as stocks and bonds, perhaps because their returns have increased), foreigners will need to acquire more of the currency, and it will rise in value (appreciate).

## CHAPTER OUTLINE
I.  Exchange Rates (Sec. 10.1)
    A.  Nominal exchange rates
        1.  The nominal exchange rate tells you how much foreign currency you can obtain with one unit of the domestic currency
            a.  For example, if the nominal exchange rate is 110 yen per dollar, one dollar can be exchanged for 110 yen
            b.  Transactions between currencies take place in the foreign exchange market
            c.  Denote the nominal exchange rate (or simply, exchange rate) as $e_{nom}$ in units of the foreign currency per unit of domestic currency
        2.  Under a flexible-exchange-rate system or floating-exchange-rate system, exchange rates are determined by supply and demand and may change every day; this is the current system for major currencies
        3.  In the past, many currencies operated under a fixed-exchange-rate system, in which exchange rates were determined by governments
            a.  The exchange rates were fixed because the central banks in those countries offered to buy or sell the currencies at the fixed exchange rate
            b.  Examples include the gold standard, which operated in the late 1800s and early 1900s, and the Bretton Woods system, which was in place from 1944 until the early 1970s

    c.   Even today, though major currencies are in a flexible-exchange-rate system, some smaller countries fix their exchange rates

B.   Real exchange rates
1.   The real exchange rate tells you how much of a foreign good you can get in exchange for one unit of a domestic good
2.   If the nominal exchange rate is 110 yen per dollar, and it costs 1100 yen to buy a hamburger in Tokyo compared to 2 dollars in Vancouver, the price of a Canadian hamburger relative to a Japanese hamburger is 0.2 Japanese hamburgers per Canadian hamburger
3.   The real exchange rate is the price of domestic goods relative to foreign goods, or
$e = e_{nom}P/P_{For}$   (10.1)
4.   To simplify matters, we'll assume that each country produces a unique good
5.   In reality, countries produce many goods, so we must use price indexes to get $P$ and $P_{For}$
6.   If a country's real exchange rate is rising, its goods are becoming more expensive relative to the goods of the other country

C.   Appreciation and depreciation
1.   In a flexible-exchange-rate system, when $e_{nom}$ falls, the domestic currency has undergone a nominal depreciation (or it has become weaker); when $e_{nom}$ rises, the domestic currency has become stronger and has undergone a nominal appreciation
2.   In a fixed-exchange-rate system, a weakening of the currency is called a devaluation, a strengthening is called a revaluation
3.   We also use the terms real appreciation and real depreciation to refer to changes in the real exchange rate

D.   Purchasing power parity
1.   To examine the relationship between the nominal exchange rate and the real exchange rate, think first about a simple case in which all countries produce the same goods, which are freely traded
    a.   If there were no transportation costs, the real exchange rate would have to be $e = 1$, or else everyone would buy goods where they were cheaper
    b.   Setting $e = 1$ in Eq. (10.1) gives $P = P_{For} / e_{nom}$   (10.2)
    c.   This means that similar goods have the same price in terms of the same currency, a concept known as *purchasing power parity*, or *PPP*
    d.   Empirical evidence shows that purchasing power parity holds in the long run but not in the short run because in reality, countries produce different goods, because some goods aren't traded, and because there are transportation costs and legal barriers to trade
2.   When PPP doesn't hold, using Eq. (10.1), we can decompose changes in the real exchange rate into parts
$\Delta e/e = \Delta e_{nom}/e_{nom} + \Delta P/P - P_{For}/P_{For}$
3.   This can be rearranged as
$\Delta e_{nom}/e_{nom} = \Delta e/e + \pi_{For} - \pi$   (10.3)
4.   Thus a nominal appreciation is due to a real appreciation or a lower rate of inflation than in the foreign country
5.   In the special case in which the real exchange rate doesn't change, so that $)\Delta e/e = 0$, the resulting equation in Eq. (10.3) is called relative purchasing power parity, since nominal exchange-rate movements reflect only changes in inflation
    a.   Relative purchasing power parity works well as a description of exchange-rate movements in high-inflation countries, since in those countries, movements in relative inflation rates are much larger than movements in real exchange rates

      6. Box 10.1:  McParity
        a.   As a test of the *PPP* hypothesis, the *Economist* magazine periodically reports on the prices of Big Mac hamburgers in different countries
        b.   The prices, when translated into dollar terms using the nominal exchange rate, range from just over $1 in Malaysia to almost $4 in Switzerland (using 1999 data), so *PPP* definitely doesn't hold
        c.   The hamburger price data forecasts movements in exchange rates
           (1)  Hamburger prices might be expected to converge, so countries in which Big Macs are expensive may have a depreciation, while countries in which Big Macs are cheap may have an appreciation

E.   The real exchange rate and net exports
   1.   The real exchange rate (also called the terms of trade) is important because it represents the rate at which domestic goods and services can be traded for those produced abroad
      a.   An increase in the real exchange rate means people in a country can get more foreign goods for a given amount of domestic goods
   2.   The real exchange rate also affects a country's net exports (exports minus imports)
      a.   Changes in net exports have a direct impact on export and import industries in the country
      b.   Changes in net exports affect overall economic activity and are a primary channel through which business cycles and macroeconomic policy changes are transmitted internationally
   3.   The real exchange rate affects net exports through its effect on the demand for goods
      a.   A high real exchange rate makes foreign goods cheap relative to domestic goods, so there's a high demand for foreign goods (in both countries)
      b.   With demand for foreign goods high, net exports decline
      c.   Thus the higher the real exchange rate, the lower a country's net exports
   4.   The analysis in this chapter assumes a time period long enough that the movements along the J curve are complete, so that a real depreciation raises net exports and a real appreciation reduces net exports

F.   Application: The value of the dollar and Canadian net exports
   1.   Our theory suggests that the dollar and Canadian net exports should be inversely related
   2.   Looking at data since the early 1970s, when the world switched to floating exchange rates, confirms the theory, at least in the 1980s (text Fig. 10.1)
      a.   From 1986 to 1989 the dollar appreciated and net exports declined sharply
      b.   The dollar began depreciating in 1989. Despite this decline, Canadian net exports continued to tall until late in 1991, when they finally began to improve

(a)  The strength of the dollar for such a long period in the first half of the 1980s meant Canadian firms lost many foreign customers

(b)  Foreign firms made many inroads into Canada

(c)  This is known as the "beachhead effect," because it allowed foreign producers to establish beachheads in Canadian economy

Figure 10.1

c.  In 1996-1997, net exports fell, but then trended strongly upwards during the rest of the 1990s even though the real exchange rate was no lower than it had been during 1993 and 1994

d.  Two influences were the trade agreements with the U.S. and Mexico and the fact that the U.S. economy grew quickly during the 1990s and 2000.

II.  How Exchange Rates Are Determined: A Supply-and-Demand Analysis (Sec. 10.2)

A.  What causes changes in the exchange rate?

1.  To analyze this, we'll use supply-and-demand analysis, assuming a fixed price level

2.  Holding prices fixed means that changes in the real exchange rate are matched by changes in the nominal exchange rate

3.  The nominal exchange rate is determined in the foreign exchange market by supply and demand for the currency

4.  Demand and supply are plotted against the nominal exchange rate, just like demand and supply for any good (Fig. 10.2; like text Fig. 10.2)

Figure 10.2

a. Supplying dollars means offering dollars in exchange for the foreign currency

b. The supply curve slopes upward, because if people can get more units of foreign currency for a dollar, they'll supply more dollars

c. Demanding dollars means wanting to buy dollars in exchange for the foreign currency

d. The demand curve slopes downward, because if people need to give up a greater amount of foreign currency to obtain one dollar, they'll demand fewer dollars

5. Why do people demand or supply dollars?
   a. People need dollars for two reasons:
      (1) To be able to buy Canadian goods and services (Canadian exports)
      (2) To be able to buy Canadian real and financial assets (Canadian financial inflows)
   b. These transactions are the two main categories in the balance of payments accounts: the current account and the capital and financial account
   c. People want to sell dollars for two reasons:
      (1) To be able to buy foreign goods and services (Canadian imports)
      (2) To be able to buy foreign real and financial assets (Canadian financial outflows)

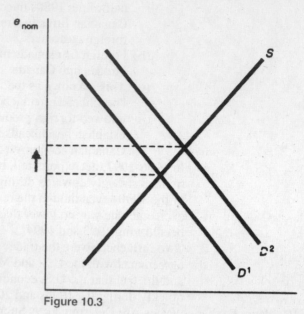

Figure 10.3

6. Factors that increase demand for Canadian exports and assets will increase demand for dollars, shifting the demand curve to the right and increasing the nominal exchange rate
   a. For example, an increase in the quality of Canadian goods relative to foreign goods will lead to an appreciation of the dollar (Fig. 10.3; like text Fig. 10.3)

B. In touch with the macroeconomy: Exchange rates
   1. Trading in currencies occurs around-the-clock, since some market is open in some country any time of day
   2. The spot rate is the rate at which one currency can be traded for another immediately
   3. The forward rate is the rate at which one currency can be traded for another at a fixed date in the future (for example, 30, 90, or 180 days from now)
   4. A pattern of rising forward rates suggests that people expect the spot rate to be rising in the future

C. Macroeconomic determinants of the exchange rate and net export demand
   1. Look at how changes in real output or the real interest rate are linked to the exchange rate and net exports, to develop an open-economy *IS-LM* model
   2. Effects of changes in output (income)
      a. A rise in domestic output (income) raises demand for goods and services, including imports, so net exports decline
      b. To increase purchases of imports, people must sell the domestic currency to buy foreign currency, increasing the supply of foreign currency, which reduces the exchange rate

       c.   The opposite occurs if foreign output (income) rises
          (1)   Domestic net exports rise
          (2)   The exchange rate appreciates

   3.   Effects of changes in real interest rates
       a.   A rise in the domestic real interest rate (with the foreign real interest rate held constant) causes foreigners to want to buy domestic assets, increasing the demand for domestic currency and raising the exchange rate
       b.   The rise in the exchange rate leads to a decline in net exports
       c.   The opposite occurs if the foreign real interest rate rises
          (1)   Domestic net exports rise
          (2)   The exchange rate depreciates

 D.   Summary Table 16: Determinants of the exchange rate (real or nominal)
   1.   A rise in domestic output (income) or the foreign real interest rate causes the exchange rate to fall
   2.   A rise in foreign output (income), the domestic real interest rate, or the world demand for domestic goods causes the exchange rate to rise

 E.   Summary Table 17: Determinants of net exports
   1.   A rise in domestic output (income) or the domestic real interest rate causes net exports to fall
   2.   A rise in foreign output (income), the foreign real interest rate, or the world demand for domestic goods causes net exports to rise

III.  The *IS-LM* Model for an Open Economy (Sec. 10.3)
 A.   Only the *IS* curve is affected by having an open economy instead of a closed economy; the *LM* curve and *FE* line are the same
   1.   Note that we don't use the *AD-AS* model because we need to know what happens to the real interest rate, which has an important impact on the exchange rate
   2.   The *IS* curve is affected because net exports are part of the demand for goods
   3.   The *IS* curve remains downward sloping
   4.   Any factor that shifts the closed-economy *IS* curve shifts the open-economy *IS* curve in the same way
   5.   Factors that change net exports (given domestic output and the domestic real interest rate) shift the *IS* curve
       a.   Factors that increase net exports shift the *IS* curve up
       b.   Factors that decrease net exports shift the *IS* curve down

 B.   The open-economy *IS* curve
   1.   The goods-market equilibrium condition is $S^d - I^d = NX$   (10.4)
       a.   This means that desired foreign lending must equal foreign borrowing
       b.   Equivalently, $Y = C^d + I^d + G + NX$   (10.5)
       c.   This means the supply of goods equals the demand for goods and is derived using the definition of national saving, $S^d = Y - C^d - G$
   2.   Plotting $S^d - I^d$ and *NX* illustrates goods-market equilibrium (Fig. 10.4; like text Fig. 10.4)

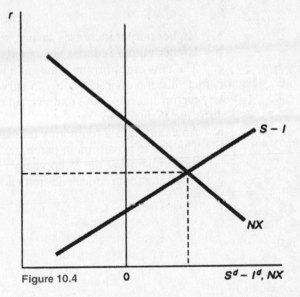

Figure 10.4

    a.   Net exports can be positive or negative

    b.   The net export curve slopes downward, because a rise in the real interest rate increases the real exchange rate and thus reduces net exports

    c.   The $S - I$ curve slopes upward, because a rise in the real interest rate increases desired national saving and reduces desired investment

    d.   Equilibrium occurs where the curves intersect

  3.   To get the open-economy $IS$ curve, we need to see what happens when domestic output changes (Fig. 10.5; like text Fig. 10.5)

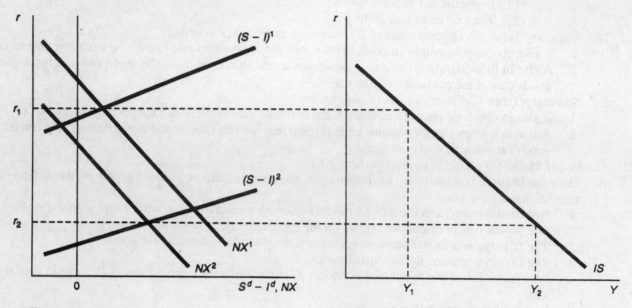

**Figure 10.5**

    a.   Higher output increases saving, so the $S - I$ curve shifts to the right

    b.   Higher output reduces net exports, so the $NX$ curve shifts to the left

    c.   The new equilibrium occurs at a lower real interest rate, so the $IS$ curve is downward sloping

C.   Factors that shift the open-economy $IS$ curve

  1.   Any factor that raises the real interest rate that clears the goods market at a constant level of output shifts the $IS$ curve up

    a.   An example is a temporary increase in government purchases (Fig. 10.6; like text Fig. 10.6)

    b.   The rise in government purchases reduces desired national saving, shifting the $S - I$ curve to the left, shifting the $IS$ curve up

    c.   Anything that reduces desired national saving relative to investment shifts the $IS$ curve up

**Figure 10.6**

2.   Anything that raises a country's net exports, given domestic output and the domestic real interest rate, will shift the open-economy *IS* curve up (Fig. 10.7; like text Fig. 10.7)
   a.   The increase in net exports is shown as a shift to the right in the *NX* curve
   b.   This raises the real interest rate for a fixed level of output, shifting the *IS* curve up
   c.   Three things could increase net exports for a given level of output and real interest rate
      (1)   An increase in foreign output, which increases foreigners' demand for domestic exports
      (2)   An increase in the foreign real interest rate, which makes people want to buy foreign assets, causing the exchange rate to depreciate, which in turn causes net exports to rise
      (3)   A shift in worldwide demand toward the domestic country's goods, for example, as occurs if the quality of domestic goods improves

Figure 10.7

3. Summary Table 18: International factors that shift the *IS* curve
   a. An increase in foreign output, the foreign real interest rate, or the demand for domestic goods relative to foreign goods all shift the *IS* curve up
   D. The international transmission of business cycles
   1. The impact of foreign economic conditions on the real exchange rate and net exports is one of the principal ways by which cycles are transmitted internationally
   2. What would be the effect on Japan of a recession in Canada?
      a. The decline in Canadian output would reduce demand for Japanese exports, shifting the Japanese *IS* curve down
      b. In a Keynesian model, or in the classical misperceptions model, this leads to recession in Japan
      c. In a classical (*RBC*) model, the decline in net exports wouldn't affect Japanese output
   3. A similar effect could occur because of a shift in preferences (or trade restrictions) for Japanese goods
IV. Macroeconomic Policy in a Small Open Economy with Flexible Exchange Rates (Sec. 10.4)
   A. Two key questions
   1. How do fiscal and monetary policy affect a country's real exchange rate and net exports?
   2. How do the macroeconomic policies of one country affect the economies of other countries?
   B. Three steps in analyzing these questions
   1. Use the domestic economy's *IS-LM* diagram to see the effects on domestic output and the domestic real interest rate
   2. See how changes in the domestic real interest rate and output affect the exchange rate and net exports

3. Use the foreign economy's *IS-LM* diagram to see the effects of domestic policy on foreign output and the foreign real interest rate

C. A fiscal expansion

1. Look at a temporary increase in domestic government purchases using the classical (*RBC*) model

a. The rise in government purchases shifts the *IS* curve up and the *FE* line to the right (Fig. 10.8; like text Fig. 10.8)

b. The *LM* curve shifts up to restore equilibrium as the price level rises

c. Both the real interest rate and output rise in the domestic country

d. Higher output reduces the exchange rate, while a higher real interest rate increases the exchange rate, so the effect on the exchange rate is ambiguous

e. Higher output and a higher real interest rate both reduce net exports, supporting the twin deficits idea

2. How do these changes affect a foreign country's economy?

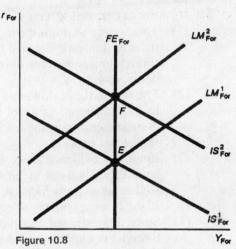

a. The decline in net exports for the domestic economy means a rise in net exports for the foreign country, so the foreign country's *IS* curve shifts up

b. In the classical model, the *LM* curve shifts up as the price level rises to restore equilibrium, thus raising the foreign real interest rate, but foreign output is unchanged

Figure 10.8

c. In a Keynesian model, the shift of the *IS* curve would give the foreign country higher output temporarily

3. In either the classical or Keynesian model, a temporary increase in domestic government purchases raises domestic income (temporarily) and the domestic real interest rate, as in a closed economy

a. It also reduces domestic net exports, so government spending crowds out both investment and net exports

b. The effect on the exchange rate is ambiguous

c. The foreign real interest rate and price level rise

e.   In the Keynesian model, foreign
output rises temporarily

D.   A monetary contraction
1.   Look at a reduction in the domestic money
supply in a Keynesian model
2.   Short-run effects on the domestic and foreign
economies (Fig. 10.9; like text
Fig. 10.9)
a.   The domestic *LM* curve shifts up
b.   In the short run, domestic output is lower
and the real interest rate is higher
c.   The exchange rate appreciates, because
lower output reduces demand for exports,
thus reducing the supply of the domestic
currency to the foreign exchange market,
and because a higher real interest rate
increases demand for the domestic
currency
d.   How are net exports affected?
(1)   The decline in domestic income
reduces domestic demand for
foreign goods, tending to increase
net exports
(2)   The rise in the real interest rate
leads to an appreciation of the
domestic currency and tends to
reduce net exports
(3)   Empirical evidence suggests that the
latter effect is weak in the short run,
so that net exports increase
e.   How is the foreign country affected?
(1)   Since domestic net exports increase,
foreign net exports must decrease,
shifting the foreign *IS* curve down
(2)   Output and the real interest rate in
the foreign country decline
(3)   So a domestic monetary contraction
leads to recession abroad
3.   Long-run effects on the domestic and foreign
economies
a.   In the long run, wages and prices in the
domestic economy decline and the *LM*
curve returns to its original position
b.   All real variables, including net exports and the real exchange rate, return to their original
levels
c.   As a result, the foreign *IS* curve returns to its original level as well
d.   Thus there is no long-run effect on any real variables, either domestically or abroad

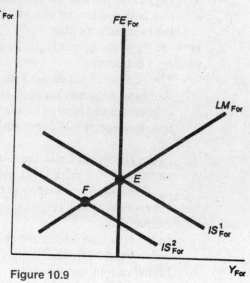

Figure 10.9

      e.   This result holds in the long run in the Keynesian model, but it holds immediately in the classical (*RBC*) model; monetary contraction affects only the price level even in the short run

      f.   Though a monetary contraction doesn't affect the real exchange rate, it does affect the nominal exchange rate because of the change in the domestic price level

      g.   Since $e_{nom} = eP_{For}/P$, the decline in $P$ raises the nominal exchange rate by the same percentage as the decline in the price level and the money supply

  E.   The Mundell-Fleming Model

    1.   Model rests on the assumption that for a small open economy the domestic interest rate always equals the foreign interest rate, even in the short-run. This assumption will be used to see how the effects of monetary policy and fiscal policy depend on a country's integration with the rest of the world.

    2.   The equality between the domestic interest rate $r$ and the foreign interest rate $r_{FOR}$ is brought about as follows:

      a.   If the domestic interest rate $r$ falls below the foreign interest rate $r_{FOR}$ this leads to an immediate capital outflow so that the domestic interest rate rises.

      b.   If the domestic interest rate $r$ rises above the foreign interest rate $r_{FOR}$ this leads to an immediate capital inflow so that the domestic interest rate falls.

    3.   These effects on capital flows are illustrated on the open-economy *IS* curve through the behaviour of net exports.

      a.   If $r > r_{FOR}$, there will be a capital inflow. A capital inflow leads to an appreciation of the domestic currency which, in turn, leads to a fall in net exports.

      b.   If $r < r_{FOR}$ there will be a capital outflow. A capital outflow leads to a depreciation of the domestic currency which, in turn, leads to a rise in net exports

    4.   Net exports are extremely elastic in response to changes in the interest rate around the foreign level. As a result, the open-economy *IS* curve is perfectly flat when $r$ cannot deviate from $r_{FOR}$.

    5.   Recall analysis of Figure 10.8 in the text. Analysis showed that a fiscal expansion in a small open economy leads to an appreciation and a fall in net exports. In the Mundell-Fleming Model, if $r = r_{FOR}$, fiscal policy is ineffective when there is a floating exchange rate and no possible international interest rate differential.

    6.   In the case of monetary policy, the situation is quite different. See Figure 10.10 in the text. $r_{FOR}$ (which is equal to $r$) is shown by a horizontal line. Initially general equilibrium is a point E. A decrease in the money supply shifts the *LM* curve up and to the left from $LM^1$ shifts to $LM^2$. The short-run equilibrium in the Keynesian model is at point F, with lower output and net exports, and a higher real exchange rate. In the long run, prices fall and the economy returns to equilibrium at point E.

    7.   Analysis of Figure 10.10 in the text suggests that in the long run money is neutral.

V.   Macroeconomic Policy in a Large Open Economy with Flexible Exchange Rates (Sec. 10.5)

  A   Foreign Fiscal Expansion

    1.   A foreign fiscal expansion is shown by Figure 10.11 in the text. Figure 10.11(a) represents the effects of a fiscal expansion in the United States. Figure 10.11(b) represents the small trading partner which represents the domestic economy or Canada.

    2.   See Figure 10.11(a). The effects of a foreign fiscal expansion are transmitted through the change in net exports. The effects of an increase in foreign government purchases shifts the *IS* curve up and to the right from $IS^1_{FOR}$ to $IS^2_{FOR}$. In the short-run Keynesian model, foreign output and the foreign real interest rate both rise. Net exports fall and the exchange rate rises (though the exchange rate could fall if it were more responsive to output than the real interest rate).

    3.   In the long run classical model, price adjustment restores general equilibrium at point H, with a higher foreign real interest rate and exchange rate, and lower foreign net exports than at point E.

    4.   See Figure 10.11(b). Because the foreign economy's net exports are the domestic economy's imports, the decrease in the foreign economy's net exports is equivalent to a rise in the domestic economy's net exports. This increase shifts the domestic *IS* curve up, from $IS^1$ to $IS^2$. In the Keynesian model, price stickiness causes a temporary increase in domestic output at point F before price adjustment restores equilibrium at point H.

B.  A Foreign Monetary Contraction
   1.  We can use the same two-country model to analyze the effect on the Canadian economy of a monetary contraction in the United States.  See Figure 10.12 in the text.  Figure 10.12(a) shows the foreign monetary contraction (similar to Figure 10.9 in the text).  Figure 10.12(b) shows the effect on Canada.
   2.  Figure 10.12(a).  A foreign monetary contract shifts the foreign *LM* curve up and to the left, from $LM^1_{FOR}$ to $LM^2_{FOR}$.  In the short-run Keynesian model, output falls and the foreign real interest rate rises.  The exchange rate rise, but net exports can rise or fall.  In this example, the effect of lower output dominates, and foreign net exports rise.
   3.  Figure 10.12(b).  Because the foreign economy's net exports rise, the domestic economy's net exports fall, and the domestic *IS* curve shifts down, from $IS^1$ to $IS^2$.  Thus, output falls in the domestic economy in the short run.  In the long-run, or classical model, foreign output and the foreign real interest rate return to their original levels, the domestic *IS* curve shifts back to $IS^1$, and both economies return to equilibrium at point E.
   4.  The results of the analysis in Figure 10.12 show that in the long run money is neutral.
C.  Application:  Golden Fetters
   1.  The most dramatic example of how the choice of the exchange rate system affects an economy occurred during the Great Depression of the 1930s.
   2.  During the late 1920s, most western economies participated in the gold standard, a system of fixed exchange rates, with all currency values set in terms of gold.  The system broke down during the Depression, as one by one, these countries left the gold standard and allowed their exchange rates to float.
   3.  Countries that left the gold standard recovered from the Depression more quickly, while no country recovered while remaining on the gold standard.  A country that left the gold standard increased its money supply so that its currency depreciated.
      a.  This pattern of floating exchange rates and macroeconomic recovery is evidence of the importance of monetary factors in the business cycle.
      b.  Some economic historians have argued that the Depression was also caused by monetary factors.
         (1)  For example, monetary policy in the US became contractionary in 1928, to curb speculation on the stock market.  In that year the Fed began to raise interest rates so that speculators had to pay more to invest with borrowed money.
         (2)  The analysis in the text shows, this contraction in the US money supply would cause an appreciation of the US dollar and hence depreciations in other currencies.
         (3)  Under the system of fixed exchange rates, other countries responded by contracting their own monetary policies to maintain the value of their currencies.  Thus, the contractionary monetary policy was spread around the world.
   4.  As the Depression began, the international monetary system also transmitted a second shock.  In 1931, a series of banking panics led to increases in money demand in several countries, as asset-holders preferred holding money to holding less liquid non-monetary assets.
      a.  Like the decrease in the money supply, this increase in money demand shifted the *LM* curve back in countries with banking panics.  Once again the result was an exchange-rate appreciation, which then spread as countries tried to maintain fixed exchange rates.
   5.  How did these monetary factors cause the Great Depression?  Bernanke who studied 24 countries during the period from 1932 to 1935 has reviewed statistical evidence on the relation between allowing the exchange rate to float and recovering from the Depression.  Bernanke found that output was 31% higher for countries that adopted flexible exchange rates.
   6.  Eichengreen, however, found that economic conditions in 1929 and 1930 were similar across countries that adopted flexible exchange rates soon after those that did not.
   7.  The experience of countries with flexible exchange rates during the Depression does not imply that a flexible exchange rate regime should always be chosen, for the following reasons:
      a.  Not all international shocks are monetary shocks, and a flexible exchange rate may not insulate a small open economy against foreign fiscal shocks, for example.
      b.  There are other arguments for adopting a fixed exchange rate, for example to constrain domestic monetary policy that is too expansionary or to promote trade.

VI. Fixed Exchange Rates (Sec. 10.6)
   A. Fixing the exchange rate
      1. The government sets the exchange rate, perhaps in agreement with other countries
      2. What happens if the official rate differs from the rate determined by supply and demand?
         a. Supply and demand determine the fundamental value of the exchange rate (Fig. 10.10; like text Fig. 10.13)
         b. When the official rate is above its fundamental value, the currency is said to be overvalued
         c. The country could devalue the currency, reducing the official rate to the fundamental value
         d. The country could restrict international transactions to reduce the supply of its currency to the foreign exchange market, thus raising the fundamental value of the exchange rate
            (1) If a country prohibits people from trading the currency at all, the currency is said to be inconvertible
         e. The government can supply or demand the currency to make the fundamental value equal to the official rate
            (1) If the currency is overvalued, the government can buy its own currency
               (a) This is done by the nation's central bank using its official reserve assets to buy the domestic currency in the foreign exchange market

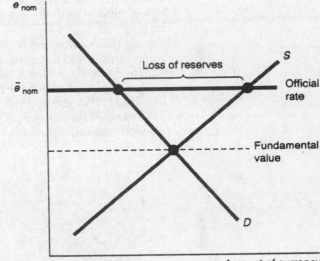

Figure 10.10

               (b) Official reserve assets include gold, foreign bank deposits, and special assets created by agencies like the International Monetary Fund
               (c) The decline in official reserve assets is equal to a country's balance of payments deficit
            (2) A country can't maintain an overvalued currency forever, as it will run out of official reserve assets
               (a) In the gold standard period, countries sometimes ran out of gold and had to devalue their currencies
               (b) A speculative run (or speculative attack) may end the attempt to support an overvalued currency
                  i) If investors think a currency may soon be devalued, they may sell assets denominated in the overvalued currency, increasing the supply of that currency on the foreign exchange market
                  ii) This causes even bigger losses of official reserves from the central bank and speeds up the likelihood of devaluation, as occurred in Mexico in 1994 and Asia in 1997-1998
                      See Application: The crises in Mexico, East Asia and Russia in Chapter 5
            (3) Thus an overvalued currency can't be maintained for very long
      3. Similarly, in the case of an undervalued currency, the official rate is below the fundamental value
         a. In this case, a central bank trying to maintain the official rate will acquire official reserve assets
         b. If the domestic central bank is gaining official reserve assets, foreign central banks must be losing them, so again the undervalued currency can't be maintained for long

B.   Monetary policy and the fixed exchange rate
1.   The best way for a country to make the fundamental value of a currency equal the official rate is through the use of monetary policy
2.   Rewrite Eq. (10.1) as $e_{nom} = eP_{For}/P$    (10.6)
3.   For an overvalued currency, a monetary contraction is desirable
   a.   In a Keynesian model, a monetary contraction causes a real (and nominal) exchange rate appreciation in the short run and a nominal exchange rate appreciation in the long run (with no long-run effect on the real exchange rate)
   b.   Conversely, a monetary expansion causes a nominal exchange rate depreciation in both the short run and the long run
   c.   Plotting the relationship between the money supply and the nominal exchange rate shows the level of the money supply for which the fundamental value of the exchange rate equals the official rate (Fig. 10.11; like text Fig. 10.17)
      (1)   A higher money supply yields an overvalued currency
      (2)   A lower money supply yields an undervalued currency

Figure 10.11

4.   This implies that countries can't both maintain the exchange rate and use monetary policy to affect output

Using expansionary monetary policy to fight a recession would lead to an overvalued currency

So under fixed exchange rates, monetary policy can't be used for macroeconomic stabilization

5.   However, a group of countries may be able to coordinate their use of monetary policy
   a.   If two countries increase their money supplies together to fight joint recessions, there needn't be an overvaluation
   b.   One country increasing its money supply by itself would lead to a depreciation
   c.   But when the other country increases its money supply, it provides an offsetting effect
   d.   If the money supplies expand in each country, they offset each other, so the exchange rate needn't change

6.   Overall, fixed exchange rates can work well if countries in the system have similar macroeconomic goals and can coordinate changes in monetary policy
   a.   But the failure to cooperate can lead to severe problems

C.   Application: Policy coordination failure and the collapse of fixed exchange rates—the cases of Bretton Woods and the EMS

1.   The Bretton Woods system worked well from 1959 to 1971
   a.   The system fixed exchange rates, with the U.S. dollar serving as an official reserve asset throughout the world
   b.   The dollar was fixed at $35 per ounce of gold
   c.   But U.S. monetary policy became expansionary in the 1960s, and the dollar became overvalued
   d.   Canada avoided the loss of official reserves by persuading foreign governments to acquire dollar assets
   e.   But foreign countries began complaining about holding so many U.S. assets and wanted the United States to slow down its monetary expansion
   f.   Instead, U.S. policymakers encouraged other countries to expand their money supplies
   g.   Countries like Germany refused and began to demand gold in exchange for their dollars
   h.   The United States didn't want all its gold to drain away, so it announced in August 1971 that it was going off the system and wouldn't exchange gold for dollars

2.   The European Monetary System (EMS) set up fixed exchange rates among Western European countries
   a.   Germany, the leader of the EMS, got into trouble in 1992 because reunification brought higher inflation, leading Germany to tighten monetary policy
   b.   This undervalued the mark, putting pressure on other EMS members to tighten monetary policy as well, but those countries were in recessions and didn't want to tighten policy
   c.   In September 1992 there was a speculative run on the British pound, as investors didn't think the British government would tighten monetary policy enough to maintain the exchange rate
      (1)   At first the government spent a lot of official reserves trying to defend the pound
      (2)   But eventually Great Britain decided to leave the EMS and allow the exchange rate to float
   d.   Other countries also decided not to tighten monetary policy and either devalued their currencies or left the system
   e.   The result was a delay in progress toward a single European currency, which had been in the planning stages

3.  In both the Bretton Woods and EMS cases, the failure of the dominant country in the system to pursue monetary policies that were desired by other countries posed a threat to the system of fixed exchange rates

D.  Fixed versus flexible exchange rates
1.  Flexible-exchange-rate systems also have problems, because the volatility of exchange rates introduces uncertainty into international transactions
2.  There are two major benefits of fixed exchange rates
    a.  Stable exchange rates make international trades easier and less costly
    b.  Fixed exchange rates help discipline monetary policy, making it impossible for a country to engage in expansionary policy; the result may be lower inflation in the long run
3.  But there are some disadvantages to fixed exchange rates
    a.  They take away a country's ability to use expansionary monetary policy to combat recessions
    b.  Disagreement among countries about the conduct of monetary policy may lead to the breakdown of the system
4.  Which system is better may thus depend on the circumstances
    a.  If large benefits can be gained from increased trade and integration, and when countries can coordinate their monetary policies closely, then fixed exchange rates may be desirable
    b.  Countries that value having independent monetary policies, either because they face different macroeconomic shocks or hold different views about the costs of unemployment and inflation than other countries, should have a floating exchange rate

E.  Currency unions
1.  Under a *currency union*, countries agree to share a common currency
    a.  They often cooperate economically and politically as well, as was the case with the 13 original U.S. colonies
2.  To work effectively, a currency union must have just one central bank
    a.  Since countries don't usually want to give up control over monetary policy by not having their own central banks, currency unions are very rare
    b.  But a currency union has advantages over fixed exchange rates because having a single currency reduces the costs of trading goods and assets across countries and because speculative attacks on a national currency can no longer occur
3.  But the major disadvantage of a currency union is that all countries share a common monetary policy, a problem that also arises with fixed exchange rates
    a.  Thus if one country is in recession while another is concerned about inflation, monetary policy can't help both, whereas with flexible exchange rates, the countries could have monetary policies that help their particular situation
4.  Application:  European monetary union:  lessons for North America
    a.  In 1991, countries in the European Community adopted the Maastricht treaty, which provides for a common currency
        (1)  The currency, called the euro, came into being on January 1, 1999
        (2)  Eleven countries took part in the union
    b.  Monetary policy is determined by the Governing Council of the European Central Bank
    c.  European monetary union is an important development, whose long-term implications are unknown
        (1)  There are many advantages
            (a)  Easier movement of goods, capital, and labour among European countries
            (b)  Lower costs of financial transactions
            (c)  Greater political and economic cooperation
            (d)  An integrated market similar in size and wealth to the Canadian market

        (e)  The possibility that the euro could become the preferred currency for international transactions, displacing the dollar

    (2)  But there are some disadvantages

        (a)  Countries may strongly disagree about what monetary policy should do

        (b)  For example, in 1999, the countries faced varying degrees of recession, and the European Central Bank faced a tough decision about what to do

VII. Appendix 10.A: An Algebraic Version of the Open-Economy *IS-LM* Model

  A.  The *IS* curve is modified, but the *LM* curve and *FE* line are unchanged

    1.  Desired consumption and investment are given by

      a.  $C^d = c_0 + c_Y[Y - (t_0 + tY)] - c_r r$   (10.A.1)

      b.  $I^d = i_0 - i_r r$   (10.A.2)

    2.  Net exports depend negatively on domestic income $Y$ and the domestic real interest rate $r$, and positively on foreign income $Y_{For}$ and the foreign real interest rate $r_{For}$

$$NX = x_0 - x_Y Y + x_{YF} Y_{For} - x_r r + x_{rF} r_{For}\quad(10.A.3)$$

    3.  The goods market equilibrium condition is $S^d = I^d + NX$ or

$$Y = C^d + I^d + G + NX\quad(10.A.4)$$

    4.  Plugging Eqs. (10.A.1), (10.A.2), and (10.A.3) into (10.A.4) gives the *IS* curve

$$[1 - (1-t)c_Y + x_Y]Y = c_0 + i_0 + G - c_Y t_0 + x_0 + x_{YF} Y_{For} + x_{rF} r_{For} - (c_r + i_r + x_r)r\quad(10.A.6)$$

    5.  Writing this more simply,

$$r = \alpha'_{IS} - \beta'_{IS} Y\quad(10.A.7)$$

$$\alpha'_{IS} = (c_0 + i_0 + G - c_Y t_0 + x_0 + x_{YF} Y_{For} + x_{rF} r_{For})/(c_r + i_r + x_r)\quad(10.A.8)$$

$$\beta'_{IS} = [1 - (1-t)c_Y + x_Y]/(c_r + i_r + x_r)\quad(10.A.9)$$

    6.  These equations confirm the points made about the *IS* curve in the text

      a.  The *IS* curve slopes downward, since $\beta'_{IS}$ is positive

      b.  Any factor that shifts the closed-economy *IS* curve also shifts the open-economy *IS* curve through changes in $\alpha'_{IS}$

      c.  For a given output and real interest rate, any factor that increases net exports shifts the open-economy *IS* curve up, as it increases the intercept term $\alpha'_{IS}$

  D.  General equilibrium is determined in the same way as for a closed economy, but using the open-economy *IS* curve instead of the closed-economy *IS* curve

    1.  Using Appendixes 10.A and 12.B, you just replace the equations there that have the coefficients $\alpha_{IS}$ and $\beta_{IS}$ with the open-economy coefficients $\alpha'_{IS}$ and $\beta'_{IS}$

    2.  The exchange rate increases if there is an increase in foreign income or the domestic interest rate, or if there is a decrease in domestic income or the foreign real interest rate, so the exchange rate is determined by the equation

$$e = e_0 - e_Y Y + e_{YF} Y_{For} + e_r r - e_{rF} r_{For}\quad(10.A.10)$$

    3.  The nominal exchange rate is then determined by the equation

$$e_{nom} = e P_{For}/P\quad(10.A.11)$$

  C.  An illustration: monetary expansion in the Keynesian model

    1.  The rise in the money supply increases domestic output, lowers the domestic real interest rate, and has no effect on the price level in the short run

    2.  Equations (10.A.10) and (10.A.11) imply that these changes will cause both a real and nominal depreciation

    3.  In the long run money is neutral, so output, the real interest rate, and the real exchange rate are unaffected, but the nominal exchange rate falls because the price level rises

## MULTIPLE-CHOICE QUESTIONS

1.  The exchange rate is
    a.   the price of one currency in terms of another.
    b.   the price of domestic goods relative to foreign goods.
    c.   the quantity of gold that can be purchased by one unit of currency.
    d.   the difference in interest rates between two countries.

2.  The international monetary system in which the exchange rate is determined by the market forces of supply and demand is called
    a.   a managed float.
    b.   a flexible-exchange-rate system.
    c.   an adjustable-peg system.
    d.   a fixed-exchange-rate system.

3.  In the post-World War II period, prior to the collapse of the Bretton Woods system in the early 1970s, the exchange rate of the dollar was
    a.   determined in a flexible-exchange-rate system.
    b.   determined by the market forces of supply and demand.
    c.   fixed at $35 per ounce of gold.
    d.   determined by a managed float.

4.  During the period of the Bretton Woods system, the U.S. government prevented a revaluation of the dollar by
    a.   offering to sell dollars at the fixed exchange rate.
    b.   allowing the dollar to appreciate.
    c.   liberalizing its trade policies.
    d.   decreasing the money supply.

5.  The European Monetary System is an example of
    a.   a flexible-exchange-rate system.
    b.   a floating-exchange-rate system.
    c.   a fixed-exchange-rate system.
    d.   an exchange-rate union.

6.  The real exchange rate is
    a.   the number of foreign goods that can be obtained in exchange for one unit of the domestic good.
    b.   the nominal exchange rate minus the rate of inflation.
    c.   the amount of foreign currency that can be obtained in exchange for one unit of the domestic currency.
    d.   the amount of domestic currency that can be obtained in exchange for one unit of the foreign currency.

7.  Three-wheel cars made in North Edsel are sold for 5000 pounds.  Four-wheel cars made in South Edsel are sold for 10,000 marks.  The nominal exchange rate between the two countries is three marks per pound.  The real exchange rate is
    a.   0.50 three-wheel cars per four-wheel car.
    b.   0.66 three-wheel cars per four-wheel car.
    c.   1.50 three-wheel cars per four-wheel car.
    d.   2.00 three-wheel cars per four-wheel car.

8. For a given nominal exchange rate, an increase in the price of foreign goods relative to the price of domestic goods causes
   a. domestic residents to buy more foreign goods.
   b. domestic residents to buy fewer domestic goods.
   c. the real exchange rate to decline.
   d. an increase in the number of units of the foreign goods needed to buy a unit of the domestic goods.

9. When the nominal exchange rate falls,
   a. the domestic currency buys more units of foreign currency and the domestic currency has depreciated.
   b. the domestic currency buys fewer units of foreign currency and the domestic currency has depreciated.
   c. the domestic currency buys more units of foreign currency and the domestic currency has appreciated.
   d. the domestic currency buys fewer units of foreign currency and the domestic currency has appreciated.

10. For a given real exchange rate, a nominal appreciation of the domestic currency will result from
    a. a decline in the terms of trade.
    b. an increase in the price of the foreign good.
    c. an increase in the price of the domestic good.
    d. an increase in the domestic rate of inflation.

11. A fall in the real exchange rate is called
    a. a real depreciation.
    b. a real appreciation.
    c. a real revaluation.
    d. a real devaluation.

12. When the nominal exchange rate in terms of dollars per yen rises,
    a. the dollar buys more yen and the dollar has depreciated.
    b. the dollar buys fewer yen and the dollar has depreciated.
    c. the dollar buys more yen and the dollar has appreciated.
    d. the dollar buys fewer yen and the dollar has appreciated.

13. If the real exchange rate rises 2%, domestic inflation is 3%, and foreign inflation is 4%, what is the percent change in the nominal exchange rate?
    a. 5%
    b. 3%
    c. 1%
    d. -1%

14. Suppose the French franc rises against the British pound but falls against the German mark. What happens to the prices of goods imported into France?
    a. Both British and German goods fall in price.
    b. Both British and German goods rise in price.
    c. British goods rise in price while German goods fall in price.
    d. British goods fall in price while German goods rise in price.

15. If the nominal exchange rate rises 2%, domestic inflation is 3%, and foreign inflation is 4%, what is the percent change in the real exchange rate?
    a. 5%
    b. 3%
    c. 1%
    d. -1%

16. Suppose purchasing power parity holds. If in 1997 the price level in Canada is 100, the price level in Japan is 10,000, and the nominal exchange rate is 100 yen per dollar, while in 1998 the price level in Japan rises to 10,500 and the nominal exchange rate rises to 105, then the price level in Canada in 1998 must be
    a. 95.
    b. 100.
    c. 105.
    d. 110.25.

17. Suppose the pound/yen exchange rate rises while the dollar/yen exchange rate falls. What happens to the price of goods imported into Japan?
    a. British goods become more expensive while Canadian goods become cheaper.
    b. British goods become cheaper while Canadian goods become more expensive.
    c. Both British and Canadian goods become more expensive.
    d. Both British and Canadian goods become cheaper.

18. When the British pound rises in value relative to other currencies, then
    a. goods imported into Britain rise in price.
    b. British exports rise in price.
    c. neither British exports nor imports rise in price.
    d. both British exports and imports rise in price.

19. Suppose the dollar/franc exchange rate rises. Then
    a. French firms will import more from Canada into France.
    b. Canadian firms will export less to France.
    c. the dollar is more valuable relative to the franc.
    d. the franc is less valuable relative to the dollar.

20. A decline in the domestic real interest rate would cause a _____ in net exports and a _____ in the exchange rate.
    a. rise; rise
    b. rise; fall
    c. fall; rise
    d. fall; fall

21. Which of the following statements is true?
    a.   The open-economy *IS* curve is derived in the same way that the closed-economy *IS* curve is derived.
    b.   The closed-economy *IS* curve is downward sloping, but the open-economy *IS* curve is upward sloping.
    c.   Some factors that shift the *IS* curve in the closed economy in one direction will shift the *IS* curve in the open economy in the opposite direction.
    d.   Factors that raise a country's current net exports, given domestic output and the domestic real interest rate, shift the open-economy *IS* curve up.

22. In a Keynesian model, a temporary decrease in government purchases would cause output to _____ and the domestic real interest rate to _____.
    a.   not change; increase
    b.   not change; decrease
    c.   decrease; increase
    d.   decrease; decrease

23. A classical *IS-LM* model of the world economy can be used to show that in a flexible-exchange-rate system, a temporary increase in government purchases will cause
    a.   output and the real interest rate to rise, which reduces net exports but has an ambiguous effect on the real exchange rate.
    b.   output and the real interest rate to rise, which increases net exports but has an ambiguous effect on the real exchange rate.
    c.   output to rise and the real interest rate to fall, which reduces net exports and causes the exchange rate to depreciate.
    d.   the real interest rate to fall, which causes the exchange rate to rise, which reduces net exports.

24. Assume Canada is currently running a current account deficit. The most effective way of eliminating this current account deficit would be to temporarily _____ government purchases and _____ the domestic money supply.
    a.   increase; increase
    b.   increase; decrease
    c.   decrease; increase
    d.   decrease; decrease

25. An overvalued currency arises when
    a.   the demand for the currency exceeds the supply.
    b.   the central bank gains reserves while maintaining the exchange rate.
    c.   the central bank keeps the official rate above the fundamental value.
    d.   the central bank keeps the official rate below the fundamental value.

26. In a fixed-exchange-rate system, if the government takes no action, an increase in the world demand for domestic goods will
    a.   increase net exports and create an undervalued domestic currency.
    b.   reduce net exports and create an overvalued domestic currency.
    c.   reduce net exports and create an undervalued domestic currency.
    d.   increase net exports and create an overvalued domestic currency.

27.  An important advantage of a fixed-exchange-rate system is that it
    a.  prevents an exchange rate from becoming an overvalued exchange rate.
    b.  prevents an exchange rate from becoming an undervalued exchange rate.
    c.  protects the domestic economy from being hit by foreign shocks.
    d.  promotes the growth of international trade and international financial transactions, by reducing the risk to market participants that exchange rates will change unexpectedly and substantially.

28.  Compared to a system of flexible exchange rates, currency unions have the disadvantage of
    a.  requiring all its members to share a common monetary policy.
    b.  allowing exchange rates to float.
    c.  requiring every country to share a common fiscal policy.
    d.  decreasing the sacrifice ratio.

## REVIEW QUESTIONS

1.  How is the real exchange rate related to the nominal exchange rate?

2.  Briefly explain the difference between a revaluation and a real depreciation of the exchange rate.

3.  Under what conditions would the real exchange rate change by the same percentage as the nominal exchange rate?

4.  Identify changes in two variables that would shift the supply curve of dollars to the right.  Identify changes in two variables that would shift the demand curve for dollars to the right.

5.  Briefly explain how a change in the domestic economy is transmitted to the foreign country in a two-country model of the world.

## NUMERICAL PROBLEMS

1.  Given goods market equilibrium in an open economy with $Y = \$7000$ billion, calculate:
    (a) $S^d$ and $NX$, when $C^d = 60\%$ of output, $I^d = 15\%$ of output, and $G = 20\%$ of output;
    (b) $NX$, when $S^d = 25\%$ of output and $I^d = 10\%$ of output.

## ANALYTICAL QUESTIONS

1.  When the real exchange rate rises, what happens to net exports in the short run? In the long run? What explains the difference between the short-run effect and the long-run effect?

2.  What happens to the exchange rate and net exports in each of the following cases?
    a.  The foreign real interest rate rises.
    b.  Foreign output falls.
    c.  Foreign demand for domestic goods falls.
    d.  Domestic output falls.
    e.  The domestic real interest rate rises.

3.  In a Keynesian model, what are the short-run effects on output, the real interest rate, and the real exchange rate, for both the domestic economy and a foreign economy, of a decline in investment?

4.  In a Keynesian model, what are the short-run effects on output, the real interest rate, and the real exchange rate, for both the domestic economy and a foreign economy, of a decline in foreign demand for domestic goods?

## ANSWERS TO MULTIPLE-CHOICE QUESTIONS

| Number | Answer | | Number | Answer | | Number | Answer |
|--------|--------|---|--------|--------|---|--------|--------|
| 1 | a | | 11 | a | | 21 | d |
| 2 | b | | 12 | b | | 22 | d |
| 3 | c | | 13 | b | | 23 | a |
| 4 | a | | 14 | d | | 24 | d |
| 5 | c | | 15 | c | | 25 | c |
| 6 | a | | 16 | b | | 26 | a |
| 7 | b | | 17 | b | | 27 | d |
| 8 | c | | 18 | b | | 28 | a |
| 9 | b | | 19 | a | | | |
| 10 | b | | 20 | b | | | |

## ANSWERS TO REVIEW QUESTIONS

1.    The real exchange rate is $e = e_{nom}P/P_{For}$.

2.    A revaluation is an increase in the exchange rate in a fixed-exchange-rate system. A real depreciation is a decline in the real exchange rate in a flexible-exchange-rate system.

3.    The percent change in the nominal exchange rate = the percent change in the real exchange rate + the foreign inflation rate - the domestic inflation rate. When the difference between the foreign inflation rate and the domestic inflation rate remains constant, the percent increase in the nominal exchange rate equals the percent increase in the real exchange rate.

4.    An increase in Canadian output or an increase in the foreign real interest rate will cause the supply curve for dollars to shift to the right. A rightward shift in the supply curve causes the exchange rate to depreciate in a flexible-exchange-rate system.

   An increase in foreign output or an increase in the Canadian real interest rate will cause the demand curve for dollars to shift to the right. A rightward shift in the demand curve causes the exchange rate to depreciate in a flexible-exchange-rate system.

5.    Domestic economy changes are transmitted to the foreign economy through changes in the exchange rate and through changes in net exports. An economic change in the domestic economy that changes net exports shifts the *IS* curve in the foreign country. In a two-country model, the exports of one country are the imports of the other; an increase in domestic net exports is also a decline in foreign net exports.

## ANSWERS TO NUMERICAL PROBLEMS

1.    The goods market equilibrium condition for an open economy is $NX = S^d - I^d$. Since $S^d = Y - C^d - G$, an alternative equation for goods market equilibrium is $NX = Y - C^d - I^d - G$.

   (a)   $C^d = .60$ x $7000 billion = $4200 billion.
         $I^d = .15$ x $7000 billion = $1050 billion.
         $G = .20$ x $7000 billion = $1400 billion.
         $S^d = $7000 billion - $4200 billion - $1400 billion = $1400 billion.
         $NX = $1400 billion - $1050 billion = $350 billion.

   (b)   $S^d = .25$ x $7000 billion = $1750 billion.
         $I^d = .10$ x $7000 billion = $700 billion.
         $NX = $1750 billion - $700 billion = $1050 billion.

## ANSWERS TO ANALYTICAL QUESTIONS

1.  In the short run, net exports rise, while in the long run net exports fall. The difference is the J curve effect, because quantities are slower to adjust than prices.

2.  a.  Exchange rate falls, net exports rise
    b.  Exchange rate falls, net exports fall
    c.  Exchange rate falls, net exports fall
    d.  Exchange rate rises, net exports rise
    e.  Exchange rate rises, net exports fall

3.  The $IS$ curve shifts down, causing $Y$ to decline and $r$ to decline, as the left panel of Figure 10.12 shows.  The decline in $Y$ causes imports to decline and $NX$ to increase.  The effect on the exchange rate is ambiguous, because the increase in $NX$ causes the exchange rate to rise, while the decline in $r$ causes it to fall.  The increase in $NX$ causes $NX_{For}$ to decline, which causes the foreign $IS$ curve to shift down, causing $Y_{For}$ and $r_{For}$ to decline, as shown in the right panel.

**Figure 10.12**

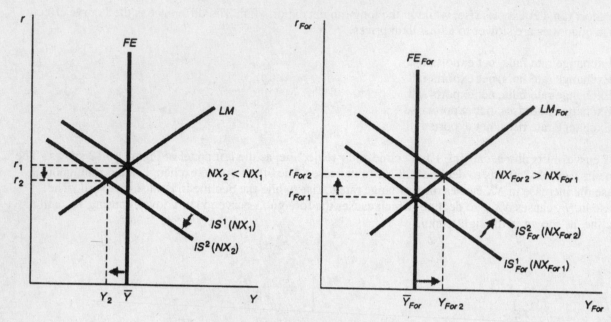

**Figure 10.13**

4.   The decline in foreign imports causes $NX_{For}$ to increase, causing the foreign *IS* curve to shift up, causing $Y_{For}$ and $r_{For}$ to increase, as shown in the right panel of Figure 10.13. An increase in $NX_{For}$ is a decline in *NX*. The decline in *NX* and the increase in $r_{For}$ cause the exchange rate to depreciate. The decline in *NX* causes the domestic *IS* curve to shift down, causing *Y* and *r* to decline, as shown in the left panel.

# CHAPTER 11: CLASSICAL BUSINESS CYCLE ANALYSIS: MARKET-CLEARING MACROECONOMICS

## INTRODUCTION

This chapter uses a version of the *IS-LM* model with rapidly adjusting wages and prices to represent the classical model. Section 11.1 introduces real business cycle theory, the modern version of the classical model, and discusses some of the current research that uses it. Then, Section 11.2 looks at the role of money in the classical model, and the issues involved in modeling it. Section 11.3 presents the misperceptions theory, a model in which people's expectations about prices matter. Appendix 11.A provides an algebraic model of the misperceptions theory.

Some of the hottest research in macroeconomics today is taking place using classical business cycle analysis. Many researchers are working with real business cycle models to create better empirical models of Canadian economy. So, if you want to get a good handle on the most recent work in macroeconomics, read Section 11.1 very carefully. Also, the misperceptions model of Section 11.3 represents an older strand of classical analysis, but was very important in leading macro researchers to the real business cycle model in use today. The distinction between anticipated changes in the money supply and unanticipated changes is important.

## CHAPTER OUTLINE

I.    Business Cycles in the Classical Model (Sec. 11.1)
    A.   The real business cycle theory
        1.   Two key questions about business cycles
            a.   What are the underlying economic causes?
            b.   What should government policymakers do about them?
        2.   Any business cycle theory has two components
            a.   A description of the types of shocks believed to affect the economy the most
            b.   A model that describes how key macroeconomic variables respond to economic shocks
        3.   Real business cycle (*RBC*) theory (Kydland and Prescott)
            a.   Real shocks to the economy are the primary cause of business cycles
                (1)   Examples: Shocks to the production function, the size of the labour force, the real quantity of government purchases, the spending and saving decisions of consumers (affecting the *IS* curve or the *FE* line)
                (2)   Nominal shocks are shocks to money supply or demand (affecting the *LM* curve)
            b.   The largest role is played by shocks to the production function, which the text has called supply shocks, and *RBC* theorists call *productivity shocks*
                (1)   Examples: Development of new products or production techniques, introduction of new management techniques, changes in the quality of capital or labour, changes in the availability of raw materials or energy, unusually good or bad weather, changes in government regulations affecting production
                (2)   Most economic booms result from beneficial productivity shocks; most recessions are caused by adverse productivity shocks

    c.   The recessionary impact of an adverse productivity shock
       (1)  Results from Chapter 3: Real wage, employment, output, consumption, and investment decline, while the real interest rate and price level rise
       (2)  So an adverse productivity shock causes a recession (output declines), whereas a beneficial productivity shock causes a boom (output increases); but output always equals full-employment output
    d.   Real business cycle theory and the business cycle facts
       (1)  The *RBC* theory is consistent with many business cycle facts
          (a)  If the economy is continuously buffeted by productivity shocks, the theory predicts recurrent fluctuations in aggregate output, which we observe
          (b)  The theory correctly predicts procyclical employment and real wages
          (c)  The theory correctly predicts procyclical average labour productivity. If booms weren't due to productivity shocks, we would expect average labour productivity to be countercyclical because of diminishing marginal productivity of labour
       (2)  The theory predicts countercyclical movements of the price level, which seems to be inconsistent with the data
          (a)  But Kydland and Prescott, when using some newer statistical techniques for calculating the trends in inflation and output, find evidence that the price level is countercyclical.
          (b)  Though the Great Depression appears to have been caused by a sequence of large, adverse aggregate demand shocks, Kydland and Prescott argue that since World War II, large adverse supply shocks have caused the price level to rise while output fell
          (c)  The surge in inflation during the recessions associated with the oil price shocks of 1973–1974 and 1979–1980 is consistent with *RBC* theory
  4.  Application: Calibrating the business cycle
    a.   A major element of *RBC* theory is that it attempts to make quantitative, not just qualitative, predictions about the business cycle
    b.   RBC theorists use the method of calibration to work out a detailed numerical example of the theory
       (1)  First they write down specific functions explaining the behavior of people in the economy; for example, they might choose as the production function for the economy, $Y = AK^a N^{1-a}$
       (2)  Then they use existing studies of the economy to choose numbers for parameters like a in the production function; for example, $a = 0.3$
       (3)  Next they simulate what happens when the economy is hit by various shocks to different sectors of the economy
       (4)  Prescott's computer simulations (text Figs. 11.1 and 11.2) match post–World War II data fairly well
  5.  Are productivity shocks the only source of recessions?
    a.   Critics of the *RBC* theory suggest that except for the oil price shocks of 1973, 1979, and 1990, there are no productivity shocks that one can easily identify that caused recessions
    b.   One *RBC* response is that it doesn't have to be a big shock; instead, the cumulation of many small shocks can cause a business cycle (text Fig. 11.3)

6. Does the Solow residual measure technology shocks?
   a. RBC theorists measure productivity shocks as the Solow residual
      (1) Named after Robert Solow, the originator of modern growth theory
      (2) Given a production function, $Y = AK^a N^{1-a}$, and data on $Y$, $K$, and $N$, the Solow residual is $A = Y/(K^a N^{1-a})$    (11.1)
      (3) It's called a residual because it can't be measured directly
   b. The Solow residual is strongly procyclical in Canadian data
      (1) This accords with RBC theory, which says the cycle is driven by productivity shocks
   c. But should the Solow residual be interpreted as a measure of technology?
      (1) If it's a measure of technology, it should not be related to factors that don't directly affect scientific and technological progress, like government purchases or monetary policy
      (2) But statistical studies show a correlation between these
   d. Measured productivity can vary even if the actual technology doesn't change
      (1) Capital and labour are used more intensively at times
      (2) More intensive use of inputs leads to higher output
      (3) Define the utilization rate of capital $u_K$ and the utilization rate of labour $u_N$
      (4) Define capital services as $u_K K$ and labour services as $u_N N$
      (5) Rewrite the production function as $Y = AF(u_K K, u_N N) = A(u_K K)^a (u_N N)^{1-a}$    (11.2)
      (6) Use this to substitute for $Y$ in Eq. (11.1) to get
         Solow residual = $A u_K^a u_N^{-a}$    (11.3)
      (7) So the Solow residual isn't just $A$, but depends on $u_K$ and $u_N$
      (8) Utilization is procyclical, so the measured Solow residual is more procyclical than is the true productivity term $A$
         (a) Burnside-Eichenbaum-Rebelo evidence on procyclical utilization of capital
         (b) Fay-Medoff and Braun-Evans evidence on procyclical utilization of labour
            i) Labour hoarding: firms keep workers in recessions to avoid incurring hiring and firing costs
            ii) Hoarded labour doesn't work as hard, or performs maintenance
            iii) The lower productivity of hoarded labour doesn't reflect technological change, just the rate of utilization
   e. Conclusion: Changes in the measured Solow residual don't necessarily reflect changes in technology
7. Also, the critics suggest that shocks other than productivity shocks, such as wars and military buildups, have caused business cycles

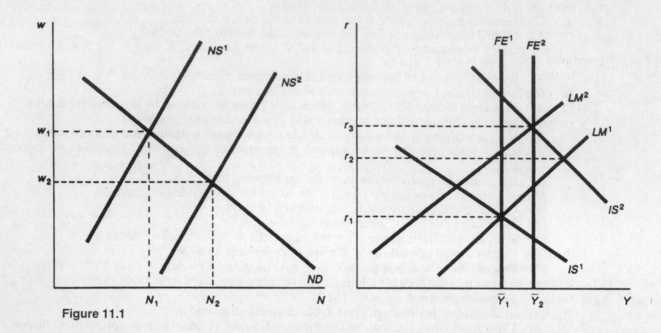

**Figure 11.1**

B.  Fiscal policy shocks in the classical model
   1.  The effects of a temporary increase in government expenditures (Fig. 11.1; like text Fig. 11.5)
      a.  The current or future taxes needed to pay for the government expenditures effectively reduce people's wealth, causing an income effect on labour supply
      b.  The increased labour supply leads to a fall in the real wage and a rise in employment
      c.  The rise in employment increases output, so the *FE* line shifts to the right
      d.  The temporary rise in government purchases shifts the *IS* curve up as national saving declines
      e.  It's reasonable to assume that the shift of the *IS* curve is bigger than the shift of the *FE* line, so prices must rise to shift the *LM* curve up to restore equilibrium
      f.  Since employment rises, average labour productivity declines; this helps match the data better, since without fiscal policy the *RBC* model shows a correlation between output and average labour productivity that is too high
      g.  So adding fiscal policy shocks to the model increases its ability to match the actual behavior of the economy
   2.  Should fiscal policy be used to dampen the cycle?
      a.  Classical economists oppose attempts to dampen the cycle, since prices and wages adjust quickly to restore equilibrium
      b.  Besides, fiscal policy increases output by making workers worse off, since they face higher taxes
      c.  Instead, government spending should be determined by cost-benefit analysis
      d.  Also, there may be lags in enacting the correct policy and in implementing it
         (1)  So choosing the right policy today depends on where you think the economy will be in the future

        (2)   This creates problems, because forecasts of the future state of the economy are imperfect

    e.   It's also not clear how much to change fiscal policy to get the desired effect on employment and output

C.   Unemployment in the classical model

    1.   In the classical model there is no unemployment; people who aren't working are voluntarily not in the labour force

    2.   In reality measured unemployment is never zero, and it is the problem of unemployment in recessions that concerns policymakers the most

    3.   Classical economists have a more sophisticated version of the model to account for unemployment

        a.   Workers and jobs have different requirements, so there is a matching problem

        b.   It takes time to match workers to jobs, so there is always some unemployment

        c.   Unemployment rises in recessions because productivity shocks cause increased mismatches between workers and jobs

        d.   A shock that increases mismatching raises frictional unemployment and may also cause structural unemployment if the types of skills needed by employers change

        e.   So the shock causes the natural rate of unemployment to rise; there's still no cyclical unemployment in the classical model

    4.   Baldwin, Dunn and Haltiwanger show that there is a tremendous amount of churning of jobs both within and across industries

    5.   But this worker match theory can't explain all unemployment

        a.   Many workers are laid off temporarily; there's no mismatch, just a change in the timing of work

        b.   If recessions were times of increased mismatch, there should be a rise in help-wanted ads in recessions, but in fact they fall

    6.   So can the government use fiscal policy to reduce unemployment?

        a.   Doing so doesn't improve the mismatch problem

        b.   A better approach is to eliminate barriers to labour-market adjustment by reducing burdensome regulations on businesses or by getting rid of the minimum wage

II.   Money in the Classical Model (Sec. 11.2)

   A.   Monetary policy and the economy

        Money is neutral in both the short run and the long run in the classical model, because prices adjust rapidly to restore equilibrium

   B.   Monetary nonneutrality and reverse causation

    1.   If money is neutral, why does the data show that money is a leading, procyclical variable?

        a.   Increases in the money supply are often followed by increases in output

        b.   Reductions in the money supply are often followed by recessions

    2.   The classical answer: Reverse causation

        a.   Just because changes in money growth precede changes in output doesn't mean that the money changes cause the output changes

        b.   Example: People put storm windows on their houses before winter, but it's the coming winter that causes the storm windows to go on, the storm windows don't cause winter

        c.   Reverse causation means money growth is higher because people expect higher output in the future; the higher money growth doesn't cause the higher future output

        d.   If so, money can be procyclical and leading even though money is neutral

3.   Why would higher future output cause people to increase money demand?
   a.   Firms, anticipating higher sales, would need more money for transactions to pay for materials and workers
   b.   The Bank of Canada would respond to the higher demand for money by increasing money supply; otherwise, the price level would decline

C.   The nonneutrality of money: Additional evidence
   1.   Friedman and Schwartz have extensively documented that often monetary changes have had an independent origin; they weren't just a reflection of changes or future changes in economic activity
      a.   These independent changes in money supply were followed by changes in income and prices
      b.   The independent origins of money changes include such things as gold discoveries, changes in monetary institutions, and changes in the leadership of the Federal Reserve
   2.   More recently, Romer and Romer documented additional episodes of monetary nonneutrality since 1960
      a.   One example is the Bank of Canada's tight money policy begun in 1979 that was followed by a minor recession in 1980 and a deeper one in 1981
      b.   That was followed by monetary expansion in 1982 that led to an economic boom
   3.   So money does not appear to be neutral
   4.   There is a version of the classical model in which money isn't neutral—the misperceptions theory discussed next

D.   Box 11.1: Money and Economic Activity at Christmastime
   1.   According to the reverse causation argument, the association of higher-than-normal money growth with economic booms and lower-than normal money growth with recessions occurs because money growth responds to changes in output.
   2.   An example of reverse causation is provided by the behaviour of money and economic activity at Christmastime as shown in the table in Box 11.1 of the text.
      a.   In Canada, both the money supply and retail sales grow rapidly in December. Clearly, the sharp increase in December retail sales (measured in real terms) results from Christmas gift buying and not from the December increase in the money supply
      b.   Therefore, at Christmastime, higher economic activity must cause a higher money supply, rather than vice versa.
      c.   The extra money comes from the Bank of Canada that regularly increases the money supply in December to meet the demands of merchants and shoppers. The existence of reverse causation from output to money in December does not rule out monetary non-neutrality, but it does mean that we have to be cautious in interpreting the positive association between money and output over the course of the business cycle.

III.   The Misperceptions Theory and the Nonneutrality of Money (Sec. 11.3)
A.   Introduction to the misperceptions theory
   1.   In the classical model, money is neutral since prices adjust quickly
      a.   In this case, the only relevant supply curve is the long-run aggregate supply curve
      b.   So movements in aggregate demand have no effect on output
   2.   But if producers misperceive the aggregate price level, then the relevant aggregate supply curve in the short run isn't vertical
      a.   This happens because producers have imperfect information about the general price level
      b.   As a result, they misinterpret changes in the general price level as changes in relative prices
      c.   This leads to a short-run aggregate supply curve that isn't vertical
      d.   But prices still adjust rapidly
B.   The misperceptions theory is that the aggregate quantity of output supplied rises above the full-employment level $\bar{Y}$ when the aggregate price level $P$ is higher than expected

1.  This makes the *AS* curve slope upward
2.  Example: A bakery that makes bread
    a.  The price of bread is the baker's nominal wage; the price of bread relative to the general price level is the baker's real wage
    b.  If the relative price of bread rises, the baker may work more and produce more bread
    c.  If the baker can't observe the general price level as easily as the price of bread, he or she must estimate the relative price of bread
    d.  If the price of bread rises 5% and the baker thinks inflation is 5%, there's no change in the relative price of bread, so there's no change in the baker's labour supply
    e.  But suppose the baker expects the general price level to rise by 5%, but sees the price of bread rising by 8%; then the baker will work more in response to the wage increase

**Figure 11.2**

3.  Generalizing this example, if everyone expects prices to increase 5% but they actually increase 8%, they'll work more
4.  So an increase in the price level that is higher than expected induces people to work more and thus increases the economy's output
5.  Similarly, an increase in the price level that is lower than expected reduces output
6.  The equation $Y = \bar{Y} + b(P - P^e)$  [Eq. (11.4)] summarizes the misperceptions theory
7.  In the short run, the aggregate supply (*SRAS*) curve slopes upward and intersects the long-run aggregate supply (*LRAS*) curve at $P = P^e$ (Fig. 11.2; like text Fig. 11.6)

C.  Application: international evidence on the slope of the short-run aggregate supply curve
    1.  When $P$ is higher than $P^e$, output exceeds its full-employment level $\bar{Y}$
    2.  How much output increases depends on how much producers think their relative prices have risen
        a.  If they think the increase in relative prices is small, they won't increase output much, and the coefficient $b$ in Eq. (11.4) will be small; so the line as plotted in Fig.11.2 will be steep, showing not much change in output (the slope of the line, $1/b$, will be large)
        b.  If producers think the increase in relative prices is large, then $b$ will be large, and the slope $1/b$ will be small
    3.  What determines the degree to which producers think a rise in the general price level represents a rise in relative prices?
        a.  Lucas suggested that if the aggregate price level is stable, producers are more easily fooled into thinking a general rise in prices is a rise in relative prices
        b.  So in countries with stable prices, the short-run aggregate supply curve is likely to be relatively flat
        c.  But in countries with highly variable prices, producers are less likely to think there's been a change in relative prices, so the short-run aggregate supply curve will be relatively steep
    4.  So, a test of the misperceptions theory is to look at data from different countries to see if the short-run aggregate supply curve is indeed flatter in countries with more stable prices
        a.  Lucas did this, and found that in Argentina and Paraguay, which had very unstable inflation rates, the *SRAS* curve was ten times as steep as the *SRAS* curve in countries with relatively stable inflation rates
        b.  So Lucas found strong evidence supporting the misperceptions theory

D.  Monetary policy and the misperceptions theory
1.  Because of misperceptions, unanticipated monetary policy has real effects; but anticipated monetary policy has no real effects because there are no misperceptions
2.  Unanticipated changes in the money supply (Fig. 11.3; like text Fig. 11.7)

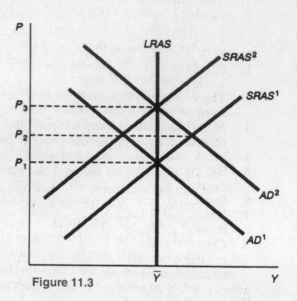

Figure 11.3

   a.  Initial equilibrium where $AD^1$ intersects $SRAS^1$ and $LRAS$
   b.  Unanticipated increase in money supply shifts $AD$ curve to $AD^2$
   c.  The price level rises to $P_2$ and output rises above $\overline{Y}$ so money isn't neutral
   d.  As people get information about the true price level, their expectations change, and the $SRAS$ curve shifts left to $SRAS^2$, with output returning to $\overline{Y}$
   e.  So unanticipated money isn't neutral in the short run, but it is neutral in the long run
3.  Anticipated changes in the money supply
   a.  If people anticipate the change in the money supply and thus in the price level, they aren't fooled, there are no misperceptions, and the $SRAS$ curve shifts immediately to its higher level
   b.  So anticipated money is neutral in both the short run and the long run
E.  Rational expectations and the role of monetary policy
1.  The only way the Bank of Canada can use monetary policy to affect output is to surprise people
2.  But people realize that the Bank of Canada would want to increase the money supply in recessions and decrease it in booms, so they won't be fooled
3.  The rational expectations hypothesis suggests that the public's forecasts of economic variables are well-reasoned and use all the available data
4.  If the public has rational expectations, the Bank of Canada won't be able to surprise people in response to the business cycle; only random monetary policy has any effects
5.  So even if smoothing the business cycle were desirable, the combination of misperceptions theory and rational expectations suggests that the Bank of Canada can't systematically use monetary policy to stabilize the economy
6.  Propagating the effects of unanticipated changes in the money supply
   a.  It doesn't seem like people could be fooled for long, since money supply figures are reported weekly and inflation is reported monthly
   b.  Classical economists argue that *propagation mechanisms* allow short-lived shocks to have long-lived effects
   c.  Example of propagation: The behavior of inventories
      (1)  Firms hold a normal level of inventories against their normal level of sales
      (2)  An unanticipated increase in the money supply increases sales
      (3)  Since the firm can't produce many more goods immediately, it draws down its inventories

  (4) Even after the money supply change is known, the firm must produce more to restore its inventory level

  (5) Thus the short-term monetary shock has a long-lived effect on the economy

F. Box 11.2: Are price forecasts rational?

 1. Economists can test whether price forecasts are rational by looking at surveys of people's expectations

 2. The forecast error of a forecast is the difference between the actual value of the variable and the forecast value

 3. If people have rational expectations, forecast errors should be unpredictable random numbers; otherwise, people would be making systematic errors and thus not have rational expectations

 4. Many statistical studies suggest that people don't have rational expectations

 5. But people who answer surveys may not have a lot at stake in making forecasts, so couldn't be expected to produce rational forecasts

 6. Instead, professional forecasters are more likely to produce rational forecasts

 7. Keane and Runkle, using a survey of professional forecasters, find evidence that these forecasters do have rational expectations

 8. Croushore used inflation forecasts made by the general public, as well as economists, and found evidence broadly consistent with rational expectations, though expectations tend to lag reality when inflation changes sharply

IV. Appendix 11.A: An Algebraic Version of the Classical *AD-AS* Model with Misperceptions

B. The aggregate demand curve

 1. From Appendix 9.A, the AD curve is

$$Y = [\alpha_{IS} - \alpha_{LM} + (1/\ell_r)(M/P)]/[\,\beta_{IS} + \beta_{LM}]\quad(11.A.1)$$

C. The aggregate supply curve (*SRAS*)

 1. Based on the misperceptions theory: $Y = \overline{Y} + b(P - P^e)$ (11.A.2)

D. General equilibrium

 1. The *AD* curve intersects the *SRAS* curve at the point found by setting the right-hand sides of Eqs. (11.A.1) and (11.A.2) equal and rearranging terms to get $a_2 P^2 + a_1 P - a_0 = 0$ (11.A.3), where $a_2 = (\beta_{IS} + \beta_{LM})b$, $a_1 = (\beta_{IS} + \beta_{LM})(\overline{Y} - bP^e) - \alpha_{IS} + \alpha_{LM}$ and $a_0 = M/\ell_r$

 2. The solution for P is given by the quadratic formula, $P = [-a_1 + (a_1^2 + 4a_2 a_0)^{1/2}]/2a_2$ (11.A.4)

 3. Then output is determined by taking this value of *P* and using it in Eqs. (11.A.1) or (11.A.2)

 4. It's easy to see that an increase in the nominal money supply increases $a_0$ and thus P

 5. If the increase in money supply in unanticipated, so that $P^e$ doesn't chPange, then output rises in the short run, according to Eq. (11.A.2)

 6. In the long run, of course, $P = P^e$, so from Eq. (11.A.2) $Y = \overline{Y}$

## MULTIPLE-CHOICE QUESTIONS

1.  According to real business cycle theory, which of the following events is least likely to cause a recession?
    a.   A decline in the money supply
    b.   A decline in the capital stock
    c.   A decline in productivity
    d.   A decline in labour supply

2.  Which of the following would *not* be an example of a productivity shock?
    a.   The introduction of new management techniques
    b.   A change in government regulations affecting production
    c.   A change in the level of government transfer programs
    d.   A spell of unusually good or unusually bad weather

3.  A temporary adverse productivity shock would
    a.   shift the labour supply curve upward.
    b.   reduce the level of employment.
    c.   decrease future income.
    d.   decrease the expected future marginal product of capital.

4.  What do *RBC* economists mean by the term calibration?
    a.   Modifying the structure of an economic theory to strengthen its logic
    b.   Changing a theory as the economy changes
    c.   Working out a detailed numerical example of a more general theory
    d.   Writing out the implications of a theory for all the main economic variables

5.  Research on productivity shocks has shown that
    a.   productivity shocks have only nominal effects.
    b.   there have been no identifiable productivity shocks in the Canadian economy since World War II.
    c.   small productivity shocks can explain large business cycle fluctuations.
    d.   large productivity shocks produce only small deviations in aggregate output.

6.  The most common measure of productivity shocks used by real business cycle theorists is
    a.   the Solow residual.
    b.   average labour productivity.
    c.   the change in the capital stock.
    d.   unit labour costs.

7.  In Canadian data, the Solow residual is
    a.   strongly countercyclical.
    b.   strongly procyclical.
    c.   weakly procyclical.
    d.   weakly countercyclical.

8.  If the utilization rates of capital and labour are procyclical, then
    a.   output will rise in recessions and decline in expansions.
    b.   measured productivity will be constant.
    c.   the Solow residual will be procyclical.
    d.   prices will be countercyclical.

9.  When, because of hiring and firing costs,  firms retain workers in a recession that they would otherwise lay off, there is said to be
    a.  labour hoarding.
    b.  a decline in capacity utilization.
    c.  voluntary unemployment.
    d.  involuntary unemployment.

10. An increase in government purchases in the classical model would
    a.  shift the production function.
    b.  shift the marginal product of labour curve.
    c.  shift the labour demand curve.
    d.  shift the labour supply curve.

11. Assuming that money is neutral, a reduction in the nominal money supply would cause
    a.  an excess demand for goods.
    b.  a decrease in the real money supply.
    c.  a fall in the price level.
    d.  a rise in nominal wages.

12. Assuming money neutrality in the classical model, a 11% increase in the nominal money supply would cause
    a.  a 11% increase in the real money supply.
    b.  a 11% decrease in the real money supply.
    c.  no change in the real money supply.
    d.  a less than 11% change in the price level due to a shift in the aggregate supply curve.

13. A decline in the money supply usually precedes a decline in business cycle activity; according to *RBC* theorists, this shows that the Bank of Canada
    a.  intentionally causes most recessions.
    b.  should not be allowed to control the money supply.
    c.  does not know what it is doing.
    d.  reduces the money supply when money demand falls prior to a recession.

14. Research by Friedman and Schwartz on the monetary history of the United States for 1867–1960, suggests that
    a.  reverse causality can explain why the nominal money supply is a leading, procyclical variable.
    b.  the Federal Reserve can accurately forecast turning points in the business cycle created by small, random changes in productivity.
    c.  money is often nonneutral in the short run.
    d.  money is often nonneutral in the long run.

15. Misperceptions theory best explains why
    a.  the aggregate demand curve is negatively sloped.
    b.  the aggregate supply curve is vertical.
    c.  the *SRAS* curve is positively sloped.
    d.  the *LM* curve is positively sloped.

16. According to the misperceptions theory, when the aggregate price level is higher than expected,
    a.  the aggregate quantity of output supplied rises above the full-employment level.
    b.  the aggregate quantity of output supplied falls below the full-employment level.
    c.  the aggregate quantity of output demanded falls below the full-employment level.
    d.  the aggregate quantity of output demanded rises above the full-employment level.

17. In the misperceptions model, a 5% decline in the money supply that is unanticipated will
    a.  cause both output and employment to decline in the short run.
    b.  cause output to increase in the long run.
    c.  cause employment to decline in the long run.
    d.  not change employment in the short run or long run.

18. You are likely to think that the relative price of your good has declined and you should decrease your output
    if
    a.  you expected inflation of 11% and the price of your good rose 7%.
    b.  you expected inflation of 11% and the price of your good rose 11%.
    c.  you expected inflation of 11% and the price of your good rose 13%.
    d.  you expected inflation of 0% and the price of your good rose 11%.

19. The misperceptions theory and the rational expectations hypothesis together suggest that systematic attempts
    by the Bank of Canada to increase aggregate output will
    a.  cause the price level to exceed the expected price level in the short run.
    b.  not have any real economic effects.
    c.  not increase the price level.
    d.  cause the $AD$ curve to shift to the right along a fixed $SRAS$ curve.

20. In the extended classical model, some kind of propagation mechanism is needed to explain
    a.  the persistence of a recession caused by a nominal shock.
    b.  imperfect information.
    c.  why money is neutral.
    d.  the difference between correlation and causation.

21. According to the misperceptions theory, when $P < P^e$, output is _____ its full-employment level and the
    short-run aggregate supply curve must shift to the _____ to restore full employment.
    a.  below; left
    b.  below; right
    c.  above; left
    d.  above; right

22. According to the misperceptions theory, after an unanticipated increase in the money supply has occurred,
    the $SRAS$ must shift to the _____ to restore general equilibrium; as it does so, the price level _____.
    a.  right; rises
    b.  right; falls
    c.  left; rises
    d.  left; falls

23. The Bank of Canada had announced to Parliament that it would allow M2 to grow by 8% this year, and M2 did grow by 8% this year. You would *not* expect
    a.  money to be neutral in the short run.
    b.  money to be neutral in the long run.
    c.  output to remain unchanged.
    d.  a movement along the short-run aggregate supply curve.

## REVIEW QUESTIONS

1.  According to the real business cycle theory, what is the principal cause of business cycle fluctuations?

2.  Define real shocks, define nominal shocks, and give an example of each.

3.  How do *RBC* theorists answer the objection that there have been few examples of large and easily measurable real shocks to the Canadian economy in recent decades?

4.  During a recession, would classical economists propose that changes in government spending or taxes be used to improve economic conditions? Briefly explain.

5.  How do *RBC* theorists answer the objection that the money supply is a leading, procyclical variable?

6.  During a recession, would classical economists propose that changes in the money supply be used to improve economic conditions? Briefly explain.

7.  In the misperceptions model, is money neutral? Can nominal shocks create business cycle fluctuations? Briefly explain.

8.  Briefly state the rational expectations hypothesis.

9.  Does the extended classical model explain the persistence of business cycle contractions and expansions? Briefly explain.

## ANALYTICAL QUESTIONS

1.  Use the classical (*RBC*) IS-LM-FE model to show the effects on the economy of a temporary *decrease* in government spending. You should show the impact on the real wage, employment, output, the real interest rate, consumption, investment, and the price level.

2.  What are the effects of an unanticipated decline in the money supply in the short run and long run in the misperceptions model?

3.  What are the effects of an anticipated decline in the money supply in the short run and long run in the misperceptions model?

## ANSWERS TO MULTIPLE-CHOICE QUESTIONS

| Number | Answer | Number | Answer | Number | Answer |
|--------|--------|--------|--------|--------|--------|
| 1 | a | 11 | c | 21 | b |
| 2 | c | 12 | c | 22 | c |
| 3 | b | 13 | d | 23 | d |
| 4 | c | 14 | c | | |
| 5 | c | 15 | c | | |
| 6 | a | 16 | a | | |
| 7 | b | 17 | a | | |
| 8 | c | 18 | a | | |
| 9 | a | 19 | b | | |
| 10 | d | 20 | a | | |

## ANSWERS TO REVIEW QUESTIONS

1.  According to the real business cycle theory, real shocks, especially productivity shocks, are the principal cause of business cycle fluctuations in aggregate economic activity.

2.  Real shocks are changes that disturb labour market equilibrium or goods market equilibrium. Nominal shocks are changes that disturb the asset market. A change in aggregate saving is an example of a real shock. A change in the money supply is an example of a nominal shock.

3.  Computer simulations of RBC statistical models have shown that frequent, small, randomly generated productivity shocks can produce large business cycle fluctuations. Therefore large business cycle fluctuations occur even in the absence of large productivity shocks.

4.  No. Classical economists do not endorse changes in government spending or taxes designed to offset business cycle fluctuations; the classical model shows that such policy attempts are not likely to improve macroeconomic conditions. From a classical viewpoint, government spending and tax decisions should be long-run decisions based on cost-benefit analysis.

5.  The money supply is a leading, procyclical variable, but correlation does not prove causation. One plausible explanation is that the Bank of Canada anticipates changes in the business cycle, then reduces the money supply prior to a recession, and increases it prior to an expansion to achieve its policy goal of maintaining price level stability.

6.  No. In the classical model, an increase in the money supply cannot improve economic conditions, because it has no real economic effects. Money is neutral in the classical model.

7. In the misperceptions model, money is neutral in the long run. In the short run, anticipated changes in the money supply are neutral, but unanticipated changes in the money supply are nonneutral.

8. The rational expectations hypothesis states that market actors will use all available information in predicting the values of important economic variables, and they will learn to improve the accuracy of their predictions over time.

9. No. Although the model shows that a monetary surprise can create short-run business cycle fluctuations in aggregate economic activity, the frequent publication of money supply data and price level data suggests that these errors will not persist. The persistence of a business cycle contraction requires some additional propagation mechanism to explain it. One such propagation mechanism is the process of adjusting inventories to their desired level once misperceptions have been corrected.

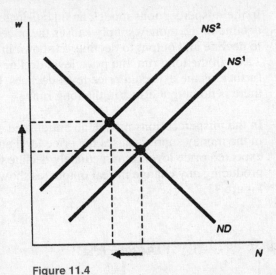

Figure 11.4

## ANSWERS TO ANALYTICAL QUESTIONS

1. The decrease in government spending reduces current or future taxes, so there's a positive wealth effect that increases people's desire for leisure and reduces their labour supply, as shown in Figure 11.4.

   The decline in labour supply leads to a rise in the real wage and a decline in employment. The fall in employment leads to less output, so the *FE* line shifts left, as shown in Figure 11.5. However, the decline in government spending increases national saving, so the *IS* curve shifts down, most likely by more than the *FE* line does. As a result, the price level must decline to restore equilibrium by shifting the *LM* curve down. This results in a decline in the real interest rate, so investment increases. The effect on consumption is ambiguous.

Figure 11.5

2.  In the misperceptions model, an unanticipated decline in the money supply causes the price level to decline and output to decline, as shown in Figure 11.6. In the long run, the price level declines further, as the expected price level declines, but there is no output effect in the long run.

3.  In the misperceptions model, an anticipated decline in the money supply causes the price level and the expected price level to immediately decline without producing any change in real output, as shown in Figure 11.7.

Figure 11.6

Figure 11.7

# CHAPTER 12: KEYNESIANISM:
# THE MACROECONOMICS OF WAGE AND PRICE RIGIDITY

## INTRODUCTION

This chapter presents the central ideas of Keynesian macroeconomics. Basically, the Keynesian model of the economy is one in which wages and prices don't adjust quickly to restore general equilibrium, the economy may be in disequilibrium for long periods of time, and the government should act to stabilize the economy. The chapter also discusses the potential causes of wage and price rigidity that lead to these results.

The chapter begins with a discussion of real-wage rigidity in Section 12.1, developing a theory that firms pay workers what are known as "efficiency wages." Then, Section 12.2 discusses price stickiness—the reasons why firms are slow to change their prices. Section 12.3 discusses policy—both monetary and fiscal. Section 12.4 shows how well the Keynesian model fits the business cycle facts and looks at the possibility of using policy to stabilize the economy.

The classical model in chapter 11 is identical to the Keynesian model in the long run. In the short run, the Keynesian model differs in two major aspects: (1) the labour market is characterized by efficiency wages, which are a bit different than the usual supply and demand model of the labour market; and (2) prices are sticky, so the short-run aggregate supply curve is horizontal. Given these differences, however, the type of analysis that is done is the same as you saw in chapter 11. When there's some shock to the economy, you need to identify which curve or curves are affected and which direction they shift, then see what happens as the economy moves to the new equilibrium.

## CHAPTER OUTLINE

I. Real-Wage Rigidity (Sec. 12.1)
   A. Wage rigidity is important in explaining unemployment
      1. In the classical model, unemployment is due to mismatches between workers and firms
      2. Keynesians are skeptical, believing that recessions lead to substantial cyclical employment
      3. To get a model in which unemployment persists, Keynesian theory posits that the real wage is slow to adjust to equilibrate the labour market
   B. Some reasons for real-wage rigidity
      1. For unemployment to exist, the real wage must exceed the market-clearing wage
      2. If the real wage is too high, why don't firms reduce the wage?
         a. One possibility is that the minimum wage and labour unions prevent wages from being reduced
            (1) But most Canadian workers aren't minimum wage workers, nor are they in unions
            (2) The minimum wage would explain why the nominal wage is rigid, but not why the real wage is rigid
            (3) This might be a better explanation in Europe, where unions are far more powerful
         b. Another possibility is that a firm may want to pay high wages to get a stable labour force and avoid turnover costs—costs of hiring and training new workers
         c. A third reason is that workers' productivity may depend on the wages they're paid—the efficiency wage model

C. The Efficiency Wage Model
   1. Workers who feel well treated will work harder and more efficiently (the "carrot"); this is Akerlof's *gift exchange motive*
   2. Workers who are well paid won't risk losing their jobs by shirking (the "stick")
   3. Both the gift exchange motive and shirking model imply that a worker's effort depends on the real wage (Fig. 12.1)
   4. The effort curve, plotting effort against the real wage, is S-shaped
      a. At low levels of the real wage, workers make hardly any effort
      b. Effort rises as the real wage increases
      c. As the real wage becomes very high, effort flattens out as it reaches the maximum possible level

Figure 12.1

D. Wage determination in the efficiency wage model
   1. Given the effort curve, what determines the real wage firms will pay?
   2. To maximize profit, firms choose the real wage that gets the most effort from workers for each dollar of real wages paid
   3. This occurs at point *B* in Fig. 12.1, where a line from the origin is just tangent to the effort curve
   4. The wage rate at point *B* is called the efficiency wage
   5. The real wage is rigid, as long as the effort curve doesn't change

E. Employment and Unemployment in the Efficiency Wage Model
   1. The labour market now determines employment and unemployment, depending on how far above the market-clearing wage is the efficiency wage (Fig. 12.2)
   2. The labour supply curve is upward sloping, while the labour demand curve is the marginal product of labour when the effort level is determined by the efficiency wage
   3. The difference between labour supply and labour demand is the amount of unemployment

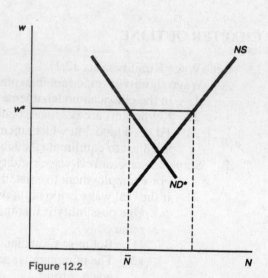

Figure 12.2

4. The fact that there's unemployment puts no downward pressure on the real wage, since firms know that if they reduce the real wage, effort will decline

5. Does the efficiency wage theory match up with the data?
   a. It seems to have worked for Henry Ford in 1914
   b. Plants that pay higher wages appear to experience less shirking
   c. But the theory implies that the real wage is completely rigid, whereas the data suggests that the real wage moves over time and over the business cycle
   d. It is possible to jazz up the model to allow for the efficiency wage to change over time
      (1) Workers would be less likely to shirk and would work harder during a recession if the probability of losing their jobs increased
      (2) This would cause the effort curve to rise and may cause the efficiency wage to decline somewhat
      (3) This would lead to a lower real wage rate in recessions, which is consistent with the data

F. Efficiency wages and the *FE* line
   1. The *FE* line is vertical, as in the classical model, since full-employment output is determined in the labour market and doesn't depend on the real interest rate
   2. But in the Keynesian model, changes in labour supply don't affect the *FE* line, since they don't affect equilibrium employment
   3. A change in productivity does affect the *FE* line, since it affects labour demand

II. Price Stickiness (Sec. 12.2)
A. Price stickiness is the tendency of prices to adjust slowly to changes in the economy
   1. The data suggests that money is not neutral, so Keynesians reject the classical model (without misperceptions)
   2. Keynesians developed the idea of price stickiness to explain why money isn't neutral
   3. An alternative version of the Keynesian model (discussed in Appendix 12.A) assumes that nominal wages are sticky, rather than prices; that model also suggests that money isn't neutral

B. Sources of price stickiness: Monopolistic competition and menu costs
   1. Monopolistic competition
      a. If markets had perfect competition, the market would force prices to adjust rapidly; sellers are price takers, because they must accept the market price
      b. In many markets, sellers have some degree of monopoly; they are price setters under monopolistic competition
      c. Keynesians suggest that many markets are characterized by monopolistic competition
      d. In monopolistically competitive markets, sellers do three things
         (1) They set prices in nominal terms and maintain those prices for some period
         (2) They adjust output to meet the demand at their fixed nominal price
         (3) They readjust prices from time to time when costs or demand change significantly
      e. Menu costs and price stickiness
         (1) The term menu costs comes from the costs faced by a restaurant when it changes prices—it must print new menus
         (2) Even small costs like these may prevent sellers from changing prices often
         (3) Since competition isn't perfect, having the wrong price temporarily won't affect the seller's profits much
         (4) The firm will change prices when demand or costs of production change enough to warrant the price change

    f.   Empirical evidence on price stickiness

        (1)  Industrial prices seem to be changed more often in competitive industries, less often in more monopolistic industries (Carlton study)

        (2)  Blinder and his students found a high degree of price stickiness in their survey of firms

          (a)  The main reason for price stickiness was managers' fear that if they raised their prices, they'd lose customers to rivals

        (3)  But catalogue prices also don't seem to change much from one issue to the next and often change by only small amounts, suggesting that while prices are sticky, menu costs may not be the reason (Kashyap)

    g.   Meeting the demand at the fixed nominal price

        (1)  Since firms have some monopoly power, they price goods at a markup over their marginal cost of production: $P = (1 + \eta)MC$   (12.1)

        (2)  If demand turns out to be larger at that price than the firm planned, the firm will still meet the demand at that price, since it earns additional profits due to the markup

        (3)  Since the firm is paying an efficiency wage, it can hire more workers at that wage to produce more goods when necessary

        (4)  This means that the economy can produce an amount of output that is not on the *FE* line during the period in which prices haven't adjusted

    h.   Effective labour demand

        (1)  The firm's labour demand is thus determined by the demand for its output

        (2)  The effective labour demand curve, $ND^{e}(Y)$, shows how much labour is needed to produce the output demanded in the economy (Fig. 12.3)

        (3)  It slopes upward from left to right because a firm needs more labour to produce additional output

Figure 12.3

III.  Monetary and Fiscal Policy in the Keynesian Model (Sec. 12.3)

    A.   Monetary policy

        1.  Monetary policy in the Keynesian *IS-LM* model

          a.  The Keynesian *FE* line differs from the classical model in two respects

            (1)  The Keynesian level of full employment occurs where the efficiency wage line intersects the labour demand curve, not where labour supply equals labour demand, as in the classical model

            (2)  Changes in labour supply don't affect the *FE* line in the Keynesian model; they do in the classical model

          b.  Since prices are sticky in the short run in the Keynesian model, the price level doesn't adjust to restore general equilibrium

            (1)  Keynesians assume that when not in general equilibrium, the economy lies at the intersection of the *IS* and *LM* curves, and may be off the *FE* line

       (2)  This represents the assumption that firms meet the demand for their products by adjusting employment

  c.  Analysis of an increase in the nominal money supply (Fig. 12.4)

       (2)  *LM* curve shifts down from $LM^1$ to $LM^2$

       (2)  Output rises and the real interest rate falls

       (3)  Firms raise employment and production due to increased demand

       (4)  The increase in money supply is an expansionary monetary policy (easy money); a decrease in the money supply is contractionary monetary policy (tight money)

       (5)  Easy money increases real money supply, causing the real interest rate to fall to clear the money market

          (a)  The lower real interest rate increases consumption and investment

          (b)  With higher demand for output, firms increase production and employment

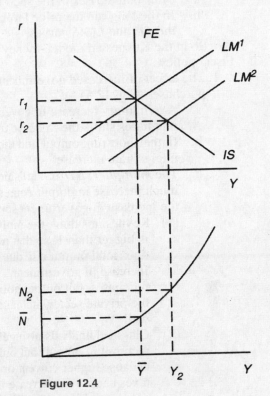

Figure 12.4

       (6)  Eventually firms raise prices, the *LM* curve shifts back to its original level, and general equilibrium is restored

       (7)  Thus money is neutral in the long run, but not in the short run

B.  Monetary Policy in the Keynesian *AD-AS* framework

  1.  We can do the same analysis in the *AD-AS* framework, as was done in text Fig. 9.14

  2.  The main difference between the Keynesian and classical approaches is the speed of price adjustment

    a.  The classical model has fast price adjustment, so the *SRAS* curve is irrelevant

    b.  In the Keynesian model, the short-run aggregate supply (*SRAS*) curve is horizontal, because monopolistically competitive firms face menu costs

3.  The effect of a 10% increase in money supply is to shift the *AD* curve up by 10%
    a.  Thus output rises in the short run to where the *SRAS* curve intersects the *AD* curve
    b.  In the long run the price level rises, causing the *SRAS* curve to shift up such that it intersects the *AD* and *LRAS* curves
4.  So in the Keynesian model, money is not neutral in the short run, but it is neutral in the long run

C.  Fiscal policy
1.  The effect of increased government purchases (Fig. 12.5)

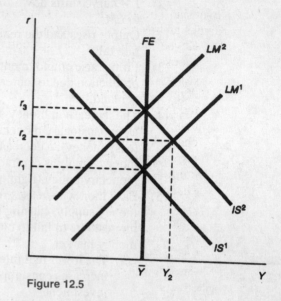

**Figure 12.5**

    a.  A temporary increase in government purchases shifts the *IS* curve up
    b.  In the short run, output and the real interest rate increase
    c.  The *multiplier*, $\Delta Y/\Delta G$, tells how much increase in output comes from the increase in government spending
        (1)  Keynesians think the multiplier is bigger than 1, so that not only does total output rise due to the increase in government purchases, but output going to the private sector increases as well
        (2)  Classical analysis also gets an increase in output, but only because higher current or future taxes caused an increase in labour supply, a shift of the *FE* line
        (3)  In the Keynesian model, the *FE* line doesn't shift, only the *IS* curve does
    d.  When prices adjust, the *LM* curve shifts up and equilibrium is restored at the full-employment level of output with a higher real interest rate than before
    e.  Similar analysis comes from looking at the *AD-AS* framework (Fig. 12.6)
2.  The effect of lower taxes
    a.  Keynesians believe that a reduction of (lump-sum) taxes is expansionary, just like an increase in government purchases

**Figure 12.6**

b.  Keynesians reject Ricardian equivalence, believing that the reduction in taxes increases consumption spending, reducing desired national saving and shifting the *IS* curve up

c.  The only difference between lower taxes and increased government purchases is that when taxes are lower, consumption increases as a percentage of full-employment output, whereas when government purchases increase, government purchases become a larger percentage of full-employment output

IV.  The Keynesian Theory of Business Cycles and Macroeconomic Stabilization (Sec. 12.4)

  A.  Keynesian business cycle theory

  1.  Keynesians think aggregate demand shocks are the primary source of business cycle fluctuations

  2.  Aggregate demand shocks are shocks to the *IS* or *LM* curves, such as fiscal policy, changes in desired investment arising from changes in the expected future marginal product of capital, changes in consumer confidence that affect desired saving, and changes in money demand or supply

  3.  A recession is caused by a shift of the aggregate demand curve to the left, either from the *IS* curve shifting down, or the *LM* curve shifting up

  4.  The Keynesian theory fits certain business cycle facts

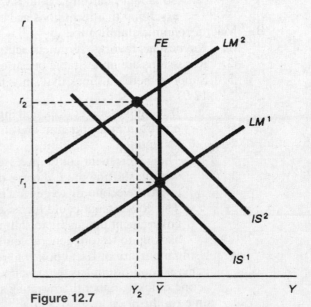

  a.  There are recurrent fluctuations in output

  b.  Employment fluctuates in the same direction as output

  c.  Money is procyclical and leading

Figure 12.7

  d.  Investment and durable goods spending is procyclical and volatile

  (1)  This is explained by the Keynesian model if shocks to investment and durable goods spending are a main source of business cycles

  (2)  Keynes believed in "animal spirits," waves of pessimism and optimism, as a key source of business cycles

e.   Inflation is procyclical and lagging

(1)  The Keynesian model fits the data on inflation, because the price level declines after a recession has begun, as the economy moves toward general equilibrium

5.   Procyclical labour productivity and labour hoarding

a.   As discussed in Sec. 12.1, firms may hoard labour in a recession rather than fire workers, because of the costs of hiring and training new workers

b.   Such hoarded labour is used less intensively, being used on make-work or maintenance tasks that don't contribute to measured output

c.   Thus in a recession, measured productivity is low, even though the production function is stable

d.   So labour hoarding explains why labour productivity is procyclical in the data without assuming that recessions and expansions are caused by productivity shocks

B.   Macroeconomic stabilization

1.   Keynesians favor government actions to stabilize the economy

2.   Recessions are undesirable because the unemployed are hurt

3.   Suppose there's a shock that shifts the *IS* curve down, causing a recession (Fig. 12.8; like text Fig. 12.9)

a.   If the government does nothing, eventually the price level will decline, restoring general equilibrium. But output and employment may remain below their full-employment levels for some time

b.   The government could increase the money supply, shifting the *LM* curve down to move the economy to general equilibrium

c.   The government could increase government purchases to shift the *IS* curve back up to restore general equilibrium

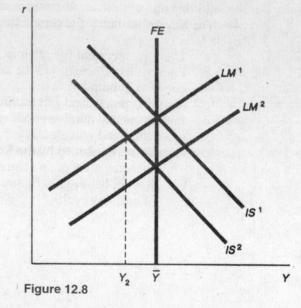

4.   Using monetary or fiscal policy to restore general equilibrium has the advantage of acting quickly, rather than waiting some time for the price level to decline

5.   But the price level is higher in the long run when using policy than it would be if the government took no action

6.   The choice of monetary or fiscal policy affects the composition of spending

a.   An increase in government purchases crowds out consumption and investment spending, because of a higher real interest rate

b.   Tax burdens are also higher when government purchases increase, further reducing consumption

**Figure 12.8**

7.   Difficulties of macroeconomic stabilization

a.   *Macroeconomic stabilization* is the use of monetary and fiscal policies to moderate the business cycle; also called *aggregate demand management*

b.   In practice, macroeconomic stabilization hasn't been terribly successful

c.   One problem is in gauging how far the economy is from full employment, since we can't measure or analyze the state of the economy perfectly

      d.   Another problem is that we don't know the quantitative impact on output of a change in policy

      e.   Also, because policies take time to implement and take effect, using them requires good forecasts of where the economy will be six months or a year in the future; but our forecasting ability is quite imprecise

      f.   These problems suggest that policy shouldn't be used to "fine tune" the economy, but should be used to combat major recessions

   8.  Application: fiscal and monetary policy in the great Japanese slump

      a.   From 1960 to 1990, Japan's economy grew over 6% per year and became the envy of the world

      b.   But the Japanese economy slumped in the 1990s, with growth near zero

         (1)   Stock and land prices fell from excessive levels, hurting banks

         (2)   Bank's financial distress caused lending to fall, reducing investment

      c.   The Keynesian solution was to use expansionary monetary and fiscal policies, which Japan tried

      d.   But the economy didn't respond because of a liquidity trap

         (1)   Nominal interest rates became zero

         (2)   Since nominal interest rates can't go below zero, monetary policy was ineffective

      e.   Critics argue that the Japanese government didn't do enough to stimulate the economy

         (1)   Fiscal stimulus could have been greater, combined with more expansionary monetary policy

         (2)   Even with a flat *LM* curve, shifting the *IS* curve up enough will get the economy back to full employment

C.  Supply shocks in the Keynesian model

   1.  Until the mid-1970s, Keynesians focused on demand shocks as the main source of business cycles

   2.  But the oil price shock that hit the economy beginning in 1973 forced Keynesians to reformulate their theory

   3.  Now Keynesians concede that supply shocks can cause recessions, but they don't think supply shocks are the main source of recessions

4.  An adverse oil price shock shifts the
    *FE* line left (Fig. 12.9; like text Fig.
    12.11)
    a.  The average price level rises,
        shifting the *LM* curve up (from
        *LM*¹ to *LM*²), because the large
        increase in the price of oil
        outweighs the menu costs that
        would otherwise hold prices fixed
    b.  The *LM* curve could shift farther
        than the *FE* line, as in the figure,
        though that isn't necessary
    c.  So in the short run, inflation rises
        and output falls
    d.  There's not much that
        stabilization policy can do about
        the decline in output that occurs,
        because of the lower level of full-
        employment output
    d.  Inflation is already increased due
        to the shock; expansionary policy to
        increase output would increase
        inflation further

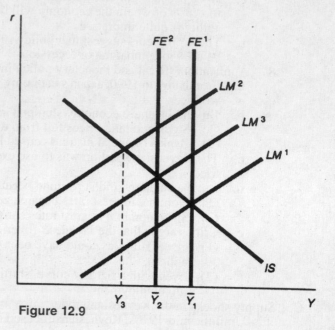

Figure 12.9

V.  Appendix 12.A: Labour Contracts and Nominal-
    Wage Rigidity
    A.  Some Keynesians think the nonneutrality of money is because of nominal-wage rigidity, not nominal-
        price rigidity
        1.  Nominal wages could be rigid because of long-term contracts between firms and unions
        2.  With nominal-wage rigidity, the short-run aggregate supply curve slopes upward instead of being
            horizontal
        3.  Even so, the main results of the Keynesian model still hold
    B.  The short-run aggregate supply curve with labour contracts
        1.  Canadian labour contracts usually specify employment conditions and the nominal wage rate for
            three years
        2.  Employers decide on workers' hours and must pay them the contracted nominal wage
        3.  The result is an upward-sloping short-run aggregate supply curve
            a.  As the price level rises, the real wage declines, since the nominal wage is fixed
            b.  As the real wage declines, firms hire more workers and thus increase output
    C.  Nonneutrality of money
        1.  Money isn't neutral in this model, because as the money supply increases, the *AD* curve shifts
            along the fixed (upward-sloping) *SRAS* curve (text Fig. 12.A.1)
        2.  As a result, output and the price level increase
        3.  Over time, workers will negotiate higher nominal wages and the *SRAS* curve will shift left to
            restore general equilibrium
        4.  Thus money is nonneutral in the short run but neutral in the long run

5.  There are several objections to this theory
    a.  Less than one-third of the Canadian labour force is unionized and covered by long-term wage contracts; however, some nonunion workers get wages similar to those in union contracts, and other workers may have implicit contracts that act like long-term contracts
    b.  Some labour contracts are indexed to inflation, so the real wage is fixed, not the nominal wage; however, most contracts aren't completely indexed
    c.  The theory predicts that real wages will be countercyclical, but in fact they are procyclical; however, if there are both aggregate supply shocks and aggregate demand shocks, real wages may turn out on average to be procyclical, but could still be countercyclical for demand shocks

## MULTIPLE-CHOICE QUESTIONS

1. The existence of labour unions could contribute to real-wage rigidity, except that in Canada
   a. labour unions are outlawed.
   b. most workers aren't in unions.
   c. unions are interested in benefits, not wages.
   d. unions try to increase employment rather than negotiating over wages.

2. In the efficiency wage model, an increase in productivity will cause
   a. no change in the real wage.
   b. an increase in the real wage.
   c. a decrease in the real wage.
   d. an increase in both the real wage and the level of employment.

3. The effort curve is
   a. horizontal, because work effort is independent of the real wage.
   b. negatively sloped, because of diminishing marginal returns to labour.
   c. positively sloped, because of the law of increasing cost.
   d. s-shaped, because a small increase in the real wage will increase work effort more at an intermediate wage than at a low wage or at a high wage.

4. Real-wage rigidity in the Keynesian efficiency wage diagram of the labour market is depicted by
   a. a vertical labour supply curve at the efficient level of employment.
   b. a vertical labour demand curve at the efficient level of employment.
   c. a horizontal line at the efficiency wage.
   d. a steep, positively sloped labour supply curve depicting various efficiency wages at various employment levels.

5. A firm faces the following relationship between the real wage it pays and the effort exerted by its workers:

   | Real wage | Effort ($E$) |
   |-----------|--------------|
   | 10        | 14           |
   | 14        | 20           |
   | 18        | 27           |
   | 22        | 32           |
   | 26        | 36           |

   The marginal product of labour for this firm is given by $MPN = E (50 - N)/3$. The firm will choose to pay a wage equal to
   a. 10.
   b. 14.
   c. 18.
   d. 22.

6. According to the efficiency wage model, during a recession firms
   a. will not reduce real wages, because unions would go on strike, reducing profitability.
   b. will not reduce real wages, because this would reduce worker effort and productivity.
   c. will reduce real wages to restore profitability to the firm.
   d. will reduce both real wages and the level of employment to restore profitability to the firm.

7.  In the Keynesian model, the full-employment level of output is the amount of output produced when
    a.  the quantity of labour demanded equals the quantity of labour supplied.
    b.  the market wage exceeds the efficiency wage.
    c.  labour is paid an efficiency wage, and the real wage equals the marginal product of labour.
    d.  the real wage exceeds the nominal wage.

8.  In the efficiency wage model, an increase in productivity would
    a.  increase output but decrease the real wage.
    b.  decrease the real wage but have no effect on output.
    c.  increase output but have no effect on the real wage.
    d.  have no effect on either output or the real wage.

9.  A firm is a price taker if it
    a.  always sells its output at the industry-determined price.
    b.  takes consumer demand into consideration in setting its price.
    c.  takes its production costs into consideration in setting its price.
    d.  uses a pricing strategy to gain market share.

10. In an economy where firms in most industries are purely competitive firms, individual firms in each industry would produce _____ products and have a _____ share of industry output.
    a.  differentiated; large
    b.  differentiated; small
    c.  standardized; large
    d.  standardized; small

11. In the Keynesian model, firms are best characterized as
    a.  perfectly competitive.
    b.  irrational.
    c.  price takers.
    d.  monopolistically competitive.

12. In the Keynesian model, a firm's high menu costs cause
    a.  real-wage rigidity.
    b.  full employment.
    c.  price stickiness.
    d.  efficiency wages.

13. If the menu cost theory is true, then firms that change prices less frequently than other firms are likely to be in
    a.  more competitive industries.
    b.  service, rather than manufacturing, industries.
    c.  growing, rather than declining, industries.
    d.  less competitive industries.

14. If firms are price setters, a small decline in the demand for their outputs will cause them to
    a.  reduce price and reduce the level of output produced.
    b.  reduce output in the short run, but reduce price in the long run.
    c.  reduce price in the short run, but reduce output only in the long run.
    d.  increase price in the short run to offset the effect on profits of a decline in output.

15. The cost to a firm of producing one more unit of output
    a.    usually exceeds the firm's price.
    b.    is significantly less than the firm's price for purely competitive firms operating in long-run equilibrium.
    c.    usually equals the firm's price for monopolistically competitive firms.
    d.    is the firm's marginal cost.

16. Firms that charge a price for their output in excess of marginal cost in the short run
    a.    are not maximizing profits.
    b.    cannot find buyers for their output.
    c.    are charging a markup.
    d.    will suffer huge losses.

17. As the economy moves down an effective labour demand curve,
    a.    output declines and employment declines.
    b.    output declines and employment rises.
    c.    output rises and employment rises.
    d.    output rises and employment declines.

18. In the Keynesian model, if equilibrium output is less than the full-employment level of output in the short run,
    a.    the price level will rise in the long run.
    b.    the price level will decline in the long run.
    c.    the *LM* curve will shift up in the long run.
    d.    the *FE* line will shift to the left in the long run.

19. Because of price stickiness in the Keynesian model, a decline in investment demand will not cause the
    a.    *LM* curve to shift down in the short run.
    b.    *LM* curve to shift in the long run.
    c.    *IS* curve to shift down in the short run.
    d.    *IS* curve to shift in the long run.

20. In the Keynesian model in the short run, an increase in the money supply will cause
    a.    an increase in output and a decrease in the real interest rate.
    b.    a decrease in the real interest rate but no change in output.
    c.    an increase in the real interest rate and an increase in output.
    d.    no change in either the real interest rate or output.

21. In the Keynesian model in the long run, an increase in the money supply will cause
    a.    an increase in output and a decrease in the real interest rate.
    b.    a decrease in the real interest rate but no change in output.
    c.    an increase in the real interest rate and an increase in output.
    d.    no change in either the real interest rate or output.

22. In the Keynesian model, the short run aggregate supply curve is
    a.    perfectly horizontal.
    b.    upward sloping, but relatively flat.
    c.    upward sloping, but relatively steep.
    d.    perfectly vertical.

23. In the Keynesian model in the long run, an increase in the money supply will cause _____ in the real interest rate and _____ in the price level.
    a.   an increase; an increase
    b.   a decrease; an increase
    c.   no change; an increase
    d.   no change; no change

24. Using the Keynesian model, the effect of an increase in corporate taxes would be to cause _____ in the real interest rate and _____ in output in the short run.
    a.   a decrease; a decrease
    b.   a decrease; no change
    c.   a decrease; an increase
    d.   no change; a decrease

25. In the Keynesian model in the long run, a decrease in taxes causes the price level to _____ and the real interest rate to _____.
    a.   fall; rise
    b.   fall; fall
    c.   rise; rise
    d.   rise; fall

26. The early 1990s were characterized by _____ monetary policy and _____ fiscal policy.
    a.   tight; easy
    b.   tight; tight
    c.   easy; easy
    d.   easy; tight

27. During a severe and persistent recession, Keynesians would most likely propose
    a.   tax increases.
    b.   a tight money policy.
    c.   annually balanced federal budgets.
    d.   macroeconomic stabilization.

28. Keynesians explain the procyclical behavior of average labour productivity by introducing the concept of
    a.   menu costs.
    b.   sticky prices.
    c.   sticky wages.
    d.   labour hoarding.

29. In the short run in the Keynesian model, an oil price shock would leave the economy with a _____ level of output and a _____ real interest rate.
    a.   higher; lower
    b.   lower; higher
    c.   lower; lower
    d.   higher; higher

30.  In practice, one of the principal problems with aggregate demand management is that
    a.   changes in aggregate demand do not affect output.
    b.   changes in aggregate demand cannot reduce unemployment.
    c.   changes in aggregate demand are highly inflationary.
    d.   stabilization policies could increase aggregate demand too much and at the wrong times.

## REVIEW QUESTIONS

1.   Why might firms pay an efficiency wage rather than a market-clearing wage?

2.   How do Keynesians explain real-wage rigidity during a recession?

3.   Briefly define price stickiness.

4.   Briefly explain how monopolistic competition and high menu costs can explain price stickiness.

5.   Do the real effects of aggregate demand shocks differ in the short run and long run in the Keynesian sticky-price model from the effects of these shocks in the classical model of perfectly flexible prices? Briefly explain.

6.   Is money neutral in both the classical model and the Keynesian model?  Briefly explain.

7.   Could monetary stabilization policy be used to reduce or offset the negative short-run output effect of a temporary decline in consumption spending?  Briefly explain.

8.   What is the principal goal of macroeconomic stabilization, and how can fiscal policy be used to achieve this goal?

9.   Do  Keynesians and classicals agree on the effectiveness and desirability of macroeconomic stabilization? Briefly explain.

10.  What critique does the real business cycle theory make of the Keynesian belief that most recessions are caused by aggregate demand shocks?

11.  What are the major difficulties the government faces in attempting to stabilize the economy?

12.  Discuss the major problems that arise in practice in attempting to use aggregate demand management to stabilize the economy.

## ANALYTICAL QUESTIONS

1.   In the Keynesian model, what are the short-run effects and long-run effects (on output, employment, the real interest rate, and the price level) of a temporary decline in investment spending?

2.   In the Keynesian model, what are the short-run effects and long-run effects (on output, employment, the real interest rate, and the price level) of a temporary increase in consumption spending?

3.  In the Keynesian model, what are the effects (on output, the real interest rate, and the price level) of an adverse productivity (i.e., aggregate supply) shock?

4.  According to the Keynesian *IS-LM* model, what is the effect of each of the following on output, the real interest rate, employment, and the price level? Distinguish between the short run and the long run.
    a.  Expected inflation declines
    b.  Wealth declines
    c.  Labour supply increases due to a change in demographics
    d.  The future marginal product of capital increases

## ANSWERS TO MULTIPLE-CHOICE QUESTIONS

| Number | Answer | | Number | Answer | | Number | Answer |
|--------|--------|---|--------|--------|---|--------|--------|
| 1 | b | | 11 | d | | 21 | d |
| 2 | a | | 12 | c | | 22 | a |
| 3 | d | | 13 | d | | 23 | c |
| 4 | c | | 14 | b | | 24 | a |
| 5 | c | | 15 | d | | 25 | c |
| 6 | b | | 16 | c | | 26 | d |
| 7 | c | | 17 | a | | 27 | d |
| 8 | c | | 18 | b | | 28 | d |
| 9 | a | | 19 | a | | 29 | b |
| 10 | d | | 20 | a | | 30 | d |

## ANSWERS TO REVIEW QUESTIONS

1. An efficiency wage is better than a market-clearing wage in that it maximizes effort per dollar of wage income paid to labour. This means that labour productivity per dollar spent on labour is maximized, which means that labour cost per unit of output is minimized. The gift-exchange motive and the shirking model provide two explanations for why an efficiency wage that is above the market-clearing wage may increase productivity per wage dollar. The gift-exchange motive suggests that workers who believe their employer is treating them fairly will want to do a good job. The shirking model views the wage as the reward that workers risk losing if they are so unproductive that they get fired; a higher wage increases productivity by increasing the expected cost of shirking (i.e., having low productivity).

2. In the Keynesian efficiency wage model, firms pay each worker the efficiency wage. A recession reduces labour demand, which causes employment to decline, but firms do not lower the wage. Since the efficiency wage is the wage that maximizes effort per dollar of real wage paid to labour, reducing the real wage would reduce the productivity of labour, which would increase production cost. Another problem with lowering the wage enough to induce the desired number of workers to quit during a recession is that the most productive workers are the most likely workers to quit.

3. Price stickiness means that prices are not perfectly flexible; they do not quickly adjust to long-run market-clearing levels. If prices are slow to adjust to changes in market conditions, they may be viewed, for analytic purposes, as fixed or rigid for some short-run time period.

4. Unlike perfectly competitive firms, monopolistically competitive firms set their prices in nominal terms and leave them set for some time; they meet the demand at their fixed price; and they readjust price from time to time. Since monopolistically competitive firms incur menu costs when they change their prices, they don't change them often. Thus prices are sticky.

5. In the Keynesian model, aggregate demand shocks affect real output, employment, and unemployment in the short run. There is no short-run adjustment period in the classical model, since economic shocks cause prices to adjust immediately to their long-run, general equilibrium values. Keynesian and classical economists agree that aggregate demand shocks have no real output or employment effects in the long run.

6.   Money is neutral in the classical model, which is a long-run model with perfectly flexible wages and prices. In the Keynesian model of imperfectly flexible wages and prices, money is nonneutral in the short run, but it is still neutral in the long run. In the Keynesian model, quantities adjust in the short run (e.g., employment and output), rather than wages and prices.

7.   Yes, an increase in the money supply would shift the $LM$ curve down to the right and shift $AD$ up to the right to offset the output effect of a decline in consumer spending. The increase in the money supply returns the $AD$ curve to its original position, at the full-employment level of output.

8.   The principal goal of macroeconomic stabilization is to maintain aggregate demand ($AD$) at the full- employment level of output. Countercyclical changes in government purchases, and possibly taxes, can be used to offset the output effects of private sector $AD$ shocks, to maintain $AD$ at the full-employment level of output. For example, a downward shift in $IS$ and $AD$, caused by a decline in investment spending, can be offset by a temporary increase in government purchases, causing $IS$ and $AD$ to shift back to their original positions.

9.   No, Keynesians and classical economists disagree on the effectiveness and desirability of macroeconomic stabilization. In the classical model, business cycles fluctuations are the optimal response of the economy to various shocks that hit the economy; thus they should not be offset by macroeconomic policy. In the Keynesian model, large and persistent business cycle fluctuations are usually caused by aggregate demand shocks in the presence of price stickiness. Macroeconomic stabilization policies can effectively reduce business cycle fluctuations, so these policies are desirable in that they can help the economy to maintain output at the full-employment level.

10.   As classical economists, real business cycle theorists believe that aggregate supply shocks cause most business cycle fluctuations. $RBC$ theorists highlight the importance of productivity shocks. $RBC$ theorists believe that Keynesians are wrong in their contention that aggregate demand shocks cause most recessions, because aggregate demand shocks would cause productivity to be countercyclical, when in fact it is procyclical.

11.   It's difficult to tell how far the economy is from full employment, there's uncertainty about how much the economy responds to monetary and fiscal policy, and there's a need to know where the economy will be in six months to a year.

12.   There are problems in gauging how far the economy is from full employment, knowing how much output responds to a change in monetary or fiscal policy, and forecasting the economy reasonably well.

## ANSWERS TO ANALYTICAL QUESTIONS

1.  See Figure 12.10.  Point *A* is the starting point, point *B* shows the short-run equilibrium after the change, and point *C* shows the long-run equilibrium after the change.  When there's a decline in investment spending, in the short run, the aggregate demand curve shifts to the left, while the aggregate supply curve doesn't shift, so output declines and the price level doesn't change.  Since output declines, employment declines.  The decline in investment spending shifts the *IS* curve to the left, so that, in addition to the decline in output, the real interest rate falls.  In the long run, the price level declines to restore general equilibrium.  This shifts the short-run aggregate supply curve down, returning output to its full-employment level.  Since there's no change in output in the long run, there's no change in employment, either. As the price level falls, the *LM* curve shifts to the right, so that it intersects the *IS* curve at the full-employment level of output.  As a result, the real interest rate declines further.

Figure 12.10

2.    See Figure 12.11.  Point *A* is the starting point, point *B* shows the short-run equilibrium after the change, and point *C* shows the long-run equilibrium after the change.  When there's an increase in consumption spending, in the short run, the aggregate demand curve shifts to the right, while the aggregate supply curve doesn't shift, so output increases and the price level doesn't change.  Since output rises, employment increases.  The increase in consumption spending shifts the *IS* curve up, so that, in addition to the rise in output, the real interest rate rises.  In the long run, the price level rises to restore general equilibrium.  This shifts the short-run aggregate supply curve up, returning output to its full-employment level.  Since there's no change in output in the long run, there's no change in employment, either.  As the price level rises, the *LM* curve shifts up, so that it intersects the *IS* curve at the full-employment level of output.  As a result, the real interest rate rises further.

Figure 12.11

3.   See Figure 12.12.  Point $A$ is the starting point, point $B$ shows the short-run equilibrium after the change, and point $C$ shows the long-run equilibrium after the change.  When there's an adverse productivity shock, the long run aggregate supply curve shifts to the left, while the aggregate demand curve doesn't shift, and the short-run aggregate supply curve shifts up as well.  As a result, output decreases and the price level rises (assuming the short run aggregate supply curve shifts sufficiently far up).  The productivity shock shifts the $FE$ line to the left, while the rise in the price level shifts the $LM$ curve up.  At the new intersection of the $IS$ and $LM$ curves, the real interest rate is higher.  Assuming the $LM$ curve shifts sufficiently far, in the long run, the price level must fall to restore general equilibrium.  This reduces the real interest rate somewhat, but it remains higher than it was initially.  The fall in the price level shifts the short run aggregate supply curve down, so output rises somewhat, but remains less than it was initially.  The price level also remains higher than it was initially.

4.   a.   Short run: $Y$ and $N$ decline, $r$ rises, $P$ is unchanged. Long run: $P$ declines; $Y$, $r$, and $N$ are unchanged.

     b.   Short run: $Y$, $r$, and $N$ decline; $P$ is unchanged. Long run: $r$ and $P$ decline; $Y$ and $N$ are unchanged.

     c.   Nothing happens to any of the variables.

     d.   Short run: $Y$, $r$, and $N$ rise; $P$ is unchanged. Long run: $r$ and $P$ rise; $Y$ and $N$ are unchanged.

Figure 12.12

# CHAPTER 13: UNEMPLOYMENT AND INFLATION

## INTRODUCTION

This is the first chapter of Part 4, the section of the textbook that explains how macroeconomic policy works and how it can best be used. This chapter discusses unemployment and inflation, Chapter 10 looks at policy in an open economy—international trade and finance, Chapter 14 covers monetary institutions and policy, and Chapter 15 discusses fiscal institutions and policy.

In this chapter, we study unemployment and inflation together because they are the most important macroeconomic problems and because they are related, according to the Phillips curve relationship. In Section 13.1, we study this relationship between inflation and unemployment, looking at whether it has changed over time and if there really is a trade-off. In the following two sections, we study the costs of unemployment (Section 13.2) and inflation (Section 13.3) and consider the implications for macroeconomic policy making.

The only analytical concept that may prove difficult in this chapter is the expectations-augmented Phillips curve in Section 13.1. You should be sure you understand why the Phillips curve shifts with changes in expected inflation. Note that the unemployment rate equals the natural rate of unemployment at the point at which inflation equals expected inflation.

## CHAPTER OUTLINE

I.  Unemployment and Inflation: Is There a Trade-off? (Sec. 13.1)
    A.  Many people think there is a trade-off between inflation and unemployment
        1.  The idea originated in 1958 when A.W. Phillips showed a negative relationship between unemployment and nominal wage growth in Britain
        2.  Since then economists have looked at the relationship between unemployment and inflation
        3.  In the 1950s and 1960s many nations seemed to have a negative relationship between the two variables
        4.  Canada appears to be on one Phillips curve in the 1960s (text Fig. 13.1)
        5.  This suggested that policymakers could choose the combination of unemployment and inflation they most desired
        6.  But the relationship fell apart in the following three decades (text Fig. 13.2)
        7.  The 1970s were a particularly bad period, with both high inflation and high unemployment, inconsistent with the Phillips curve
    B.  The expectations-augmented Phillips curve
        1.  Friedman and Phelps: The *cyclical* unemployment rate (the difference between actual and natural unemployment rates) depends only on *unanticipated* inflation (the difference between actual and expected inflation)
            a.  This theory was made before the Phillips curve began breaking down in the 1970s
            b.  It suggests that the relationship between inflation and the unemployment rate isn't stable

2.  How does this work in the extended classical model?
    a.  First case: anticipated increase in money supply (Fig. 13.1; like text Fig. 13.3)
        (1)  *AD* shifts up and *SRAS* shifts up, with no misperceptions
        (2)  Result: *P* rises, *Y* unchanged
        (3)  Inflation rises with no change in unemployment
    b.  Second case: unanticipated increase in money supply (Fig. 13.2; like text Fig. 13.4)
        (1)  *AD* expected to shift up to
        (2)  $AD^{2,\ old}$ (money supply expected to rise 10%), but unexpectedly money supply rises 15%, so *AD* shifts further up to $AD^{2,\ new}$
        (3)  SRAS shifts up based on expected 10% rise in money supply
        (4)  Result: *P* rises and *Y* rises as misperceptions occur
        (5)  So higher inflation occurs with lower unemployment
        (6)  Long run: *P* rises further, *Y* declines to full-employment level
    c.  Expectations-augmented Phillips curve:
        $$\pi = \pi^e - h(u - \bar{u}) \qquad (13.1)$$
        (1)  When $\pi = \pi^e$, $u = \bar{u}$
        (2)  When $\pi < \pi^e$, $u > \bar{u}$
        (3)  When $\pi > \pi_e$, $u < \bar{u}$

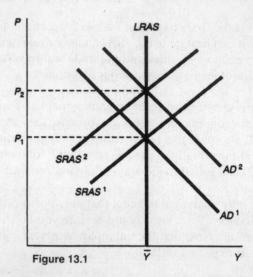

Figure 13.1

C.  The shifting Phillips curve
    1.  The Phillips curve shows the relationship between unemployment and inflation for a given expected rate of inflation and natural rate of unemployment
    2.  Changes in the expected rate of inflation (Fig. 13.3; like text Fig. 13.5)
        a.  For a given expected rate of inflation, the Phillips curve shows the trade-off between cyclical unemployment and actual inflation

Figure 13.2

      b.   The Phillips curve is drawn such that
           $\pi = \pi^e$ when $u = \bar{u}$

      c.   Higher expected inflation implies a
           higher Phillips curve

3.   Changes in the natural rate of unemployment (Fig. 13.4; like text Fig. 13.6)

      d.   For a given natural rate of unemployment, the Phillips curve shows the trade-off between unemployment and unanticipated inflation

      e.   A higher natural rate of unemployment shifts the Phillips curve to the right

**Figure 13.3**

4.   Supply shocks and the Phillips curve

      a.   A supply shock increases both expected inflation and the natural rate of unemployment

          (1)  A supply shock in the classical model increase the natural rate of unemployment, because it increases the mismatch between firms and workers

          (2)  A supply shock in the Keynesian model reduces the marginal product of labour and thus reduces labour demand at the fixed real wage, so the natural unemployment rate rises

      b.   So an adverse supply shock shifts the Phillips curve up and to the right

      c.   The Phillips curve will be unstable in periods with many supply shocks

5.   The shifting Phillips curve in practice

      a.   Why did the original Phillips curve relationship apply to many historical cases?

          (1)  The original relationship between inflation and unemployment holds up as long as expected inflation and the natural rate of unemployment are approximately constant

          (2)  This was true in Canada in the 1960s, so the Phillips curve appeared to be stable

      b.   Why did the Canadian Phillips curve disappear after 1970?

          (1)  Both the expected inflation rate and the natural rate of unemployment varied considerably more in the 1970s than they did in the 1960s

          (2)  Especially important were the oil price shocks of 1973–1974 and 1979–1980

**Figure 13.4**

(3)    Also, the composition of the labour force changed in the 1970s and there were other structural changes in the economy as well, raising the natural rate of unemployment

(4)    Monetary policy was expansionary in the 1970s, leading to high and volatile inflation

(5)    Plotting unanticipated inflation against cyclical unemployment shows a fairly stable relationship since 1970 (text Fig. 13.7)

D.    Macroeconomic policy and the Phillips curve

1.    Can the Phillips curve be exploited by policymakers? Can they choose the optimal combination of unemployment and inflation?

a.    Classical model: NO

(1)    The unemployment rate returns to its natural level quickly, as people's expectations adjust

(2)    So unemployment can change from its natural level only for a very brief time

(3)    Also, people catch on to policy games; they have rational expectations and try to anticipate policy changes, so there is no way to fool people systematically

b.    Keynesian model: YES, temporarily

(1)    The expected rate of inflation in the Phillips curve is the forecast of inflation at the time the oldest sticky prices were set

(2)    It takes time for prices and expected prices to adjust, so unemployment may differ from the natural rate for some time

2.    Box 13.1: The Lucas critique

a.    When the rules of the game change, behavior changes

b.    For example, if batters in baseball were called out after two strikes instead of three, they'd swing more often when they have one strike than they do now

c.    Lucas applied this idea to macroeconomics, arguing that historical relationships between variables won't hold up if there's been a major policy change

d.    The Phillips curve is a good example—it fell apart as soon as policymakers tried to exploit it

e.    Evaluating policy requires an understanding of how behavior will change under the new policy, so both economic theory and empirical analysis are necessary

E.    The long-run Phillips curve

1.    Long run: $u = \bar{u}$ for both Keynesians and classicals

2.    The long-run Phillips curve is vertical, since when $\pi = \pi^e$, $u = \bar{u}$ (Fig. 13.5; like text Fig. 13.8)

3.    Changes in the level of money supply have no long-run real effects; changes in the growth rate of money supply have no long-run real effects, either

4.    Even though expansionary policy may reduce unemployment only temporarily, policymakers may want to do so if, for example, timing economic booms right before elections helps them (or their political allies) get reelected

**Figure 13.5**

F.  The political environment: macroeconomic performance and opinion
    1.  Among the many issues affecting the popularity of successive federal governments, macroeconomic policy and performance are among the most important.  There seems to be little doubt that the 1990-92 recession severely damaged the re-election prospects of the federal Progressive Conservatives.
    2.  Richards tried to measure the effect of macroeconomic performance on the support for the incumbent party from 1957-1990.  Support was measured as the percentage of voters who told Gallup Poll Canada each quarter that they would vote for the party in power if an election were soon held.
    3.  Two macroeconomic variables seemed to have a significant effect on a government's popularity
        a.  Voter support fell when GDP was volatile around its trend level .  One interpretation of this finding is that voters believe there is a role for stabilization policy, as described in Chapter 12
        b.  Voters withdraw their support from the government if the inflation rate is too high or too low.
    4.  The results were apparent during the following time periods:
        a.  In 1963 when a weak economy helped Pearson Liberals defeated the Diefenbaker Conservatives
        b.  In 1984 when the Mulroney Conservatives replaced the Trudeau-Turner Liberals
        c.  In the 1990s, support for the federal Progressive Conservatives was 25 percentage points below the value it would have taken without a recession and disinflation
    5.  If voter support depends on macroeconomic performance, why don't government alter their policies to maximize their support?  According to the theory of "political business cycles" we should see that governments practicing expansionary policies in election years.  However, historical evidence does not provide much support for this type of cycle in macroeconomic policy.
    6.  Problems with "political business cycle theory"
        a.  Assumption that incumbents are motivated only by the prospects of re-election, which ignores the possibility that politicians have other goals, such as promoting policies that they favour.  If different parties have different goals, in addition to re-election then their macroeconomic policies may differ.
        b.  The theory may not allow for rational expectations.  As we have seen in studying the expectations-augmented Phillips curve, it may be only unexpected changes in policy that affect output and unemployment.
II. The Problem of Unemployment (Sec. 13.2)
    A.  The costs of unemployment
        1.  Loss in output from idle resources
            a.  Workers lose income
            b.  Society pays for unemployment benefits and makes up lost tax revenue
            c.  Using Okun's Law (each percentage point of cyclical unemployment is associated with a loss equal to 2.0% of full-employment output), if full-employment output is $1000 billion, each percentage point of unemployment sustained for one year costs $20 billion
        2.  Personal or psychological cost to workers and their families
            a.  Especially important for those with long spells of unemployment
        3.  There are some offsetting factors
            a.  Unemployment leads to increased job search and acquiring new skills, which may lead to increased future output
            b.  Unemployed workers have increased leisure time, though most wouldn't feel that the increased leisure compensated them for being unemployed
    B.  The long-term behavior of the unemployment rate
        1.  The changing natural rate
            a.  How do we calculate the natural rate of unemployment?
            b.  Economic Council of Canada estimates: 7.5% today; 3 percentage points higher than in the 1950s and 1960s; 4% to 5%

        c.   Why did the natural rate rise from the 1950s to the late 1970s?
           (1)   Partly demographics; more teenagers, blacks, and women
               (a)   Their unemployment rates are higher because of discrimination, language problems, lower educational attainment, interruptions of careers to have children
               (b)   Their proportion of the labour force increased from WWII to about 1980
        d.   Since 1980, demographic forces have increased the natural rate of unemployment
           (1)   The proportion of the labour force aged 15-24 years rose

    2.   Hysteresis in unemployment
        a.   Europe's unemployment rates rose dramatically from the 1970s to the 1980s (text Fig. 13.11)
        b.   Hysteresis: The natural rate of unemployment rises as the actual unemployment rate rises
        c.   Caused partly by deteriorating skills of the unemployed, which increases the mismatch problem
        d.   Caused partly by restrictions on firms' ability to fire workers, making them reluctant to hire workers in good times
        e.   Caused partly by union-firm bargaining, as suggested by insider-outsider theory
           (1)   Unions try to maximize wage rates to benefit insiders; outsiders then can't get jobs at wage rates that exceed market-clearing levels
           (2)   Canadian labour markets are much more unionized than U.S. labour markets, so the effect is much stronger there
        f.   Box 13.2: The effect of unemployment insurance on unemployment
           (1)   The rise in the natural rate of unemployment is caused partly by the unemployment insurance (UI) system
           (2)   The longer duration of UI benefits in Canada than in the United States accounts for longer spells of unemployment by individual workers than in Canada
           (3)   But it doesn't look like there's much evidence that higher UI benefits increase the unemployment rate (since UI benefits were more generous in 1971-1972 in Canada, yet the gap didn't appear until the 1980s
                 Moreover, the gap persisted in the 1990s when Canadian UI become less generous
C.   Policies to reduce the natural rate of unemployment
    1.   Government support for job training and worker relocation
        a.   Firms may be reluctant to train workers because they might leave to go to other firms
        b.   Tax breaks or subsidies would encourage training
    2.   Increased labour market flexibility
        a.   Regulations (like minimum wages, working conditions, fringe benefits, etc.) increase the costs of hiring workers
        b.   Reducing regulations whose benefits are less than the costs would help reduce unemployment
    3.   Unemployment insurance reform
        a.   Unemployment insurance increases the time workers spend looking for work and increases the incentives for firms to lay off workers
        b.   Reducing incentives for unemployment would reduce unemployment
    4.   A high-pressure economy?
        a.   Using expansionary monetary and fiscal policies to create a high-pressure economy could reduce the natural rate of unemployment if there is hysteresis
        b.   Critics suggest that there is little evidence of hysteresis in Canada, and that the attempt to use expansionary policy would create a high rate of inflation

III. The Problem of Inflation (Sec. 13.3)
   A. The costs of inflation
      1. Perfectly anticipated inflation
         a. No effects if all prices and wages keep up with inflation
         b. Even returns on assets may rise exactly with inflation
         c. Shoe-leather costs: People spend resources to economize on currency holdings; the estimated cost of 10% inflation is 0.3% of GNP
         d. Menu costs: the costs of changing prices (but technology may mitigate this somewhat)
      2. Unanticipated inflation ($\pi - \pi^e$)
         a. Realized real returns differ from expected real returns
           (1) Expected $r = i - \pi^e$
           (2) Actual $r = i - \pi$
           (3) Actual $r$ differs from expected $r$ by $\pi^e - \pi$
           (4) Numerical example: $i = 6\%$, $\pi^e = 4\%$, so expected $r = 2\%$; if $\pi = 6\%$, actual $r = 0\%$; if $\pi = 2\%$, actual $r = 4\%$
         b. Similar effect on wages and salaries
         c. Result: transfer of wealth
           (1) From lenders to borrowers when $\pi > \pi^e$
           (2) From borrowers to lenders when $\pi < \pi^e$
         d. So people want to avoid risk of unanticipated inflation
           (1) They spend resources to forecast inflation
           (2) Box 13.3: Indexed contracts
              (a) People could use indexed contracts to avoid the risk of transferring wealth because of unanticipated inflation
              (b) Most Canadian financial contracts are not indexed, with the exception of some long-term contracts like adjustable-rate mortgages and inflation-indexed bonds issued by the Canadian Treasury beginning in 1997
              (c) Many Canadian labour contracts are indexed by COLAs (cost-of-living adjustments)
              (d) Indexed contracts are more prevalent in countries with high inflation
         e. Loss of valuable signals provided by prices
           (1) Confusion over changes in aggregate prices vs. changes in relative prices
           (2) People expend resources to extract correct signals from prices
      3. The costs of hyperinflation
         a. Hyperinflation is a very high, sustained inflation (for example, 50% or more per month)
           (1) Hungary in August 1945 had inflation of 19,800% per month
           (3) Bolivia had annual rates of inflation of 1281% in 1984, 11,750% in 1985, 276% in 1986
         b. There are large shoe-leather costs, as people minimize cash balances
         c. People spend many resources getting rid of money as fast as possible
         d. Tax collections fall, as people pay taxes with money whose value has declined sharply
         e. Prices become worthless as signals, so markets become inefficient
   B. Fighting inflation: The role of inflationary expectations
      1. If rapid money growth causes inflation, why do central banks allow the money supply to grow rapidly?
         a. Developing or war-torn countries may not be able to raise taxes or borrow, so they print money to finance spending
         b. Industrialized countries may try to use expansionary monetary policy to fight recessions, then not tighten monetary policy enough later
      2. Disinflation is a reduction in the rate of inflation
         a. But disinflations may lead to recessions

      b.   An unexpected reduction in inflation leads to a rise in unemployment along the Phillips curve

  3.  The costs of disinflation could be reduced if expected inflation fell at the same time actual inflation fell

  4.  Rapid versus gradual disinflation

      a.   The classical prescription for disinflation is cold turkey—a rapid and decisive reduction in money growth

          (1)   Proponents argue that the economy will adjust fairly quickly, with low costs of adjustment, if the policy is announced well in advance

          (2)   Keynesians disagree

               (a)   Price stickiness due to menu costs and wage stickiness due to labour contracts make adjustment slow

               (b)   Cold turkey disinflation would cause a major recession

               (c)   The strategy might fail to alter inflation expectations, because if the costs of the policy are high (because the economy goes into recession), the government will reverse the policy

      b.   The Keynesian prescription for disinflation is gradualism

          (1)   A gradual approach gives prices and wages time to adjust to the disinflation

          (2)   Such a strategy will be politically sustainable because the costs are low

  5.  Box 13.4:  The sacrifice ratio

      a.   When unanticipated tight monetary and fiscal policies are used to reduce inflation, they reduce output and employment for a time, a cost that must be weighed against the benefits of lower inflation

      b.   Economists use the sacrifice ratio as a measure of the costs

          (1)   The sacrifice ratio is the number of percentage points of output lost in reducing inflation by one percentage point

          (2)   For example, a study of past disinflations by Laurence Ball found that U.S. inflation fell by 8.83 percentage points in the early 1980s, with a loss in output of 16.18 percent of the nation's potential output

               (a)   The sacrifice ratio was 16.18 divided by 8.83, which equals 1.832

      c.   Ball studied the sacrifice ratios for many different disinflations around the world in the 1960s, 1970s, and 1980s

          (1)   The sacrifice ratios varied substantially across countries, from less than 1 to almost 3

          (2)   One factor affecting the sacrifice ratio is the flexibility of the labour market

          (3)   Countries with slow wage adjustment (for example, because of heavy government regulation of the labour market) have higher sacrifice ratios

          (4)   Ball also found a lower sacrifice ratio from cold turkey disinflation than from gradualism

      d.   Ball's results should be interpreted with caution, since it isn't easy to calculate the loss of output and because supply shocks can distort the calculation of the sacrifice ratio

  6.  Wage and price controls

      a.   Pro: Controls would hold down inflation, thus lowering expected inflation and reducing the costs of disinflation

      b.   Con: Controls lead to shortages and inefficiency; once controls are lifted, prices will rise again

      c.   The outcome of wage and price controls may depend on what happens with fiscal and monetary policy

          (1)   If policies remain expansionary, people will expect renewed inflation when the controls are lifted

        (2)   If tight policies are pursued, expected inflation may decline

    d.   Application: The Nixon and Trudeau wage-price controls

        (1)   Price controls from August 1971 to April 1974

        (2)   Shortages developed in many products

        (3)   Gordon's study suggested that the controls reduced inflation when they were in effect, but prices returned to where they would have been soon after the controls were lifted

        (4)   Macro policies remained expansionary, so inflation didn't decline

7.   Credibility and reputation

    a.   Key determinant of the costs of disinflation: how quickly expected inflation adjusts

    b.   This depends on credibility of disinflation policy; if people believe the government and if the government carries through with its policy, expected inflation should drop rapidly

    c.   Credibility can be enhanced if the government gets a reputation for carrying out its promises

    d.   Also, having a strong and independent central bank that is committed to low inflation provides credibility

## MULTIPLE-CHOICE QUESTIONS

1. The Phillips curve suggests that monetary policymakers could use monetary policy to
   a. reduce the unemployment rate at the expense of higher inflation.
   b. reduce the unemployment rate while reducing inflation.
   c. reduce the unemployment rate without affecting the inflation rate.
   d. reduce inflation without affecting the unemployment rate.

2. Cyclical unemployment is caused by
   a. people entering the labour force to search for jobs.
   b. technological progress, which causes some industries to expand employment and others to reduce employment.
   c. reducing international trade barriers, which causes some industries to expand employment and others to reduce employment.
   d. recessions.

3. If the expected inflation rate is 15%, the expectations-augmented Phillips curve will
   a. be the same as the Phillips curve.
   b. be the same as the long-run Phillips curve.
   c. intersect the long-run Phillips curve at the natural unemployment rate, when the inflation rate is 15%.
   d. be horizontal at an expected inflation rate of 15%.

4. In the extended classical model, an anticipated increase in the money supply would cause output to _____ and the price level to _____ in the short run.
   a. increase; increase
   b. increase; not change
   c. not change; increase
   d. decrease; increase

5. In the extended classical model, an unanticipated increase in the money supply would cause output to _____ and the price level to _____ in the short run.
   a. increase; increase
   b. increase; not change
   c. not change; increase
   d. decrease; increase

6. In the expectations-augmented Phillips curve $\pi = \pi^e - 3(u - .06)$, when $\pi = .06$ and $\pi^e = .03$, the unemployment rate is
   a. .03.
   b. .05.
   c. .07.
   d. .09.

7. Suppose most people had anticipated that inflation would increase by 10% in the coming year because the Bank of Canada would increase the money supply by 10%. Instead, the Bank of Canada increases the money supply by only 5%. In the short run, this would cause actual output to be _____ full-employment output and prices to increase by _____ 5%.
   a. above; more than
   b. above; less than
   c. below; more than
   d. below; less than

8. If the expected inflation rate is unchanged, a rise in the natural rate of unemployment would
   a. shift the Phillips curve to the right.
   b. not shift the Phillips curve.
   c. shift the Phillips curve to the left.
   d. shift the Phillips curve to the left and shift the long-run Phillips curve to the right.

9. An adverse supply shock would cause
   a. a movement up the short-run Phillips curve.
   b. a movement down the short-run Phillips curve.
   c. the short-run Phillips curve to shift upward and to the right.
   d. the short-run Phillips curve to shift downward and to the left.

10. Classicals argue that an adverse supply shock would
   a. raise neither the natural rate of unemployment nor the actual rate of unemployment.
   b. raise the actual rate of unemployment, but not the natural rate of unemployment.
   c. raise the natural rate of unemployment, but not the actual rate of unemployment.
   d. raise both the natural rate of unemployment and the actual rate of unemployment.

11. Which of the following forms of unemployment probably imposes the greatest personal costs?
   a. Frictional unemployment
   b. Structural unemployment
   c. Cyclical unemployment
   d. Voluntary unemployment

12. One reason for the rise in the natural rate of unemployment is
   a. changes in the demographic composition of the work force.
   b. the rise in inflation.
   c. increased competition from foreign workers.
   d. the depreciation of the dollar relative to foreign currencies.

13. The costs of quickly trading money for nonmonetary assets to reduce one's holdings of money are the
   a. menu costs of anticipated inflation.
   b. menu costs of unanticipated inflation.
   c. shoe-leather costs of anticipated inflation.
   d. relative price distortion costs of unanticipated inflation.

14. One cost of a perfectly anticipated inflation is that it
   a. transfers wealth from lenders to borrowers.
   b. transfers wealth from borrowers to lenders.
   c. erodes the value of currency.
   d. damages the role of prices as signals in the economy.

15. When actual inflation is greater than expected inflation
    a. unemployment rises, according to Phillips-curve analysis.
    b. cyclical unemployment rises, according to Phillips-curve analysis.
    c. there are transfers from borrowers to lenders.
    d. there are transfers from lenders to borrowers.

16. When there is a hyperinflation, all of the following occur *except*
    a. people spend a lot of time and energy getting rid of currency as fast as possible.
    b. the government finds it difficult to collect taxes.
    c. markets become inefficient because prices are no longer reliable signals.
    d. people make fixed-rate loans to protect themselves against inflation.

17. Most economists would agree that the best way to reduce hyperinflation is to
    a. reduce the nominal money supply growth rate.
    b. increase transfer payments.
    c. institute wage-price controls.
    d. reduce taxes.

18. In analyzing the disinflationary period of the early 1980s in Canada, Keynesians concluded that
    a. political business cycle theory best explains this monetary policy attempt to reduce unemployment just prior to the 1980 prime ministerial election.
    b. the rational expectations hypothesis correctly predicts that systematic monetary policies are anticipated and are neutral.
    c. the basic classical model is correct in showing that changes in the money supply have only price effects.
    d. the cold turkey approach to reducing inflation can create a costly recession with a sharp increase in cyclical unemployment.

19. Which of the following disinflationary monetary policies would classical economists prefer?
    a. A cold turkey approach that is announced and credible.
    b. A cold turkey approach that is announced, but not credible.
    c. A gradual approach that is announced and credible.
    d. A gradual approach that is unannounced.

20. The most important factor determining how quickly expected inflation adjusts when the government attempts to reduce inflation is
    a. the slope of the Phillips curve.
    b. the credibility of the government's disinflationary policy.
    c. the degree of gradualism in the government's disinflationary policy.
    d. the slope of the *IS* curve.

**REVIEW QUESTIONS**

1.  What trade-off is demonstrated by the simple Phillips curve?

2.  State and briefly explain whether or not the empirical evidence generally supports the belief that there is a fixed trade-off between unemployment and inflation, such that monetary policymakers can achieve the combination they prefer.

3.  Briefly explain why the expectations-augmented Phillips curve is superior to the Phillips curve.

4.  State and briefly explain whether or not the empirical evidence generally supports the belief that a change in expected inflation or the natural unemployment rate will shift the expectations-adjusted Phillips curve.

5.  Why did the government use expansionary monetary policies in the late 1970s, and what was the principal negative macroeconomic effect of these policies?

6.  State and briefly explain whether or not the empirical evidence generally supports the belief that government policy attempts to improve economic conditions by exploiting an existing relationship among economic variables may change the relationship in such a way as to prevent the policies from achieving their objectives.

7.  State and briefly explain whether or not the empirical evidence generally supports the belief that government policymakers will use fiscal and monetary policies to get themselves reelected rather than to reduce business cycle fluctuations.

8.  Does unemployment insurance reduce the unemployment rate or reduce the costs of unemployment?  Briefly explain.

9.  Identify and briefly explain the two principal costs of anticipated inflation.

10. Identify and briefly explain the two principal costs of unanticipated inflation.

11. Compare and contrast the classical cold turkey approach and the Keynesian gradualism approach to reducing inflation.

12. What are the pros and cons of using cold turkey disinflation compared to a policy of gradualism?

## NUMERICAL PROBLEMS

1.  Suppose Okun's Law holds and a one percentage point increase in the unemployment rate reduces real output by 2.0% of full-employment output. The expectations-augmented Phillips curve is given by

    $$\pi = \pi^e - 2\,(u - .05).$$

    Suppose $\pi = .06$ and $\pi^e = .02$.
    a.  What is the natural rate of unemployment?
    b.  What is the actual rate of unemployment?
    c.  How much is actual GDP compared to full-employment GDP?


2.  Suppose expected inflation in the economy is 5%. Banks set nominal interest rates so they'll earn a 2% expected return. Employers set nominal wages based on a 2% expected real wage increase. Suppose the nominal interest rate and nominal wages are determined this way, but actual inflation turns out to differ from the expected inflation rate. Calculate the actual real interest rate and the percent increase in the real wage for each of the following actual inflation rates: a) 2%; b) 5%, c) 10%.


## ANALYTICAL QUESTIONS

1.  Suppose the natural rate of unemployment is 6% and that the expected inflation rate is 5%. Compare and contrast the effects of an unanticipated and anticipated increase in money supply growth rate.

## ANSWERS TO MULTIPLE-CHOICE QUESTIONS

| Number | Answer | Number | Answer |
|--------|--------|--------|--------|
| 1 | a | 11 | b |
| 2 | d | 12 | a |
| 3 | c | 13 | c |
| 4 | c | 14 | c |
| 5 | a | 15 | d |
| 6 | b | 16 | d |
| 7 | c | 17 | a |
| 8 | a | 18 | d |
| 9 | c | 19 | a |
| 10 | d | 20 | b |

## ANSWERS TO REVIEW QUESTIONS

1.  The Phillips curve depicts various possible combinations of unemployment and inflation that could exist in the economy. The negative slope of the Phillips curve shows that these variables are negatively related. Therefore a trade-off exists between them; any decline in the unemployment rate increases the inflation rate. Any decline in the inflation rate increases the unemployment rate. The simple Phillips curve suggests that policymakers could choose the particular combination of unemployment and inflation that they prefer, and that they could use monetary policy to move the economy to that preferred point on the Phillips curve.

2.  The Phillips curve suggests that there is a stable set of unemployment rate and inflation rate combinations, and that monetary policymakers could achieve the combination they prefer. The macroeconomic data for the 1950s and 1960s for many countries seemed consistent with this view, but further research using data for the 1970s and 1980s failed to show that a stable trade-off exists. The empirical evidence suggests that a stable trade-off exists only during the time period in which expected inflation and the natural unemployment rate remain unchanged. The extended classical model suggests that a nonsystematic expansionary monetary policy attempt to move up a fixed expectations-augmented Phillips curve to a lower unemployment rate and higher inflation rate will achieve its objective only for the short-run period in which the increase in inflation is not anticipated. Systematic monetary policies will be anticipated, so they cannot achieve their objective of temporarily reducing unemployment below the natural unemployment rate.

3.  The expectations-augmented Phillips curve critique is that the Phillips curve fails to include the expected inflation rate as a determinant of the actual inflation rate. The Phillips curve suggests that there is a stable relationship between unemployment and inflation that policymakers can exploit, but the expectations-augmented Phillips curve shows that this relationship is not stable and therefore not exploitable. Any attempt to reduce the unemployment rate below the natural unemployment rate will be effective only if unanticipated and, even then, only during the short-run period of misperceptions or wage-price rigidities. Once expectations, wages, and prices have adjusted, the Phillips curve will shift up to the right and unemployment will return to the natural unemployment rate at a higher inflation rate.

4. The Friedman-Phelps theory suggests that a change in expected inflation or the natural unemployment rate will shift the expectations-augmented Phillips curve. The empirical evidence generally supports this theory. For example, structural and demographic changes in Canada after 1970 caused the natural unemployment rate to increase; the curve also shifted to the right when expected inflation increased, then shifted to the left when expected inflation declined.

5. In the late 1970s the Canadian government used expansionary monetary policies in an attempt to reduce the unemployment rate and to increase the growth rate of output. Relying on the Keynesian model to explain the slowdown in economic growth, policymakers concluded that aggregate demand had declined and that expansionary monetary stabilization policies could pull aggregate demand back to the full-employment level of output. However, aggregate demand had not declined. The recession was created by a decline in aggregate supply caused by an increase in the price of oil. Expansionary monetary policies caused aggregate demand to increase along the new aggregate supply curve, which caused inflation to increase further.

6. The Lucas critique is that government policy attempts to improve economic conditions by exploiting an existing relationship among economic variables may change the relationship in such a way as to prevent the policies from achieving their objectives. The empirical evidence generally supports this critique. A good example of this policy problem is the Canadian government's attempts to reduce the unemployment rate by exploiting the Phillips curve trade-off between inflation and unemployment. While successful in the 1960s, it was not effective in the 1970s because the policy attempts increased expected inflation, causing the Phillips curve to shift to the right.

7. Daniel Richards political business cycle theory suggests that government policymakers will use fiscal and monetary policies to get themselves reelected rather than to reduce business cycle fluctuations. The empirical evidence regarding this theory is mixed, in part because it is hard to properly evaluate. To the extent that attempts to reduce business cycle fluctuations are beneficial to voters, it may be good politics as well as good economics to undertake macroeconomic stabilization policies. Critics contend that the theory wrongly assumes that policymakers are concerned only with getting reelected and are not concerned with the economic welfare of their constituents. One problem with political business cycle theory is that monetary policy is controlled by the Bank of Canada, whose members are not elected and who serve for long terms. The Bank of Canada is largely independent of elected fiscal policymakers.

8. Unemployment insurance does reduce the personal cost of unemployment by redistributing the cost to other time periods and to other people. Workers and firms pay the unemployment insurance premium all the time, not just when unemployment is high. Also, all workers and firms pay the insurance premium, while only a small percentage file for unemployment insurance income payments at any given time. Unemployment insurance increases the output cost of unemployment by prolonging the duration of unemployment spells, since those receiving the income benefits have less incentive to return to work quickly. The output cost of unemployment insurance would increase with increases in the income payments provided by the insurance, increases in the number of months over which people could collect it, and increases in the eligibility of those unemployed.

9. 1) Menu costs: The costs of changing prices are called menu costs. Classical economists believe these costs are small, assuming perfectly competitive market conditions. Keynesians believe these costs are large enough to create price stickiness, assuming monopolistically competitive market conditions.

   2) Shoe leather costs: The transactions costs incurred by households and firms in reducing the share of their assets they hold as money are called shoe-leather costs. These costs are likely to be larger than menu costs.

10. 1)   Risk of redistribution of wealth cost:  Unanticipated inflation creates a redistribution of wealth; what some people and firms lose, others gain.  For example, creditors lose and debtors gain, because unanticipated inflation lowers the real interest rate on existing loans.  Although there is no aggregate income loss from redistribution, the costs incurred by market participants trying to reduce their risk of losses may be large.  For example, creditors may charge an inflation risk premium on all loans to cover their risk, even during periods when inflation is constant, thereby increasing the real interest rate in the long run.

2)   Relative price distortions cost:  Unanticipated inflation causes firms to misperceive a change in the price level as changes in the relative prices of their products.  This misperception causes firms to charge inefficient prices for their products, produce inefficient levels of output, and employ efficient amounts of labour at inefficient wages.  These relative price distortions cause inefficiencies that are costly.

11. 1)   Cold turkey approach:  Classical economists propose a  rapid reduction in money supply growth to achieve disinflation, assuming that prices, wages, and expectations adjust quickly.  Unemployment costs and inflation costs are most likely to be small if the classical assumptions about rapid market adjustments are correct, the policy is announced in advance, and the announcement is credible.  Both classical economists and Keynesians agree that the inflation costs would be smaller for a cold turkey approach than for gradualism, since inflation is being reduced more quickly.  However, Keynesians believe that the unemployment costs could be very high.

2)   Gradualism approach:  Keynesians propose a gradualism approach of slowly reducing money supply growth over several years to achieve disinflation, assuming wages, prices, and expectations adjust slowly to changes in the inflation rate.  Both classical economists and Keynesians believe that this approach would have small unemployment costs, but the inflation costs would be greater, since the inflation rate would be higher for a long period of time.  Classicals contend inflation costs could be much higher than for a cold turkey approach, since an announced gradualism approach is unlikely to be credible.

12. Cold turkey disinflation reduces inflation quickly and could be successful if expected inflation fell at the same time; that requires that policy be credible, however. But Keynesians suggest that menu costs and nominal wage contracts will prevent prices and wages from adjusting quickly, so a cold turkey strategy will cause a recession. Further, if a cold turkey strategy is begun, but people think the costs will be so large that the strategy will be abandoned, then expected inflation will not decline. For this reason, Keynesians prefer a gradualist approach to allow wages and prices more time to adjust to policy changes. Such a policy is more likely to be sustainable politically.

## ANSWERS TO NUMERICAL PROBLEMS

1.  a.  .05
    b.  .03
    c.  4% higher

2.  The real interest rate $(r)$ = the nominal interest rate - the inflation rate.  In percentage terms, the increase in the real wage $(w)$ = the increase in the nominal wage - the inflation rate.  It is given that the expected inflation rate = 5%, so the nominal interest rate on bank savings deposits = 7%, and the increase in the nominal wage = 7%.  When inflation is

    a)   2%, then $r$ = 7% - 2%= 5%, and the increase in $w$ = 7% - 2% = 5%.

    b)   5%, then $r$ = 7% - 5% = 2%, and the increase in $w$ = 7% - 5% = 2%.

    c)   10%, then $r$ = 7% - 10% = -3%, and the increase in $w$ = 7% - 10% = -3%.

## ANSWERS TO ANALYTICAL QUESTIONS

1.  Figure 13.6 shows a Phillips curve diagram in which the natural unemployment rate = 6%. The economic effects of a 3% increase in money supply growth depend on whether the increase is anticipated or unanticipated:

    1) Anticipated:  If the increase in money supply growth is anticipated, then money is neutral.  In the diagram, the economy moves quickly from point E to H.  There is no unemployment effect or output effect.  Wages, prices, and expectations quickly adjust to general equilibrium.

    2) Unanticipated:  In the short run, the 3% increase in money supply growth causes the growth rate of output to increase, the unemployment rate to decline, and the inflation rate to increase as we move from point E to F in the diagram along a fixed, short-run Phillips curve with the expected inflation rate equal to 5%.  In the long run, the expected inflation rate rises to 8%, causing the Phillips curve to shift up.  In the diagram, we move from point E to H in the long run. At point H, the inflation rate has increased to 8%, the expected inflation rate has increased to 8%, and unemployment is at the natural rate of 6%.

Figure 13.6

# CHAPTER 14
# MONETARY POLICY AND THE BANK OF CANADA

## INTRODUCTION

Chapter 14 looks at how the nation's money supply is determined. It explores the question: How should the central bank conduct monetary policy? This leads to a discussion of the following issues: (1) Should the central bank offset cyclical fluctuations? (2) Should the central bank follow simple rules? (3) How should policy-making institutions be designed?

The chapter begins with a discussion in Section 14.1 of the factors that determine the money supply, including a demonstration of how the Bank of Canada, banks, and the public all make decisions that affect the money supply. Section 14.2 covers the Bank of Canada in more detail, describing its institutional structure, how it affects the money supply, and how it develops its strategy for monetary policy. The issue of whether the Bank of Canada should use rules or discretion is taken up in Section 14.3, which includes a discussion of new research into credibility, modeling a game between the Bank of Canada and the public.

There are a couple of fairly technical parts of this chapter. First, the money supply is described by a set of equations that relate what the Bank of Canada controls (the monetary base and the required reserve ratio) to what banks and the public control (the currency-deposit ratio). These are used to develop the money multiplier, which you need to understand to be able to do many of the problems in this chapter. So spend some time working through the algebra that develops the formula and working on problems that use it. The second technical aspect is the game between the central bank and firms that is developed in Section 14.3. This is a standard example in the economic field called game theory, so you might have seen something similar in other economics courses. If you haven't seen it before, the logic can seem mysterious. However, once you work carefully through the logic of the exercise, it will make sense to you. In fact, economists are doing more and more with game theory, so it's a good idea to invest some time with it to be sure you get the main concepts.

## CHAPTER OUTLINE

I. Principles of Money Supply Determination (Sec. 14.1)
  A. Three groups affect the money supply
    1. The central bank is responsible for monetary policy
    2. Depository institutions (banks) accept deposits and make loans
    3. The public (people and firms) holds money as currency and coin or as bank deposits
  B. The money supply in an all-currency economy
    1. A trading system based on barter is inconvenient
    2. The creation of a central bank to print money can improve matters
      a. The central bank uses money it prints to buy real assets from the public; this gets money in circulation
      b. People accept the paper money if they believe other people will accept it in exchange
      c. The government often decrees that the paper money is *legal tender*, so that it can be used to pay off debts and the government will accept it for tax payments
      d. The central bank's assets are the real assets it buys from the public; its liabilities are the paper money it issued
      e. That money is called the monetary base, or high-powered money
    3. In an all-currency economy, the money supply equals the monetary base

    C.   The money supply under fractional reserve banking

        1.   As an economy becomes more sophisticated financially, banks develop

        2.   If currency is easily lost or stolen, people may want to hold all their money in bank deposits and none in currency

            a.   In this case, the consolidated balance sheet of banks has assets of all the currency in the economy and liabilities consisting of all the bank deposits

            b.   The balance sheet of the central bank is unchanged from the case in the all-currency economy

        3.   The currency that banks hold is called bank reserves

            a.   When bank reserves are equal to deposits, the system is called 100% reserve banking

            b.   To make money, banks would have to charge fees for deposits, since they earn no interest on reserves

        4.   Rather than holding reserves that earn no interest, suppose a bank lent some of the reserves

            a.   It could do this, since the flow of money in and out of the bank is fairly predictable and only a fraction of reserves are needed to meet the need for outflows

            b.   If the bank needs to keep only 25% of the amount of its deposits on reserve to meet the demand for funds, it can lend the other 75%

            c.   The reserve-deposit ratio would be 25%

            d.   When the reserve-deposit ratio is less than 100%, the system is called fractional reserve banking

        5.   When all the banks catch on to this idea, they will all make loans as the economy undergoes a *multiple expansion of loans and deposits*

        6.   The process stops only when the banks' currency holdings (reserves) are exactly 25% of their total deposits, with loans equal to 75% of total deposits

            a.   For example, if the monetary base is $1 million, banks would make $3 million in loans, so their total assets would be $4 million

            b.   In loaning the $3 million, banks create $3 million in new deposits

            c.   Adding the $3 million in new deposits to the $1 million in existing deposits gives total liabilities in the banking system of $4 million

        7.   The money supply in this economy is equal to the total amount of bank deposits ($4 million in the example)

        8.   The relationship between the monetary base and the money supply can be shown algebraically

            a.   Let $M$ = money supply, $BASE$ = monetary base, $DEP$ = bank deposits, $RES$ = bank reserves, $res$ = banks' desired reserve-deposit ratio ($RES/DEP$)

            b.   Since no currency is held by the public, $M = DEP$    (14.1)

            c.   Banks want to hold ($res$)($DEP$) in reserves, which must equal the amount of currency distributed by the central bank, so ($res$)($DEP$) = $BASE$    (14.2)

            d.   Using Eqs. (14.1) and (14.2) gives $M = DEP = BASE/res$    (14.3)

            e.   So an economy with fractional reserve banking and no currency held by the public has money supply equal to the monetary base divided by the reserve-deposit ratio

        9.   Each unit of monetary base allows $1/res$ of money to be created

       10.  The monetary base is called high-powered money because each unit of the base that is issued leads to the creation of more money

    D.   Bank runs

        1.   In the example, banks plan on never having to pay out more than 25% of their deposits

        2.   If more people wanted to get their money from the bank, the bank would be unable to give them their funds

        3.   If people think a bank won't be able to give them their money, they may panic and rush to withdraw their money, causing a bank run

E.   The money supply with both public holdings of currency and fractional reserve banking
   1.   If there is both public holding of currency and fractional reserve banking, the picture gets more complicated
   2.   The money supply consists of currency held by the public and deposits, so
        $M = CU + DEP$    (14.4)
   3.   The monetary base is held as currency by the public and as reserves by banks, so $BASE = CU + RES$    (14.5)
   4.   Taking the ratio of these two equations gives $M/BASE = (CU + DEP)/(CU + RES)$    (14.6)
   5.   This can be written as $M/BASE = [(CU/DEP) + 1]/[(CU/DEP) + (RES/DEP)]$    (14.7)
   6.   The currency-deposit ratio ($CU/DEP$, or $cu$) is determined by the public
   7.   The reserve-deposit ratio ($RES/DEP$, or $res$) is determined by banks
   8.   Rewrite Eq. (14.7) as $M = [(cu + 1)/(cu + res)]BASE$    (14.8)
   9.   The term $(cu + 1)/(cu + res)$ is the money multiplier
        a.   The money multiplier is greater than 1 for $res$ less than 1 (that is, with fractional reserve banking)
        b.   If $cu = 0$, the multiplier is $1/res$, as when all money is held as deposits
        c.   The multiplier decreases when either $cu$ or $res$ rises
F.   Open-market operations
   1.   The most direct and frequently used way of changing the money supply is by raising or lowering the monetary base through open-market operations
   2.   To increase the monetary base, the central bank prints money and uses it to buy assets in the market; this is an open-market purchase
        a.   If the central bank wishes to increase the money supply by 15%, it purchases 15% more assets and its liabilities increase by 15%, which is the currency it issues
        b.   To decrease the monetary base, the central bank sells assets in the market and retires the money it receives; this is an open-market sale
        c.   For a constant money multiplier, the decline or fall in the monetary base of 15% is matched by a decline or fall in the money supply of 15%

II.   Monetary Control in Canada (Sec. 14.2)
   A.   The Bank of Canada
      1.   The Bank of Canada began operation in 1935 for the purpose of eliminating severe financial crises
      2.   The leadership of the Bank of Canada is provided by the Board of Directors.
         a.   The board of directors consists of a governor, the senior deputy governor, the deputy minister of finance and 12 directors
         b.   The Governor of the Bank of Canada has considerable power, and has a term of seven years
   B.   The Bank of Canada's balance sheet and open-market operations
      1.   Balance sheet of the Bank of Canada (text Table 14.2)
         a.   Largest asset is holdings of government securities
         b.   Also owns gold, makes loans to banks, and holds other assets including foreign exchange and federal agency securities
         c.   Largest liability is currency outstanding
            (1)   Some is held in bank vaults and is called vault cash
            (2)   The rest is held by the public
         d.   Another liability is deposits by banks and other depository institutions
         e.   Vault cash plus banks' deposits at the Bank of Canada are banks' total reserves ($RES$)
      2.   The monetary base equals banks' reserves plus currency in circulation
      3.   The primary method for changing the monetary base is open-market operations
   C.   The Tools of Monetary Policy
      1.   Reserve requirements
         a.   The Bank of Canada sets the minimum fraction of each type of deposit that a bank must hold as reserves

    b.  An increase in reserve requirements forces banks to hold more reserves, thus reducing the money multiplier
  2.  Overnight rates
    a.  The Bank of Canada affects the Canadian money supply primarily through changes in the overnight interest rate
    b.  Changes in monetary policy are signalled with the target overnight rate, the centre of the operating band for the overnight rate.
    c.  The target overnight rate is determined as follows: the Bank of Canada announces an operating band of 0.5 percentage points for the overnight rate on eight preset dates each year (or at other times in unusual circumstances).  The centre of this band is called the target overnight rate, which is the key indicator of the stance of monetary policy
  3.  Open-Market Operations
    a.  The Bank of Canada can affect the size of the monetary base and thus the money supply through open market operations.  Open market operations consists of open-market sales and open-market purchases.
    b.  An open-market sale (in which  central bank assets are sold for currency or bank reserves) reduces the monetary base.
    c.  An open-market purchase (in which the central bank uses money to buy assets, such as government securities, from the public) increases the monetary base.
  D.  Intermediate targets
  1.  The Bank of Canada uses intermediate targets to guide policy as a step between its tools or instruments (such as open-market purchases) and its goals or ultimate targets of price stability and stable economic growth
  2.  Intermediate targets are variables the Bank of Canada can't directly control but can influence predictably, and they are related to the Bank of Canada's goals
  3.  Most frequently used are monetary aggregates such as M1 and M2, and short-term interest rates, such as the overnight rate
  4.  The Bank of Canada cannot target both the money supply and the overnight rate simultaneously
    a.  Suppose both the money supply and the overnight rate were above target, so the Bank of Canada needs to lower them
    b.  Since a decrease in the money supply shifts the $LM$ curve up, it will increase the overnight rate
  5.  In recent years the Bank of Canada has been targeting the overnight rate (Fig. 14.1; like text Fig. 14.6)
    a.  This strategy works well if the main shocks to the economy are to the $LM$ curve (shocks to money supply or money demand)
    b.  The strategy stabilizes output, the real interest rate, and the price level, as it offsets the shocks to the $LM$ curve completely
    c.  But if other shocks to the economy (such as $IS$ shocks) are more important than nominal shocks,   the policy may be destabilizing

Figure 14.1

  E.  Making monetary policy in practice
  1.  The $IS$-$LM$ model makes monetary policy look easy—just change the money supply to move the economy to the best point possible
    a.  In fact, it isn't so easy because of lags in the effect of policy and uncertainty about the ways monetary policy works

2. Lags in the effects of monetary policy
   a. It takes a fairly long time for changes in monetary policy to have an impact on the economy
   b. Interest rates change quickly, but output and inflation barely respond in the first four months after the change in money growth
   c. Tighter monetary policy causes real GDP to decline sharply after about four months, with the full effect being felt about 6 to 24 months after the change in policy
   d. Inflation responds even more slowly, remaining essentially unchanged for the first year, then declining somewhat
   e. These long lags make it very difficult to use monetary policy to control the economy very precisely
   f. Because of the lags, policy must be made based on forecasts of the future, but forecasts are often inaccurate
3. The channels of monetary policy transmission
   a. Exactly how does monetary policy affect economic activity and prices?  There are two effects discussed in the textbook so far
      (1) The interest rate channel: as seen in the *IS-LM* model, a decline in money supply raises real interest rates, reducing aggregate demand, leading to a decline in output and prices
      (2) The exchange rate channel: in an open economy, tighter monetary policy raises the real exchange rate, reducing net exports, and thus aggregate demand
      (3) The credit channel: tighter monetary policy reduces both the supply and demand for credit (see the box below)
   b. How important are these different channels?
      (1) Suppose real interest rates are high, but the dollar has been falling; is monetary policy tight or easy?  It depends on the relative importance of the different channels
      (2) Or suppose real interest rates are low, but borrowing and lending are weak
4. These practical difficulties make monetary policy "more an art than a science"
III. The Conduct of Monetary Policy: Rules Versus Discretion (Sec. 14.3)
   A. The monetarist case for rules
      1. Rules make monetary policy automatic, as they require the central bank to set policy based on a set of simple, prespecified, and publicly announced rules
      2. Examples of rules
         a. Increase the monetary base by 1% each quarter
         b. Maintain the price of gold at a fixed level
      3. The rule should be simple; there shouldn't be much leeway for exceptions
      4. The rule should specify something under the Bank of Canada's control, like growth of the monetary base, not something like fixing the unemployment rate at 4%, over which the Bank of Canada has little control
      5. The rule may also permit the Bank of Canada to respond to the state of the economy
   B. Most Keynesian economists support discretion
      1. Discretion means the central bank looks at all the information about the economy and uses its judgment as to the best course of policy
      2. Discretion gives the central bank the freedom to stimulate or contract the economy when needed; it is thus called *activist*
      3. Since discretion gives the central bank leeway to act, while rules constrain its behavior, why would anyone suggest that the central bank follow rules?
   C. Box 14.1: The Taylor rule
      1. John Taylor of Stanford University introduced a rule that allows the Bank of Canada to take economic conditions into account
      2. The rule is $i = \pi + 0.02 + 0.5y + 0.5(\pi - 0.02)$, where $i$ is the nominal overnight interest rate, $\pi$ is the inflation rate over the last 4 quarters, $y = (Y - \overline{Y})/\overline{Y}$ =the percentage deviation of output from full-employment output
      3. The rule works by having the real Fed funds rate $(i - \pi)$ respond to:
         a. $y$, the difference between output and full-employment output
         b. $\pi - 0.02$, the difference between inflation and its target of 2 percent

4.  If either $y$ or $\pi$ increase, the real overnight rate is increased, causing monetary policy to tighten (and vice-versa)
5.  Taylor showed that the rule is similar to what the Bank of Canada does in practice
6.  Taylor advocates the use of the rule as a guideline for policy, not something to be followed mechanically

D.  The monetarist case for rules
1.  *Monetarism* is an economic theory emphasizing the importance of monetary factors in the economy
2.  The leading monetarist is Milton Friedman, who has argued for many years (since 1959) that the central bank should follow rules for setting policy
3.  Friedman's argument for rules comes from four main propositions
   a.  Proposition 1: Monetary policy has powerful short-run effects on the real economy. In the longer run, however, changes in the money supply have their primary effect on the price level
      (1)  This proposition comes from Friedman's research with Anna Schwartz on monetary history
      (2)  Friedman and other monetarists think monetary policy is a main source of business cycles
   b.  Proposition 2: Despite the powerful short-run effect of money on the economy, there is little scope for using monetary policy actively to try to smooth business cycles
      (1)  First, the information lag makes it difficult to know the current state of the economy
      (2)  Second, monetary policy works with a long and variable lag, so it isn't clear how to set policy quantitatively
      (3)  Third, wage and price adjustment is fast enough that by the time a change in policy begins to affect the economy, it may be moving the economy in the wrong direction, thus destabilizing the economy
   c.  Proposition 3: Even if there is some scope for using monetary policy to smooth business cycles, the central bank cannot be relied on to do so effectively
      (1)  Friedman believes the Bank of Canada responds to political pressure and tends to stimulate the economy in election years
      (2)  Historically, monetary policy has tended to destabilize, rather than stabilize, the economy; so eliminating monetary policy as a source of instability would improve macroeconomic performance
   d.  Proposition 4: The central bank should choose a specific monetary aggregate (such as M1 or M2) and commit itself to making that aggregate grow at a fixed percentage rate every year
      (1)  The Bank of Canada needs to give up activist, or discretionary, policy completely and follow a simple rule
      (2)  Friedman prefers a constant money growth rule, since the money supply is controllable by the Bank of Canada and the Bank of Canada would not follow destabilizing monetary policies
      (3)  To reduce inflation to zero, the money growth target should be gradually lowered over time

E.  Rules and central bank credibility
1.  New arguments for rules suggest that rules are valuable even if the central bank has a lot of information and forms policy wisely
   a.  The new arguments suggest that rules improve the credibility of the central bank
   b.  The credibility of the central bank influences how well monetary policy works
2.  Dad, the kids, and the game: credible threats and commitment
   a.  Dad wants to take the kids to a ballgame and the kids want to go, too
   b.  But the kids like to fight and Dad doesn't like them fighting
   c.  To induce them not to fight, Dad says, "If you fight, we won't go to the game"
   d.  A game theory model can tell us whether the kids will fight or not and whether Dad will take them to the game or not
   e.  First, the value of different actions is specified
      (1)  For the kids, fighting is worth 1, not fighting 0, going to the game 2, not going to the game 0

(2)   For Dad, fighting is worth 0, not fighting 1, going to the game 2, not going to the game 0

f.   This means the payoffs to the combinations of whether the kids fight or not and whether they all go to the game or not can be laid out as follows

|  | | Kid's strategy | |
|---|---|---|---|
|  | | Fight | Don't fight |
| | Go to game | Dad: 2 | Dad: 3 |
| Dad's Strategy | | Kids: 3 | Kids: 2 |
| | Don't go to game | Dad: 0 | Dad: 1 |
| | | Kids: 1 | Kids: 0 |

g.   Dad's statement isn't credible, because he would be worse off if he followed it
  (1)   If the kids fight and Dad follows through on not going to the game, he gets a payoff of 0
  (2)   But if they fight and Dad backs down from his statement and takes them to the game anyway, Dad's payoff is 2
  (3)   Since the kids know that Dad will take them to the game whether they fight or not, and since they prefer to fight, they will fight

h.   Could Dad make his statement credible?
  (1)   He could if he could commit himself somehow to following through
  (2)   One possibility is to give the tickets to Mom, who doesn't care if they go to the game, who could enforce Dad's decision
  (3)   Then both fighting and going to the game would not be possible, so the kids wouldn't fight, since they prefer not fighting and going to the game over fighting and not going to the game

3.   A game between the central bank and firms
  a.   Consider a similar game between the central bank and firms
  b.   The inflation rate is 10% and the unemployment rate is 6%
  c.   The Bank of Canada tells firms that it will hold the money supply constant this year
  d.   Should the firms believe the Bank of Canada and hold prices constant, or should they doubt that the Bank of Canada will really hold the money supply constant, in which case they should raise prices?
  e.   The payoffs
    (1)   For firms, 0% inflation is worth 1, 10% inflation is worth 0; unemployment at the natural rate is worth 2, unemployment above or below the natural rate is worth 0
    (2)   For the Bank of Canada, 0% inflation is worth 1, 10% inflation is worth 0; unemployment at the natural rate is worth 0, unemployment above the natural rate is worth -1, and unemployment below the natural rate is worth 1
  f.   If the Bank of Canada holds the money supply constant
    (1)   If firms don't raise prices, then inflation is zero and the *LM* curve stays put, so unemployment remains at the natural rate
    (2)   If firms raise prices, inflation is 10%, the *LM* curve shifts up, and unemployment rises to 9%
  g.   If the Bank of Canada raises the money supply
    (1)   If firms don't raise prices, then inflation is zero and the *LM* curve shifts down, so unemployment falls to 3%
    (2)   If firms raise prices, inflation is 10%, the *LM* curve stays put, and unemployment remains at the natural rate

h.  The payoffs can thus be laid out as

|  | | Firms' strategy | |
|---|---|---|---|
|  | | Raise *P* | Don't raise *P* |
| Bank Strategy | Increase *M* | Bank: 0<br>Firms: 2 | Bank: 2<br>Firms: 1 |
|  | Don't Increase *M* | Bank: -1<br>Firms: 0 | Bank: 1<br>Firms: 3 |

i.  The payoffs are such that if firms raise prices, the Bank of Canada is better off increasing *M*, so firms reason that the Bank of Canada's threat isn't credible

j.  Further, if the firms didn't raise prices, the Bank of Canada would increase the money supply, since its payoff is larger

So firms will increase prices and the Bank of Canada will increase the money supply, leading to inflation of 10% and unemployment of 6%

1.  If the Bank of Canada's statement not to raise the money supply was credible, however, then firms would choose not to raise prices and inflation would fall to zero, with unemployment remaining at the natural rate

4.  Rules, commitment, and credibility

a.  How does a central bank (or a dad) gain credibility?

b.  One way to get credibility is by building a reputation for following through on its promises, even if it's costly in the short run

c.  Another, less costly, way is to follow a rule that is enforced by some outside agency (Mom, for example)

d   Keynesians argue that there may be a trade-off between credibility and flexibility

(1)  To be credible, a rule must be nearly impossible to change

(2)  But if a rule can't be changed, what happens in a crisis situation?

(3)  For example, if a rule is based on economic relationships that change suddenly, then the lack of flexibility may be very costly

(4)  So a rule may create unacceptable risks

F.  Application: Monetary-growth targeting and inflation targeting

1.  High unemployment and high inflation in the 1970s led central banks worldwide to experiment with alternative strategies for monetary policy, including targeting money growth and targeting inflation

2.  Money-growth targeting

a.  Germany's Bundesbank introduced money-growth targets in 1975 and used the strategy until the European Monetary Union began in 1999

(1)  The U.S., Canada, the U.K., Switzerland, and others also adopted money targets in the 1970s

b.  Money-growth targeting means the central bank announces a money-growth rate that it will aim for over the next year or so

(1)  The idea is that by having money grow at the optimal rate, inflation and output will be at desired levels

(2)  Germany had been quite successful in targeting money growth

c.  Canada began targeting money in 1975

(1)  But the Bank of Canada tried to target three monetary aggregates (M1, M2, and M3) all at the same time, and often missed its targets badly

d.  Most countries that used money-growth targeting (including Canada) were able to reduce inflation in the early 1980s, but output and employment growth were often unstable

(1)  The Bank of Canada de-emphasized money-growth targeting in 1982 because of instability in money demand

(2)  Many other countries also weakened their reliance on money-growth targets in the 1980s, except for Germany and Switzerland

3. Inflation targeting
   a. Since 1990, some countries have switched from targeting money growth to targeting inflation
      (1) New Zealand was the pioneer, announcing explicit inflation targets that had to be met or else the central bank's governor could be fired
      (2) Canada, the U.K., Sweden, Australia, Spain, and others followed with some version of inflation targeting
      (3) The new European Central Bank uses a method of inflation targeting that retains a role for money-growth targets
   b. Under inflation targeting, the central bank announces targets for inflation over the next 1 to 4 years
   c. Advantages of inflation targeting over money-growth targeting
      (1) It avoids the problem of instability in money demand
      (2) It's easy to explain inflation targets to the public (since they understand what inflation is) than money-growth targeting (which most people don't understand)
      (3) Better communication of the central bank's goals will reduce uncertainty about what the central bank will do and may increase the bank's accountability
   d. Disadvantages of inflation targeting relative to money-growth targeting
      (1) Inflation responds to policy actions with a long lag, so it's hard to judge what policy actions are needed to hit the inflation target and hard for the public to tell if the central bank is doing the right thing
      (2) Thus central banks may miss their targets badly, losing credibility

G. Other ways to achieve central bank credibility besides targeting money growth or inflation
   1. Appointing a "tough" central banker
      a. Appointing someone who has a well-known reputation for being tough in fighting inflation may help establish credibility for the central bank
      b. For example, in 1979 the appointment of Paul Volcker to be chairman of the Bank of Canada was designed to convince people that President Carter was serious about stopping inflation
      c. Even in Volcker's case, however, disinflation proved to be costly
   2. Changing central bankers' incentives
      a. People are more likely to believe a central bank is serious about disinflation if it has the incentive to care a lot about inflation
      b. In New Zealand, for example, the head of the central bank must be replaced if inflation targets aren't met; as a result, inflation was reduced significantly, but at a cost of higher unemployment
   3. Increasing central bank independence
      a. If the executive and legislative branches of government can't interfere with the central bank, people are more likely to believe that the central bank is committed to keeping inflation low and won't cause a political business cycle
      b. Looking at evidence across countries, Alesina and Summers showed that the more independent the central bank, the lower the inflation rate from 1955 to 1988; also, the long-run level of unemployment is no higher in those countries

## MULTIPLE-CHOICE QUESTIONS

1.  Monetary policy in Canada is principally controlled by
    a.   the prime minister of Canada.
    b.   the members of parliament
    c.   the Bank of Canada
    d.   fiscal policymakers.

2.  Which of the following are depository institutions?
    a.   The Bank of Canada
    b.   The U.S. Treasury and the IRS
    c.   Banks and thrifts
    d.   Investment banks and finance companies

3.  If a currency is legal tender in a country, then
    a.   the government will readily exchange it for gold.
    b.   the government will not accept it in payment of taxes.
    c.   it is the only legal form of wealth.
    d.   creditors are required to accept it in settlement of debts.

4.  The monetary base is equal to
    a.   banks' reserves plus their holdings of Treasury securities.
    b.   banks' reserves plus Fed funds.
    c.   banks' reserves plus currency in circulation.
    d.   M2 minus M1.

5.  Vault cash is equal to $2 million, deposits by depository institutions at the central bank are $3 million, the monetary base is $10 million, and bank deposits are $25 million.  Bank reserves are equal to
    a.   $ 2 million.
    b.   $ 3 million.
    c.   $ 5 million.
    d.   $10 million.

6.  Banks hold some deposits on reserve at the Bank of Canada because
    a.   the Bank of Canada pays a higher interest rate than banks can get in the private market.
    b.   the Bank of Canada will insure those deposits, but will not insure regular bank deposits.
    c.   these are membership dues for being a member bank.
    d.   these deposits meet the reserve requirements of the Bank of Canada.

7.  In a fractional reserve banking system
    a.   most deposits are used to make bank loans.
    b.   100% of deposits are held as reserves.
    c.   the money supply = high-powered money.
    d.   the money multiplier is less than one.

8.  In a fractional reserve banking system with no currency where *res* is the ratio of reserves to deposits, the money multiplier is
    a.   1 - *res*.
    b.   1 + *res*.
    c.   1/*res*.
    d.   *res*.

9. The monetary base (*BASE*) equals
    a.   $CU + RES$.
    b.   $RES$.
    c.   $CU + DEP$.
    d.   $M - CU$.

10. If the public's demand for currency increased relative to its demand for deposits,
    a.   the monetary base would decrease.
    b.   reserve requirements would decrease.
    c.   the currency-deposit ratio would decrease.
    d.   the money multiplier would decrease.

11. Currently, the currency-deposit ratio is 0.3 and the reserve-deposit ratio is 0.2. The Bank of Canada raises the reserve-deposit ratio to 0.25, as a response to a change in the public's currency-deposit ratio, to maintain the old money multiplier. What is the public's approximate new currency-deposit ratio?
    a.   0.22
    b.   0.25
    c.   0.33
    d.   0.35

12. The money supply is $10 million, currency held by the public is $2 million, and the reserve-deposit ratio is 0.2. Deposits are equal to
    a.   $1.6 million.
    b.   $2 million.
    c.   $4 million.
    d.   $8 million.

13. Assume that the currency-deposit ratio is 0.5 and the reserve-deposit ratio is 0.2. The Bank of Canada carries out open-market operations, purchasing $1,000,000 worth of bonds from banks. This action will increase the money supply by
    a.   $1,428,571.
    b.   $1,714,285.
    c.   $2,142,857.
    d.   $2,400,000.

14. Assume that the currency-deposit ratio is 0.4. The Bank of Canada carries out open-market operations, purchasing $1,000,000 worth of bonds from banks. This action increased the money supply by $1,750,000. What is the reserve-deposit ratio?
    a.   0.2
    b.   0.3
    c.   0.4
    d.   0.5

15. Suppose the Bank of Canada wanted to increase the money supply without using open-market operations. It could try to get the public to _____ their currency-deposit ratio and _____ banks' reserve requirements, which would in turn change the banks' reserve-deposit ratio.
    a.   decrease; lower
    b.   decrease; raise
    c.   increase; lower
    d.   increase; raise

16. Vault cash is equal to $2 million, deposits by depository institutions at the central bank are $3 million, the monetary base is $10 million, and bank deposits are $25 million. The money multiplier is equal to
    a.   2.5.
    b.   3.0.
    c.   4.0.
    d.   5.0.

17. If the Bank of Canada increases the monetary base by $5 million and the money multiplier is 5, M1 will
    a.   rise by $25 million.
    b.   fall by $25 million.
    c.   rise by $1 million.
    d.   fall by $1 million.

18. The Bank of Canada can increase the money supply by
    a.   increasing the currency-deposit ratio.
    b.   increasing the monetary base.
    c.   increasing reserve requirements.
    d.   increasing the discount rate.

19. Which of the following is *not* a policy instrument of the Bank of Canada?
    a.   Open-market operations
    b.   Changes in the discount rate
    c.   Changes in reserve requirements
    d.   Changes in the government deficit

20. The policy instrument most frequently used to change the money supply is
    a.   open-market operations.
    b.   changes in reserve requirements.
    c.   changes in margin requirements on stock prices.
    d.   changes in the discount rate.

21. By lending at the discount window, the Bank of Canada
    a.   insures bank deposits.
    b.   ensures that banks will make healthy profits.
    c.   eliminates the need for banks to pay market interest rates to attract deposits.
    d.   acts as a lender of last resort to enable banks to meet unexpectedly high withdrawal demands.

22. The overnight rate is
    a.   the interest rate on federal government bonds.
    b.   the interest rate banks charge other banks for short-term loans.
    c.   the interest rate the Bank of Canada charges banks who borrow from it.
    d.   the interest rate penalty on late federal tax payments.

23. In response to an unanticipated tightening of monetary policy, the overnight rate _____ at first, then _____ after 6 to 12 months.
    a.   rises; returns most of the way to its original value
    b.   falls; returns most of the way to its original value
    c.   remains roughly unchanged; rises significantly
    d.   remains roughly unchanged; falls significantly

24. The basic Keynesian argument for discretionary monetary policy is that
    a.   monetary policy is the principal cause of business cycles.
    b.   monetary policy is much more effective than fiscal policy.
    c.   aggregate demand is unstable and monetary policy can help to stabilize it.
    d.   reducing unemployment is much more important than reducing inflation.

25. A monetary policy rule proposed by monetarists is to
    a. increase the money supply at a low, constant rate of growth every year.
    b. target a constant overnight rate over long periods.
    c. adjust money supply growth often, to stabilize the economy.
    d. adjust the overnight rate often, to stabilize the economy.

26. In New Zealand, if the Reserve Bank fails to meet its inflation targets, then _____ may be fired.
    a. the country's president
    b. the country's finance minister
    c. the Reserve Bank's governor
    d. the Reserve Bank's chief economist

27. The chief disadvantage of inflation targeting is that
    a. it's hard to measure inflation.
    b. it isn't easy for the public to observe inflation.
    c. people don't understand what inflation is.
    d. it's hard for the central bank to judge what policy actions are needed.

## REVIEW QUESTIONS

1. Identify the market actors who control each of the following variables, and state whether the money supply is positively related or negatively related to each variable: the monetary base, the reserve-deposit ratio, and the currency-deposit ratio.

2. Identify the most commonly used policy instrument for changing the money supply, and explain how the Bank of Canada can use this policy instrument to increase and decrease the money supply.

3. What policy-making body within the Bank of Canada controls monetary policy? How are its members chosen?

4. From a Keynesian viewpoint, what is wrong with the monetarist argument against an activist monetary policy?

5. If you could determine the goals of the Bank of Canada, what goals would you choose? Should the Bank of Canada's policy be activist? Discuss the pros and cons.

6. What is the intermediate target recommended by monetarists? Why do they propose this target?

7. Why don't Keynesians believe the credibility argument in favor of rules for monetary policy?

8. Should the Bank of Canada be independent? Or should the Bank of Canada be required to confer with Parliament to coordinate fiscal and monetary policies? Explain the pros and cons.

9. Why is it important to policymakers that people believe them when they say they are going to reduce inflation? How can they increase their credibility?

## NUMERICAL PROBLEMS

1.    Calculate the money multiplier for each of the following cases.
    (a) $cu = .40$ and $res = .07$
    (b) $cu = .40$ and $res = .08$
    (c) $cu = .45$ and $res = .07$

2.    The money supply is $12 million, currency held by the public is $2 million, and the reserve-deposit ratio is 0.2.

    a.    What is the quantity of bank deposits?
    b.    What is the quantity of bank reserves?
    c.    What is the quantity of the monetary base?
    d.    What is the money multiplier (give a number)?

## ANALYTICAL QUESTIONS

1.    Given an economy with no currency and a reserve-deposit ratio of 10%, explain how much money the banking system creates when the Bank of Canada buys a $1000 bond from a bank.

2.    The inflation rate is 4% and the unemployment rate is 5%. The central bank tells firms that it will reduce the growth of the money supply over the next year so that prices will rise only 3% instead of 4%. Should the firms believe the central bank and raise their prices only 3%, or should they be doubtful that the central bank will really do what it says, which means firms should raise their prices 4%? The following diagram shows the payoffs.

Firms' strategy

|  | Raise prices 4% | Raise prices 3% |
|---|---|---|
| **Keep money growth same**<br><br>Central bank's strategy | **Outcome A**<br><br>Bank:  0<br>Firms:  10<br><br>$\pi = 4\%$<br>$u = 5\%$ | **Outcome B**<br><br>Bank:  10<br>Firms:  0<br><br>$\pi = 3\%$<br>$u = 4\%$ |
| **Lower money growth** | **Outcome C**<br><br>Bank: -5<br>Firms: -10<br><br>$\pi = 4\%$<br>$u = 6\%$ | **Outcome D**<br><br>Bank: 5<br>Firms:  20<br><br>$\pi = 3\%$<br>$u = 5\%$ |

a.  If the central bank can move first, what will be the outcome of this game?

b.  Now suppose the firms move first. What will be the outcome?

## ANSWERS TO MULTIPLE-CHOICE QUESTIONS

| Number | Answer | | Number | Answer | | Number | Answer |
|--------|--------|---|--------|--------|---|--------|--------|
| 1 | c | | 11 | a | | 21 | d |
| 2 | c | | 12 | d | | 22 | b |
| 3 | d | | 13 | c | | 23 | a |
| 4 | c | | 14 | c | | 24 | c |
| 5 | c | | 15 | a | | 25 | a |
| 6 | d | | 16 | b | | 26 | c |
| 7 | a | | 17 | a | | 27 | d |
| 8 | c | | 18 | b | | | |
| 9 | a | | 19 | d | | | |
| 10 | d | | 20 | a | | | |

## ANSWERS TO REVIEW QUESTIONS

1.  (1)  The monetary base (*BASE*) is positively related to the money supply; an increase in the base increases the money supply. The Bank of Canada controls the monetary base.

    (2)  The reserve-deposit ratio (*res*) is negatively related to the money supply; an increase in the reserve-deposit ratio reduces the money multiplier and thus reduces the money supply. The Bank of Canada sets the minimum reserve requirement ratio on bank deposits, but the private banks can change the reserve-deposit ratio by changing their holdings of excess reserves (i.e., reserves in excess of required reserves).

    (3)  The currency-deposit ratio (*cu*) is negatively related to the money supply; an increase in the currency-deposit ratio reduces the money multiplier and thus reduces the money supply. The public (i.e., everyone except banks, thrifts, and the Bank of Canada) controls the currency-deposit ratio by deciding how much of their money they want to retain as currency, rather than as deposits in banks and thrift institutions.

2.  Open-market operations are the most commonly used policy instrument for changing the money supply. The Bank of Canada can increase the money supply by making an open-market purchase of government securities (bonds) from the public or banks. An open-market purchase increases currency in circulation and bank reserves, which is an increase in the monetary base. An increase in the monetary base increases the money supply by the amount of the money multiplier times the increase in the money base. Alternatively, the Bank of Canada can reduce the monetary base and the money supply by making an open-market sale of government securities.

3.  The leadership of the Bank of Canada is provided by the Board of Directors. The board of directors consists of a governor, the senior deputy governor, the deputy minister of finance and 12 directors. The Governor of the Bank of Canada has considerable power, and has a term of seven years. The part-time directors are private citizens and are appointed for three-year terms. The governor is appointed by the board, with the government's approval, for a renewable seven-year term.

4.  Keynesians do not believe that the economy is stable and self-regulating. Consequently, the economy does not quickly recover from recessions. Unlike monetarists, Keynesians believe that the Bank of Canada is reasonably efficient and can use monetary stabilization policy efficiently. Keynesians contend that using monetary policy would greatly reduce the magnitude of the business cycle.

5.  Goals: Maintain low inflation and unemployment in a stable economic environment with steady interest rates and exchange rates. If you are a Keynesian, you believe that activist policy is desirable, as the Bank of Canada can offset shocks to the economy. Monetarists see activist policy as destabilizing, partly because of the long and variable lags associated with monetary policy. Classical (*RBC*) economists see no need for activist policy, since the economy is self-correcting.

6.  The monetarists recommend that the Bank of Canada choose a monetary aggregate as an intermediate target, such as M2. They propose a monetary aggregate target for several reasons. First, they do not believe that nominal shocks are an important source of instability in the economy. In the monetarist view, money demand is reasonably stable. Second, they believe that the macroeconomy is reasonably stable and self-regulating, and normally operates at full-employment output, consistent with the natural unemployment rate. Third, they believe that the money supply largely determines the level of aggregate demand, and that aggregate demand determines the price level; therefore the money supply determines the price level. Fourth, in a stable economy operating at full employment, the ultimate target of monetary policy should be to maintain price level stability (i.e., zero inflation). Fifth, to hit the price level target, the Bank of Canada needs to achieve a constant rate of money supply growth.

7.  Rules provide credibility, but there may be a need for flexibility to respond to conditions that the rules didn't anticipate.

8.  The value of Bank of Canada independence is that it prevents political pressure from influencing the money supply process. On the other hand, if fiscal and monetary policy aren't coordinated, there may be large swings in the real interest rate and/or output if the policies move in opposite directions.

9.  If policymakers are credible, inflation expectations will fall quickly, reducing the costs of disinflation. Credibility can be enhanced by building a reputation, following a rule, appointing a tough central banker, changing the incentives of the central banker, or increasing central bank independence.

## ANSWERS TO NUMERICAL PROBLEMS

1.  The money multiplier = $(cu + 1)/(cu + res)$.

    (a) For $cu = .40$ and $res = .07$, the money multiplier = $1.40/0.47 = 2.98$.
    (b) For $cu = .40$ and $res = .08$, the money multiplier = $1.40/0.48 = 2.92$.
    (c) For $cu = .45$ and $res = .07$, the money multiplier = $1.45/0.52 = 2.79$.

2.  a.  $10 million
    b.  $2 million
    c.  $4 million
    d.  3

## ANSWERS TO ANALYTICAL QUESTIONS

1.  For an economy with no currency and a reserve-deposit ratio of 10%, a $1000 open-market purchase from a bank increases the bank's excess reserves by $1000. The bank can make loans up to the limit of its excess reserves, so it makes a $1000 loan to some borrower. The borrower deposits the amount of the loan in his bank account. The bank retains 10% of the $1000 deposit as reserves and now makes a $900 loan, using its excess reserves. The amount of the $900 loan is deposited in a second bank, which retains 10% as reserves and makes a loan for the $810 balance. The borrower deposits the amount of the $810 loan in a third bank, which retains 10% as reserves and lends out the balance. When all possible loans have been made by the banking system, this multiple expansion of loans and deposits will increase the money supply by (1/.10) x $1000 = $10,000.

2.  a.  If the central bank can move first, it will reason as follows. If it keeps money growth the same, firms can raise prices 4% and earn a payoff of 10, or they can raise prices 3% and earn a payoff of 0; clearly they'll raise prices 4%. If the central bank lowers money growth, firms can raise prices 4% and earn a payoff of -10, or they can raise prices 3% and earn a payoff of 20; clearly they'll raise prices 3%. So if the central bank keeps money growth the same, firms raise prices 4%, outcome A is reached and the central bank's payoff is 0. If the central bank lowers money growth, firms raise prices 3%, outcome D is reached, and the central bank's payoff is 5. Since the central bank is better off with a payoff of 5, it will choose to lower money growth.

    b.  If firms can move first, they will reason as follows. If they raise prices 4%, the central bank can keep money growth the same and earn a payoff of 0, or lower money growth and earn a payoff of -5; clearly they'll keep money growth the same. If firms raise prices 3%, the central bank can keep money growth the same and earn a payoff of 10, or they can lower money growth and earn a payoff of 5; clearly they'll keep money growth the same. So if firms raise prices 4%, the central bank will keep money growth the same, outcome A is reached and the firms' payoff is 10. If firms raise prices 3%, the central bank will keep money growth the same, outcome B is reached, and the firms' payoff is 0. Since firms are better off with a payoff of 10, they will choose to raise prices 4%.

# CHAPTER 15: GOVERNMENT SPENDING AND ITS FINANCING

## INTRODUCTION

This chapter examines fiscal policy and its macroeconomic effects. Section 15.1 looks at definitions and facts about the government's budget. Section 15.2 examines the effects of government spending and taxes on economic activity. The burden of government debt on future generations is discussed in Section 15.3. Section 15.4 covers the link between budget deficits and inflation.

This is a very policy-oriented chapter. Pay close attention to the main facts about government debt and deficits in Section 15.1, as some are surprising, and they'll help you understand why the government debt is of such great concern to economists. Also, you'll understand a lot about how economists think about taxes if you understand the different effects of changes in marginal tax rates compared to average tax rates, which are discussed in Section 15.2. They'll help you figure out the incentive effects and distortions caused by taxes.

## CHAPTER OUTLINE

I.  The Government Budget: Some Facts and Figures (Sec. 15.1)
    A.  Government outlays
        1.  Three categories of government expenditures
            a.  Government purchases ($G$)
                (1)  Government investment, which is about 1/6 of total government purchases, consists of purchases of capital goods
                (2)  Government consumption expenditures are about 5/6 of total government purchases
            b.  Transfer payments ($TR$)
                (1)  Transfers are expenditures for which the government receives no current goods or services in return
                (2)  Examples: Old Age Security benefits, pensions for government retirees, welfare payments
            c.  Net interest payments (INT)
                (1)  Interest paid to holders of government bonds less interest received by the government
                (2)  Government makes loans to students, farmers, small businesses
        2.  Total (Federal, provincial, and local) government outlays are about one-third of GDP (text Fig. 15.1)
            a.  Government purchases increased enormously in World War II
                (1)  Government purchases rose in other wars as well
                (2)  Since the late-1940s, government purchases have been about 22% of GDP
            b.  Transfer payments have been rising steadily
                (1)  Many social programs, including Old Age Security and Employment Insurance have expanded over time
            c.  Net interest payments have also changed over time
                (1)  Interest payments rose from 2.9% of GDP in 1942 to 4.6% of GDP in 1946
                (2)  They nearly doubled in the 1980s, as both the government debt and interest rates increased sharply
                (3)  They've declined in the 1990s because of lower interest rates and government budget surpluses

3. Comparing Canadian government spending to that of other countries shows that Canada 's rate of government spending is comparable to those of Western European countries but higher than those in the United States and Japan

B. Revenue
   1. Total tax collections have increased over time, from about 18% of GDP in 1940 to 32% in 1998 (text Fig. 15.2)
   2. Three principal categories
      a. Direct taxes
      b. Indirect taxes
      c. Investment income
   3. The composition of outlays and taxes: the Federal government versus provincial and local governments
      a. To see the overall picture of government spending, we usually combine Federal, provincial, and local government spending
      b. But the composition of the Federal government budget is quite different from provincial and local government budgets (text Table 15.2)
         (1) Consumption expenditures
            (a) About two thirds of provincial and local current expenditures are purchases of goods and services
            (b) By contrast, less than 1/4 of Federal current expenditures are for purchases
            (c) Of all government purchases of nondefense goods and services, about four-fifths is done by provincial and local governments
         (2) Transfer payments
            (a) The Federal government budget is more heavily weighted to transfers than provincial and local budgets
         (3) Transfers to provinces and local governments are payments from the Federal government to provincial and local governments
         (4) Interest payments
            (a) Net interest is significant and positive for the Federal government
            (b) It is negative for provincial and local governments, because they hold substantial amounts of government bonds
         (5) Composition of revenue
            (a) Personal taxes account for about 58% of Federal receipts, but only 28% of provincial and local government receipts

C. Surpluses or Deficits
   1. When outlays exceed revenues, there is a deficit; when revenues exceed outlays, there is a surplus
   2. Formally, surplus = revenues - expenditures = tax revenue – government purchases - transfers + net interest $= T - G + TR + INT$    (15.1)

3. Another useful surplus definition is the primary government budget surplus, which excludes net interest payments: primary surplus = tax revenue − expenditures + net interest = tax revenue − government purchases - transfers = $T - G - TR$    (15.2)

4. a. The total surplus tells the amount the government must borrow to cover all its expenditures
   b. The primary surplus tells if the government's receipts are enough to cover its current purchases and transfers
   c. The primary surplus ignores interest payments, because those are payments for past government spending

5. The current surplus and primary current surplus usually move together over time (text Fig. 15.4)
   a. Large current deficits occurred in World War II, the mid-1970s, and the early 1980s
   b. The primary current deficit became a primary surplus in some years in the 1980s and 1990s, but large interest payments kept the overall deficit large until the late 1990s

II. Government Spending, Taxes, and the Macroeconomy (Sec. 15.2)
   A. Fiscal policy and aggregate demand
      1. An increase in government purchases increases aggregate demand by shifting the *IS* curve up
      2. The effect of tax changes depends on the economic model
         a. Classical economists accept the Ricardian equivalence proposition that lump-sum tax changes have no effect on national saving or on aggregate demand
         b. Keynesians think a tax cut is likely to increase consumption and decrease saving, thus increasing aggregate demand
      3. Classicals and Keynesians disagree about using fiscal policy to stabilize the economy
         a. Classicals oppose activist policy while Keynesians favor it
         b. But even Keynesians admit that fiscal policy is difficult to use
            (1) There is a lack of flexibility, because much of government spending is committed years in advance
            (2) There are long time lags, because the political process takes time to make changes
      4. Automatic stabilizers and the full-employment surplus or deficit
         a. Automatic stabilizers cause fiscal policy to be countercyclical by changing government spending or taxes automatically
         b. One example is unemployment insurance, which causes transfers to rise in recessions
         c. The most important automatic stabilizer is the income tax system, since people pay less tax when their incomes are low in recessions, and they pay more tax when their incomes are high in booms
         d. Because of automatic stabilizers, the government budget surplus falls in recessions and rises in booms
            (1) The full-employment surplus is a measure of what the government budget surplus would be if the economy were at full employment
            (2) So the full-employment surplus doesn't change with the business cycle, only with changes in government policy regarding spending and taxation
            (3) The actual budget surplus is much larger than the full-employment budget surplus in recessions (text Fig. 15.5)

5.  Federal-provincial fiscal policy coordination
    a.  In studying the macroeconomic effects of federal fiscal policy, we also need to keep track of provincial fiscal policy
        (1) If the federal government reduces income tax rates as part of tax reform or as part of expansionary policy and if provincial governments respond by raising their tax rates by the same amount, the behaviour of the private sector will not change
        (2) If the federal government reduces its planned transfers to provincial and local governments to try to reduce the deficit, two things may happen:
            (a)  Provincial governments may increase taxes in response to the decline in tax revenue (but their deficits may rise too)
            (b)  If provincial taxes do not increase, then the deficit of the public sector as a whole, may be unchanged by the change in fiscal policy at one level because the policy is not coordinated
    b.  A reduction in transfers from one level of government to another if called "off-loading"
    c.  The federal government transfers funds to provincial governments for spending on health, post-secondary education and social assistance in the form of the Canada Health and Social Transfer (CHST)
        (1) CHST was reduced as part of the federal government deficit reduction strategy in the mid-1990's
        (2) Different recipients were treated differently, with Alberta, British Columbia and Ontario receiving smaller transfers per capita
        (3) The CHST is distinct from equalization payments, which were made to provincial governments in relatively poor provinces so they may provide public services comparable with those in other provinces while keeping per capita tax burdens roughly equal across provinces
    d.  The allocation of spending and revenue between levels of government is known as "fiscal federalism"
        (1) The coordination of fiscal policy involves elements of bargaining and strategy
        (2) The most noticeable recent example is the bargaining between the federal government and most provincial governments over sales tax harmonization, reform of Canada Pension Plan and the scale of payroll taxes

B.  Government capital formation
    1.  Fiscal policy affects the economy through the formation of government capital—long-lived physical assets owned by the government, like roads, schools, and sewer systems
    2.  Also, fiscal policy affects human capital formation through expenditures on health, nutrition, and education
    3.  Data on government investment include only physical capital, not human capital
        a.  In 1996, 2/3 of federal government investment was on national defense and 1/3 on nondefense capital
        b.  Most federal government investment is in equipment, but most provincial and local government investment is for structures

C.  Incentive effects of fiscal policy
    1.  Average versus marginal tax rates
        a.  Average tax rate = total taxes / pretax income
        b.  Marginal tax rate = taxes due from an additional dollar of income
        c.  Example: Suppose taxes are imposed at a rate of 20% on income over $5000
            (1) For someone earning less than $5000, the marginal tax rate and average tax rate are both zero
            (2) Anyone earning over $5000 would have a marginal tax rate of .20
            (3) Someone earning $10,000 would pay ($10,000 - $5000) x .20 = $1000 in taxes, so he *or* she would have an average tax rate of .10
            (4) Someone earning $20,000 would pay ($20,000 - $5000) x .20 = $3000 in taxes, so he or she would have an average tax rate of .15
        d.  The distinction between average and marginal tax rates affects people's decisions about how much labour to supply

(1) If the average tax rate increases, with the marginal tax rate held constant, a person will increase labour supply
   (a) The higher average tax rate causes an income effect
   (b) With lower income, a person consumes less and wants less leisure, so he or she works more
   (c) The labour supply curve shifts right
(2) If the marginal tax rate increases, with the average tax rate held constant, a person will decrease labour supply
   (a) The higher marginal tax rate causes a substitution effect
   (b) With a lower after-tax reward for working, a person wants to work less
   (c) The labour supply curve shifts left

2. Application: The poverty trap
   a. According to the analysis in the text, a decrease in marginal tax rates should lead to an increase in labour supply. While the direction of this change in not controversial, the size of this effect is
   b. In the United States, a group of economists, politicians and journalists have argued for an approach to economic policy known as "supply-side economics"
      (1) Their basic belief is that all aspects of economic behaviour—such as labour supply, saving and investment—respond to economic incentives and to incentives provided by the tax code
      (2) Supply-siders claim that incentive effects of tax policy are much larger than most economists traditionally believed
      (3) Moreover, supply-siders argue that the amounts of labour supplied would increase substantially as a result of income tax reductions
   c. While supply-side economics has not been as influential in Canada, there has been considerable debate about Canadian marginal income tax rates
      (1) Some commentators have argued that marginal tax rates, which are higher in Canada than in the United States discourage labour supply of highly skilled workers, by encouraging them to emigrate
   d. It is surprising that some of the highest marginal tax rates are faced by relatively poor Canadians
      (1) Higher effective marginal tax rates are possible because transfers under several social programs depend on a household's income
      (2) As income increases the benefits may fall in order to limit the transfers to high-income earners
      (3) A household that earns an additional dollar in wages may lose almost as much in benefits, as its income rises above a cut-off point
      (4) According to our analysis these high marginal tax rates (combined with low average tax rates) should act to discourage labour supply. This situation is known as the "poverty trap"
   e. Eliminating the poverty trap is challenging for two reasons
      (1) Defraying the costs that low-income workers face when entering the labour force costs money
      (2) Removing the trap requires coordination between the federal government, which is responsible for most refundable income tax credits, and provincial governments, which administer social assistance

3. Tax-induced distortions and tax rate smoothing
   a. In the absence of taxes, the free market works efficiently
      (1) Taxes change economic behavior, reducing welfare
      (2) Thus tax-induced deviations from free-market outcomes are called distortions
   b. The difference between the number of hours a worker would work without taxes and the number of hours he or she actually works when there is a tax reflects the tax distortion
   c. The higher the tax rate, the greater the distortion
   d. Fiscal policymakers would like to raise the needed amount of government revenue while minimizing distortions

e.  It's better to keep the tax rate constant over time than to raise it and lower it, because the higher tax rate has a higher distortion
    (1)  For example, keeping the tax rate at a steady 15% is better than having it at 10% one year and 20% the next, since the distortions in the second year are much higher
    (2)  Keeping a constant tax rate over time is called tax rate smoothing
    (3)  Empirical studies suggest that the Federal government hasn't always smoothed tax rates as much as it could to minimize distortions
    (4)  But borrowing to finance wars, thus avoiding the need to raise taxes a lot in war years, is consistent with the idea of tax rate smoothing

III.  Government Deficits and Debt (Sec. 15.3)
    A.  The growth of the government debt
        1.  The deficit is the difference between expenditures and revenues in any fiscal year
        2.  The debt is the total value of outstanding government bonds on a given date
        3.  The deficit is the change in the debt in a year
            a.  $\Delta B$ = nominal government budget deficit    (15.3)
            b.  $B$ = nominal value of government bonds outstanding
        4.  A useful measure of government's indebtedness that accounts for the ability to pay off the debt is the debt–GDP ratio
            a.  The Canadian debt–GDP ratio (text Fig. 15.7) fell from over 100% after World War II to a low point in the mid-1970s
            b.  Since 1980 the debt–GDP ratio has risen sharply, though it's been declining a bit in recent years

5. Growth rate of debt–GDP ratio = primary deficit/$B + i$ - growth rate of nominal GDP (15.6), where $i$ is the nominal interest rate
   a. So three things cause the debt–GDP ratio to rise
      (1) A high primary deficit
      (2) A high real interest rate
      (3) A low rate of GDP growth
   b. During World War II, large primary deficits raised the debt–GDP ratio
   c. For the next 35 years, primary deficits were small or negative, so the debt–GDP ratio fell
   d. After 1980 the debt–GDP ratio rose, both because of high primary deficits and because interest rates exceeded GDP growth rates

B. The burden of the government debt on future generations
   1. People worry that their children will have to pay back the debt that past generations have accumulated
   2. But Canadian citizens own most government bonds, so future generations will just be paying themselves
   3. However, there could be a burden, because if tax rates have to be raised in the future to pay off the debt, the higher tax rates could be distortionary
   4. Also, since bondholders are richer on average than nonbondholders, when the debt was repaid there would be a large transfer from the poor to the rich
   5. Finally, government deficits reduce national saving according to many economists
      a. If so, with lower saving there will be lower investment
      b. Lower investment means a smaller capital stock
      c. A smaller capital stock means less output in the future
      d. So the future standard of living will be lower
      e. However, this assumes that government deficits reduce national saving; that is a key and unsettled question

C. Box 15.1: How large is the federal surplus?
   1. The measures of the federal surplus in this chapter are on a "national accounts" basis. In 2000, the federal surplus on this basis was $15.5 billion. However, two other ways of measuring the federal surplus are also common
      a. First, when the federal government presents its budget, it quotes the surplus on a "public accounts" or "budgetary" basis. For the 2000-2001 fiscal year, the budgetary surplus was $17.1 billion
      b. One source of the budgetary surplus in 2000-2001 was the excess of Employment Insurance (EI) premiums over benefits, which amounted to $7.3 billion. Though this amount is not in a separate fund, the size of this gap between revenue from payroll taxes and EI benefits has led some economists, and provincial governments, to argue for a reduction in EI premiums
   2. The public accounts exclude certain "non-budgetary" items, such as loans and advances by the government, the accounts of the pension plan of government employees, and revenue from the Exchange Fund Account. When these items are added to the public accounts deficit, we have a "financial requirements" surplus, which gives the amount by which debt can be reduced
   3. The main source of difference between the budgetary balance and the financial requirements balance was the Exchange Fund Account, which had a deficit of $8.8 billion
   4. The federal government's budget does not include the Canada Pension Plan. During 2000, the CPP ran a surplus of $3.5 billion, while the QPP surplus was $427 million
   5. The CPP must run surpluses today because the proportion of the population eligible for retirement benefits will be much larger in 25 years
   6. One reason to emphasize that the Canadian federal government's surplus does not include the CPP is that the situation is different in the United States
      a. There, the federal surplus does not include the Social Security system, which accounts for most of the large surpluses run by the U.S. federal government in the late 1990s
   7. These examples show how difficult it may be to interpret the deficit. For this reason, Laurence Kotlikoff, of Boston University, has argued that the current deficit is not useful as an indicator of fiscal policy. Research on alternate measures are examined in Box 15.2: Generational accounts

D.  Box 15.2: Generational accounts
   1.  For many purposes, looking at the taxes and transfers people get over their entire lifetimes is useful—generation accounting
   2.  Oreopoulos and others find that the net tax rate on each generation had been rising over time until 1960, so that earlier generations had borne less of a fiscal burden than later generations
   3.  But since 1960, the burden has fallen
   4.  Because of recent Federal government surpluses, the burden on future generations isn't much higher than that faced by other generations
       a.  But similar research a few years ago showed a much higher burden, thanks to a growing ratio of debt-GDP
E.  Budget deficits and national saving: Ricardian equivalence revisited
   1.  When will a government deficit reduce national saving?
       a.  It almost certainly does when government spending rises
       b.  But it may not for a cut in taxes or increase in transfers
   2.  Ricardian equivalence: an example
       a.  Suppose the government cuts taxes by $100 per person
       b.  Since $S = Y - C - G$, national saving declines only if consumption rises (assuming $Y$ is fixed at its full-employment level)
       c.  Consumption might not rise if people realize that a tax cut today must be financed by higher taxes in the future
          (1)  A tax cut of $100 per person could be financed by a tax increase of $(1+r)\$100$ next year
          (2)  Then taxpayers' ability to consume is the same with or without the tax cut
          (3)  People will simply save the tax cut so they can pay off the future taxes
       d.  As a result, national saving should be unaffected
   3.  Ricardian equivalence across generations
       a.  What if the higher future taxes are to be paid by future generations?
       b.  Then people might consume more today, because they wouldn't have to pay the higher future taxes
       c.  But as Barro pointed out, if people care about their children, they'll increase their bequests to their children so their children can pay the higher future taxes
          (1)  After all, if people wanted to consume at their children's expense, they could have lowered their planned bequests
          (2)  So why should the fact that the government gives people a tax cut cause them to consume at their children's expense?
F.  Departures from Ricardian equivalence
   1.  The data show that Ricardian equivalence holds sometimes, but not always
       a.  It certainly didn't hold in Canada in the 1980s, when high government deficits were accompanied by low savings
       b.  It did seem to hold in Canada and Israel sometimes
       c.  But overall, there seems to be little relationship between government budget deficits and national saving
   2.  What are the main reasons Ricardian equivalence may fail?
       a.  Borrowing constraints
          (1)  If people can't borrow as much as they would like, a tax cut financed by higher future taxes essentially lets them borrow from the government
       b.  Shortsightedness
          (1)  If people don't foresee the higher future taxes, or spend based on rules of thumb about their current after-tax income, they may increase consumption in response to a tax cut
       c.  Failure to leave bequests
          (1)  People may not leave bequests because they don't care about their children, or because they think their children will be richer than they are, so they will increase consumption spending in response to a tax cut
       d.  Non–lump-sum taxes
          (1)  When taxes aren't lump sum, changes in tax rates affect economic decisions
          (2)  However, a tax cut won't necessarily lead to an increase in consumption in this case

IV. Deficits and Inflation (Sec. 15.4)
  A.  The deficit and the money supply
    1.  Inflation results when aggregate demand rises more quickly than aggregate supply
    2.  Budget deficits could be related to inflation, but we usually think of expansionary fiscal policy as leading to a one-time jump in the price level, not a sustained inflation
    3.  The only way for a sustained inflation to occur is for there to be sustained growth in the money supply
    4.  Can government deficits lead to ongoing increases in the money supply?
      a.  Yes, if spending is financed by printing    money
      b.  The revenue that a government raises by printing money is called *seignorage*
      c.  Usually, governments don't just buy things directly with newly printed money, they do so indirectly
        (1)  The Treasury borrows by issuing government bonds
        (2)  The central bank buys the bonds with newly printed money
        (3)  The relationship between the deficit and the increase in the monetary base is

$$\text{deficit} = \Delta B = \Delta B^p + \Delta B^{cb} = \Delta B^p + \Delta BASE$$
        (15.8)

        (4)  $\Delta B$ is the increase in government debt, which is divided into government debt held by the public $B^p$ and government debt held by the central bank $B^{cb}$
        (5)  Changes in $B^{cb}$ equal changes in the monetary base $BASE$
        (6)  In an all-currency economy, the change in the monetary base is equal to the change in the money supply

(a) $\pi = 8\%$

(b) $\pi = 1\%$ and $\pi = 15\%$

Figure 15.1

5.  Why would governments use money creation to finance deficits, knowing that it causes inflation?
    a.  Developed countries rarely use seignorage, because it doesn't raise much revenue
    b.  But war-torn or developed countries are unable to raise sufficient tax revenue to cover government spending and may not be able to borrow from the public
B.  Real seignorage collection and inflation
    1.  The real revenue the government gets from seignorage is closely related to the inflation rate
    2.  Consider an all-currency economy with a fixed level of real output and a fixed real interest rate, plus constant rates of money growth and inflation
        a.  The real quantity of money demanded is constant, so real money supply must be constant
        b.  Thus $\pi = \Delta M/M$    (15.10)
        c.  Real seignorage revenue $R$ is $\Delta M/P$, but since $\pi = \Delta M/M$, $R = \Delta M/P = \pi M/P$    (15.12)
    3.  Seignorage is called the inflation tax, because the government's seignorage revenue equals the inflation rate times real money balances
        a.  So seignorage is like a tax (at the rate of inflation) on real money balances
        b.  The government collects its revenue from the inflation tax when it buys goods with newly printed money
        c.  The inflation tax is paid by everyone who holds money
    4.  Will a rise in money growth increase seignorage revenue?
        a.  As the money growth rate rises, inflation rises, but people may hold less real balances
        b.  Whether seignorage rises or falls depends on whether inflation rises more or less than the decline in real money holdings (Fig. 15.1; like text Fig. 15.8)
        c.  Real seignorage revenue is shown by the shaded rectangles in the figures, which represent $\pi M/P$
        d.  At low inflation rates, seignorage is low
        e.  As the inflation rate rises, seignorage rises
        f.  But at some inflation rate, seignorage begins to decline because of the decline in real money demand
        g.  Plotting inflation against real seignorage revenue illustrates this result (Fig. 15.2; like text Fig. 15.9)
    5.  If governments raise money supply too rapidly, they may cause hyperinflation, but get less seignorage revenue than they would get with less money growth
        1.  In Germany after World War I, inflation reached 322% per month
        2.  Cagan estimated the inflation rate that maximizes seignorage at only 20% per month

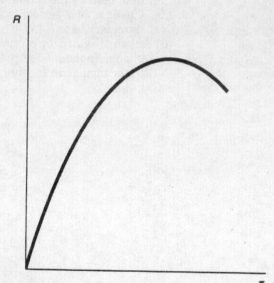

Figure 15.2

V.  Appendix 15.A: The Debt-GDP Ratio
  A.  Let $Q$ be the ratio of nominal government debt to nominal GDP: $Q = B/PY$    (15.A.1)
  B.  Transforming this into percent change form gives: $\Delta Q/Q = \Delta B/B - \Delta(PY)/PY$    (15.A.2)
  C.  The nominal budget deficit ($\Delta B$) equals the nominal primary deficit plus nominal interest payments on the debt: $\Delta B = PD^P + iB$    (15.A.3)
  D.  Use Eq. (15.A.3) to substitute for $\Delta B$ in Eq. (15.A.2) to get: $\Delta Q/Q = PD^P/B + i - \Delta(PY)/PY$  (15.A.4)
  E.  This is the same as Eq. (15.6) in the text

**MULTIPLE-CHOICE QUESTIONS**

1.  What portion of nondefense government purchases of goods and services is carried out by provincial and local governments?
    a.   One-third
    b.   One-half
    c.   Two-thirds
    d.   Five-sixths

2.  The primary deficit is
    a.   the amount by which government purchases, transfers, and net interest exceed tax revenues.
    b.   the amount by which government purchases and transfers exceed tax revenues.
    c.   the deficit plus net interest payments.
    d.   total tax revenues minus net interest minus government expenditures.

3.  The primary current deficit is
    a.   the deficit minus tax revenues.
    b.   the deficit minus net interest.
    c.   the current deficit minus tax revenues.
    d.   the current deficit minus net interest.

4.  According to Keynesian economists, the primary problem with using fiscal policy as a stabilization tool is that
    a.   fiscal policy does not have the effect on output in practice that it should have in theory.
    b.   fiscal policy will be effective only if it is funded through lump-sum tax changes.
    c.   fiscal policy will be effective only if it is funded through permanent changes in taxes.
    d.   fiscal policy is inflexible because a large portion of government spending is planned years in advance and cannot easily be changed.

5.  An example of an automatic stabilizer is
    a.   consumer spending.
    b.   inflation.
    c.   unemployment insurance.
    d.   discretionary fiscal policy.

6.  The full-employment deficit is
    a.   the number of jobs needed to restore full employment.
    b.   what the government budget deficit would be if the economy were at full employment.
    c.   the increase in government spending that would be needed to return the economy to full employment.
    d.   the extra amount paid to government workers under the National Recovery Act.

7.  The average tax rate is
    a.   the fraction of an additional dollar of income that must be paid in taxes.
    b.   the total amount of taxes paid divided by after-tax income.
    c.   the total amount of taxes paid divided by before-tax income.
    d.   the average amount of government spending that is financed by taxes.

8.  A decrease in the average tax rate, with the marginal tax rate held constant, will
    a.  increase the amount of labour supplied at any real wage.
    b.  not affect the amount of labour supplied at any real wage.
    c.  decrease the amount of labour supplied at any real wage.
    d.  increase the amount of labour supplied at any real wage if the average tax rate is above the marginal tax rate, but decrease the amount of labour supplied at any real wage if the average tax rate is below the marginal tax rate.

9.  Assuming that market prices are efficient, imposing taxes on various economic activities creates
    a.  distortions.
    b.  a budget surplus.
    c.  an efficient tax system.
    d.  tax rate smoothing.

10. If a government is highly committed to tax rate smoothing, it will
    a.  require annually balanced fiscal budgets.
    b.  reduce tax rates during a recession.
    c.  tax every activity and every source of income at the same tax rate.
    d.  not change tax rates frequently to finance fluctuations in government spending.

11. The debt-GDP ratio in Canada
    a.  steadily fell after World War II.
    b.  steadily increased after World War II.
    c.  fell from the end of World War II until around 1970 and rose thereafter.
    d.  fell from the end of World War II until around 1980 and rose thereafter.

12. Assume that the lost output due to tax distortions is proportional to the square of the tax rate. If the government increased the tax rate from 25% to 40%, the lost output would increase by a factor of
    a.  1.56.
    b.  1.60.
    c.  1.96.
    d.  2.56.

13. An expansionary fiscal policy will not cause an increase in the price level if the government
    a.  reduces the corporate income tax rate.
    b.  increases purchases in the classical model.
    c.  lowers taxes and Ricardian equivalence does not hold.
    d.  lowers taxes and Ricardian equivalence holds.

14. According to the Ricardian equivalence proposition, a government budget deficit created by a temporary tax cut
    a.  does not affect desired national saving.
    b.  does not affect expected future taxes.
    c.  reduces desired investment spending.
    d.  increases the real interest rate.

15. Suppose a temporary tax cut today is combined with a rise in tax rates on the next generation of taxpayers. This long delay in increasing future taxes would not in itself cause the Ricardian equivalence proposition to fail to accurately predict the effects of the tax cut, unless the
   a.    parents failed to leave bequests.
   b.    parents saved the tax cut.
   c.    parents invested the tax cut.
   d.    parents were far-sighted in their expectations of future tax increases.

16. A decrease in taxes on the current generation would have no effect on consumption or national saving if
   a.    individuals face borrowing constraints.
   b.    individuals increase their consumption by less than the tax cut.
   c.    consumers bequeath all of the tax cut to the next generation.
   d.    consumers are not forward looking concerning their future tax burden.

17. Which of the following would *not* be an argument that government debt imposes a burden on future generations?
   a.    Lump-sum taxes in the future may be raised to pay higher real interest costs.
   b.    Higher taxes in the future could increase the average cost of distortions to the economy created by taxes.
   c.    Higher taxes in the future to repay government debt will transfer resources from the poor to the rich.
   d.    Higher government deficits resulting from increased purchases may reduce savings, causing investment to fall.

18. In Canada, which of the following is the least involved in the federal budget process?
   a.    The Canadian prime minister
   b.    The Members of Cabinet
   c.    The Members of Parliament
   d.    The Bank of Canada

19. Real seignorage revenue is most likely to be a significant source of revenue for
   a.    international development organizations.
   b.    developing countries during times of war.
   c.    developed countries during periods of slow output growth.
   d.    periods of disinflation.

20. Assuming that output is fixed, the real revenue raised by government from printing money in an all-currency economy is
   a.    the real money supply.
   b.    the inflation rate times the real money supply.
   c.    the real interest rate times the real money supply.
   d.    the tax rate times the increase in the growth rate of output.

21. The inflation tax is primarily a tax on
   a.    government bonds.
   b.    Old Age Security recipients.
   c.    money.
   d.    real income.

22. Consider an economy that has the following monetary data:

    Currency in circulation = $ 300
    Bank reserves           = $  50
    Monetary base           = $ 350
    Deposits                = $ 700
    Money supply            = $1000

    The monetary base and the money supply are expected to grow at a constant rate of 20% per year. Inflation and expected inflation are 20% per year. Suppose that bank reserves and currency pay no interest, all currency is held by the public, and bank deposits pay no interest. What is the profit to the banks from the inflation?
    a.   $130
    b.   $140
    c.   $190
    d.   $200

23. Suppose that all workers place a value on their leisure of 75 goods per day. The production function relating output per day $Y$ to the number of people working per day $N$ is
    $$Y = 500N - 0.4 N^2$$
    and the marginal product of labour is
    $$MPN = 500 - 0.8 N.$$
    A 25% tax is levied on wages. Output per day would be
    a.   100,000.
    b.   150,000.
    c.   200,000.
    d.   250,000.

24. Suppose that all workers place a value on their leisure of 75 goods per day. The production function relating output per day $Y$ to the number of people working per day $N$ is
    $$Y = 500N - 0.4 N^2$$
    and the marginal product of labour is
    $$MPN = 500 - 0.8 N.$$
    A 25% tax is levied on wages. In terms of lost output, what is the cost of the distortion introduced by this tax?
    a.    63
    b.    531
    c.    2734
    d.    3751

25. Assume that the lost output due to tax distortions is proportional to the square of the tax rate. If the average cost of the distortion created by taxes is currently $100, and the tax rate is increased from 20% to 50%, the average cost of the distortion created by taxes will increase to
    a.   $169.
    b.   $225.
    c.   $250.
    d.   $625.

## REVIEW QUESTIONS

1.  How is the primary budget surplus related to the budget surplus?

2.  Compare and contrast automatic stabilizers and discretionary fiscal stabilization policy in terms of flexibility and policy lags.

3.  Compare and contrast the effects of automatic stabilizers during recessions on the budget deficit and on the full-employment deficit.

4.  Why do economists endorse tax rate smoothing?

5.  Why should governments smooth tax rates? If they do so, what happens to deficits over the business cycle?

6.  Identify and briefly explain two reasons why a large government debt may not be a major burden on the future generation asked to pay it off.

7.  Provincial the Ricardian equivalence proposition.

8.  Identify two conditions under which the Ricardian equivalence proposition may not hold.

## NUMERICAL PROBLEMS

1.  Suppose that for the economy of Chou,
    Tax revenues = 2000 + 0.1 GDP
    Transfers = 1500 - 0.05 GDP
    Government purchases = 3000
    Interest payments = 200
    Full employment GDP = 15,000
    Actual GDP = 16,000

    a.  How much is the budget deficit?
    b.  How much is the primary budget deficit?
    c.  How much is the full-employment budget deficit?

2.  Calculate the growth rate of debt-GDP ratio for each of the following cases, given that outstanding government debt = $5000 billion and the primary budget deficit = $250 billion.
    (a)  nominal interest rate = 8% and nominal GDP growth = 2%
    (b)  nominal interest rate = 5% and nominal GDP growth = 2%
    (c)  nominal interest rate = 15% and nominal GDP growth = 4%

3.  Calculate the real seignorage revenue in an all-currency economy, given each of the following conditions
    (a)  inflation rate = 3% and $M/P$ = $1000 billion
    (b)  inflation rate = 6% and $M/P$ = $700 billion
    (c)  inflation rate = 12% and $M/P$ = $400 billion

## ANALYTICAL QUESTIONS

1.  Compare and contrast the short-run effects of a tax cut on unemployment and output in the *AD-AS* model in which Ricardian equivalence holds, compared to a model in which Ricardian equivalence doesn't hold.

# ANSWERS TO MULTIPLE-CHOICE QUESTIONS

| Number | Answer | Number | Answer | Number | Answer |
|---|---|---|---|---|---|
| 1 | d | 11 | d | 21 | c |
| 2 | b | 12 | d | 22 | a |
| 3 | d | 13 | d | 23 | b |
| 4 | d | 14 | a | 24 | c |
| 5 | c | 15 | a | 25 | d |
| 6 | b | 16 | c | | |
| 7 | c | 17 | a | | |
| 8 | c | 18 | d | | |
| 9 | a | 19 | b | | |
| 10 | d | 20 | b | | |

# ANSWERS TO REVIEW QUESTIONS

1. The primary budget surplus = $T - G - TR$. The budget surplus = $T - G + TR + INT$. The budget surplus exceeds the primary budget surplus by the value of net interest payments on government debt.

2. Automatic stabilizers have virtually no policy lags, and they are very flexible in creating changes in government spending and taxes, because these adjustments are automatic. In contrast, discretionary fiscal stabilization policy changes in government spending and taxes have long policy lags (e.g., eighteen months) and are not very flexible.

3. During a recession, automatic stabilizers increase government spending in the form of transfer payments and reduced taxes, thereby creating a budget deficit. In contrast, automatic stabilizers do not create a full-employment deficit, because automatic stabilizers do not create a deficit at the full-employment level of output. The full-employment deficit is the amount of the budget deficit created by discretionary fiscal stabilization policy. The difference between the budget deficit and the full-employment deficit is the deficit created by automatic stabilizers.

4. Tax rate smoothing reduces the output cost of raising a given amount of tax revenue over a number of years. Imposing a tax on the return to some factor of production, output, or asset typically creates a distortion. The overall distortion is smaller if tax rates remain fairly constant over time, rather than rising and falling over the business cycle. Business cycle fluctuations in output will create budget deficits in some years and budget surpluses in other years. But the distortions caused by taxes will be lower than if the government maintained an annually balanced government budget over the business cycle by raising the income tax rate in recessions when income declines and reducing the income tax rates in booms when income rises.

5. Governments should smooth tax rates because the increase in distortions from increasing the tax rate is larger than the decrease in distortions from reducing the tax rate by the same amount. Because of that, it's better to keep tax rates constant over time and run periodic deficits and surpluses rather than raise tax rates in times when the government needs extra revenue. This means running deficits in recessions and surpluses in booms.

6.    Two reasons why a large government debt might not be a large burden on the future generation asked to pay it are: (1) this generation might have received bequests to cover the debt payments from the generation that incurred the debt; and (2) if the debt is "internal debt," then the future generation owes the debt to itself. Although some people are harmed by having to pay it off, others gain by receiving the debt payments.

7.    The Ricardian equivalence proposition provincials that a tax cut financed by the sale of bonds is not expansionary, because the effect of bond financing on the present value of lifetime resources of the public is equivalent to tax financing. The Ricardian equivalence proposition assumes that the public does not face binding borrowing constraints and that future taxes will increase enough to pay off the bonds and the interest earned on the bonds.

8.    The Ricardian equivalence proposition may not hold when either of its two principal assumptions is violated. If a significant percentage of taxpayers face binding borrowing constraints, they will spend some of the extra after-tax income they receive from the tax cut. Likewise, if people are shortsighted and consequently do not believe that their future taxes or their children's future taxes will be increased by enough to pay off the government debt, they will spend some of the extra after-tax income they receive from the tax cut. If the Ricardian equivalence proposition fails to hold, a temporary tax cut will increase aggregate spending, which is expansionary.

## ANSWERS TO NUMERICAL PROBLEMS

1.    a.    The budget deficit is $(G + TR + INT) - T = [3000 + 1500 - (0.05 \times 16{,}000) + 200] - [2000 + (0.1 \times 16{,}000)] = 300$.

b.    The primary budget deficit is $(G + TR) - T = [3000 + 1500 - (0.05 \times 16{,}000)] - [2000 + (0.1 \times 16{,}000)] = 100$.

c.    The full-employment budget deficit is what the budget deficit would be if output were at its full-employment level instead of its actual level, which is $[3000 + 1500 - (0.05 \times 15{,}000) + 200] - [2000 + (0.1 \times 15{,}000)] = 450$.

2.    The growth rate of debt-GDP ratio = (primary deficit)$/B + i$ - growth rate of nominal GDP, where $B =$ outstanding government debt and $i =$ nominal interest rate. The primary deficit = \$250 billion and $B =$ \$5000 billion, so (primary deficit)$/B =$ \$250 billion/\$5000 billion = 5%.

(a)    For $i = 8\%$, and the growth rate of nominal GDP = 2%, the growth rate of debt-GDP ratio =    5% + 8% - 2% = 11%.

(b)    For $i = 5\%$, and the growth rate of nominal GDP = 2%, the growth rate of debt-GDP ratio =    5% + 5% - 2% = 8%.

(c)    For $i = 15\%$, and the growth rate of nominal GDP = 4%, the growth rate of debt-GDP ratio =    5% + 15% - 4% = 16%.

3.    For an all-currency economy, real seignorage revenue is $R =$ (inflation rate) $\times M/P$, where $M/P$ is the real money supply.

(a)    For an inflation rate = 3%, and $M/P =$ \$1000 billion, $R = 3\% \times$ \$1000 billion = \$30 billion.

(b)    For an inflation rate = 6%, and $M/P =$ \$700 billion, $R = 6\% \times$ \$700 billion = \$42 billion.

(c)    For an inflation rate = 12%, and $M/P =$ \$300 billion, $R = 12\% \times$ \$300 billion = \$36 billion.

## ANSWERS TO ANALYTICAL QUESTIONS

1.  Given the Ricardian equivalence proposition, a temporary tax cut does not change national saving, so it doesn't shift the *IS* curve or *AD* curve, thus it has no output or employment effect. In the model without Ricardian equivalence, a temporary tax cut reduces national saving, which causes aggregate demand to increase, thus output increases and unemployment declines.